Sickness, Disability and Work: Breaking the Barriers

A SYNTHESIS OF FINDINGS ACROSS OECD COUNTRIES

OECD

ORGANISATION FOR ECONOMIC CO-OPERATION AND DEVELOPMENT

The OECD is a unique forum where governments work together to address the economic, social and environmental challenges of globalisation. The OECD is also at the forefront of efforts to understand and to help governments respond to new developments and concerns, such as corporate governance, the information economy and the challenges of an ageing population. The Organisation provides a setting where governments can compare policy experiences, seek answers to common problems, identify good practice and work to co-ordinate domestic and international policies.

The OECD member countries are: Australia, Austria, Belgium, Canada, Chile, the Czech Republic, Denmark, Finland, France, Germany, Greece, Hungary, Iceland, Ireland, Israel, Italy, Japan, Korea, Luxembourg, Mexico, the Netherlands, New Zealand, Norway, Poland, Portugal, the Slovak Republic, Slovenia, Spain, Sweden, Switzerland, Turkey, the United Kingdom and the United States. The European Commission takes part in the work of the OECD.

OECD Publishing disseminates widely the results of the Organisation's statistics gathering and research on economic, social and environmental issues, as well as the conventions, guidelines and standards agreed by its members.

ISBN 978-92-64-08884-9 (print)
ISBN 978-92-64-08885-6 (PDF)

Also available in French: *Maladie, invalidité et travail : Surmonter les obstacles – Synthèse des résultats dans les pays de l'OCDE*

Photo credits: Cover © Myriam MICHAU/Personimages.

Corrigenda to OECD publications may be found on line at: *www.oecd.org/publishing/corrigenda*.
© OECD 2010

Foreword

Sickness and disability policies are rapidly moving to centre stage in the economic policy agenda of many OECD countries. Even before the onset of the recent recession too many people of working age who were able to work relied on sickness and disability benefits as their main source of income, and the employment rate of those reporting disabling conditions was low. The economic crisis has added to this pressure by raising the possibility that many of the long-term unemployed may end up on sickness and disability benefits, similar to what happened in previous downturns. In this context, there is an urgent need to address this "medicalisation" of labour market problems by tackling the widespread use of disability benefits across the OECD and promoting labour market participation of people with disability. Many people with health problems can work and indeed want to work in ways compatible with their health condition, so any policy based on the assumption that they cannot work is fundamentally flawed. Helping people to work is potentially a "win-win" policy: It helps people avoid exclusion and have higher incomes while raising the prospect of more effective labour supply and higher economic output in the long term.

This report summarises the thematic review on Sickness, Disability and Work undertaken by the OECD over the past few years. It analyses key labour market outcomes of people with disability across the OECD and draws policy lessons from the thirteen reviewed countries (Australia, Canada, Denmark, Finland, Ireland, Luxembourg, the Netherlands, Norway, Poland, Spain, Sweden, Switzerland and the United Kingdom) in transforming their sickness and disability schemes to active support systems that promote work. The report consists of six chapters and an Executive Summary with the main conclusions and policy recommendations. Chapter 1 reviews the main trends and the short and long-term economic context in which disability policy operates. Chapter 2 sets the scale of the problems by laying out the main social and economic outcomes for people with disability and society at large across the OECD. Chapter 3 looks at the direction and extent of recent sickness and disability policy reforms, the degree of policy convergence across countries, and the impact of policies on the disability beneficiary rate. The three subsequent chapters discuss key policy areas in need of change: The disability benefit system, which is too passive in most cases, and the work incentives it provides (Chapter 4); the involvement and financial incentives of employers, especially in the critical sickness absence phase (Chapter 5); and the responsibilities for public authorities and service providers in helping people access timely employment supports (Chapter 6).

The report also provides an update, further development and deepening of the findings of the 2003 OECD report on disability policy for the working-age population, Transforming Disability into Ability, many of whose conclusions are still valid. As this new report shows, in many countries disability policy has advanced considerably during the past decade. However, changes in outcomes have not kept pace with changes in policy development. Disability appears to be a moving target for policy makers, requiring i) more rigorous implementation of rules and recent changes and ii) additional and more comprehensive reform. Moreover, things have become even more complicated in recent years because of the growing weight of a wide range of mental health problems in the inflows to sickness and disability systems. The latter phenomenon is not yet well understood and the

OECD has just launched a new country review exercise to analyse it and evaluate which policies might help to counteract it.

Work on the Sickness, Disability and Work review was a collaborative effort, carried out jointly by the Employment Analysis and Policy Division and the Social Policy Division of the OECD. The report was prepared by Christopher Prinz (team leader), Shruti Singh, Heonjoo Kim and Ana Llena-Nozal, with contributions from Allen Gomes and Veerle Slootmaekers. Tax/benefit models were provided by Dominique Paturot, statistical work by Dana Blumin and Maxime Ladaique, and administrative support by Sophie O'Gorman. John Martin, Monika Queisser and Stefano Scarpetta provided valuable comments. The report also includes comments received from the reviewed countries and is otherwise based on the comparative review reports published during 2006-10 and additional information provided by member countries.

Table of Contents

Sickness, Disability and Work: Breaking the Barriers
A Synthesis of Findings across OECD Countries
© OECD 2010

Executive Summary and Policy Conclusions

Too many workers leave the labour market permanently due to health problems or disability, and too few people with reduced work capacity manage to remain in employment. This is a social and economic tragedy that is common to virtually all OECD countries. Economic and labour market changes are increasingly proving an obstacle for people with health problems to return to work or stay in their job. In fact, until the recent recession struck the labour market in 2008, disability was much more prevalent than unemployment across the OECD countries, and spending on disability benefits was typically twice as high as spending on unemployment benefits, and even 5-10 times higher in some cases, especially in the Nordic and English-speaking countries. These facts seem counterintuitive when one considers that the health status of the working-age population has been improving over time, as shown by several health indicators.

The deep economic downturn and the associated jobs crisis have shifted the policy focus to tackling rising unemployment. However, past experience suggests that downturns tend to hit disadvantaged people more than the general population and, with a time lag of a few months or even years, increase the disability beneficiary caseload, which then typically stays on a higher structural level in the subsequent recovery. Therefore, the current jobs crisis should not be an excuse for delaying urgently needed sickness and disability reforms.

The disability problem

Disability benefit as a benefit of last resort

Working-age disability policy today is one of the biggest social and labour market challenges for policy makers. In many countries, disability benefits have become the benefit of last resort for people unable to stay in, or get into, the labour market, for reasons related to policy development and labour market changes:

- First, comprehensive reform of unemployment and social-assistance benefit schemes, with a much tighter administration of work-availability and job-search requirements, have restricted the access to these benefits and generally reduced their maximum duration. As such, these reforms contributed to the fall in unemployment in many OECD countries prior to the recent recession and, in particular, a decline in the incidence of long-term unemployment.

- Secondly, as a consequence of comprehensive pension reform and in particular the retrenchment and gradual phasing-out of early-retirement schemes or options, as well as the elimination of many special unemployment retirement pathways, older workers – who had long been encouraged to retire several years before the legal retirement age – can no longer draw on so many options to leave the labour market prematurely.

- Thirdly, skill-biased technological changes combined with globalisation pressures have had negative effects on the employment opportunities of low-skilled workers, including many workers with health problems or disability who are far more likely than others to have not completed upper secondary education, more likely to have dropped out of school prematurely and less likely to have benefitted from job-related vocational training.

One result of these changes is that disability benefits in many OECD countries have increasingly taken on the role of a benefit of last resort for many working-age people facing labour market disadvantages and having difficulties in performing continuously at the expected high level of productivity.

Social and economic outcomes of disability policy

Spending on disability benefits has become a significant burden to public finances in most OECD countries and hinders economic growth as it reduces effective labour supply.

- Public spending on disability benefits totals 2% of GDP on average across the OECD, rising to as much as 4-5% in countries such as Norway, the Netherlands and Sweden.

- Around 6% of the working-age population rely on disability benefits, on average, and up to 10-12% in some countries in the north and east of Europe.

- Employment rates of people with disability are 40% below the overall level on average, and unemployment rates are typically twice the overall level.

Most importantly, disability benefit take-up is a one-way street. People almost never leave disability benefits for a job; and if they leave the disability benefit scheme before retiring, they are far more likely to move onto another benefit.

Moreover, low employment rates of people with disability come with high social costs: Even though most non-employed people with disability receive some public benefits, they have much lower incomes and a much higher poverty risk – in some countries, twice that of the general population.

The recent economic downturn has exacerbated the situation. It is urgent now to prevent further inflows into disability benefit during the crisis to ease unemployment pressure – to avoid a structural cost to society and a social cost to those concerned. Every effort will have to be made to improve labour market opportunities for people with chronic health problems. This is also important in view of the evidence that long-term unemployment or inactivity is bad for one's health, in particular mental health, and that returning to work is generally associated with an improvement in one's health.

Mental health problems: an unresolved challenge

The fast increase in most OECD countries in the number of disability benefit claims because of mental health problems, often at a relatively young age, is an added challenge making disability a moving target for policy makers. Mental health problems are now the biggest single cause for a disability benefit claim in most countries, in Denmark, the Netherlands, Sweden and Switzerland accounting for almost half of all new claims; and employment rates of those suffering from mental ill-health are particularly low. Disability policies are not well suited to deal with mental health problems, and they do not work well for people suffering from mental ill-health (e.g. the take-up and effectiveness of employment services is even lower for this group). There is still substantial uncertainty as to the key drivers behind this development, but they seem to include changes in the acceptance of mental health problems in society and the associated changes in attitudes of doctors and disability systems in addressing problems that have long existed, as well as improved diagnostic tools.

Breaking labour market barriers

Work: the best way to help people with health problems or disability

The best way to fight benefit dependence and exclusion among people with disability is to promote their re-integration into employment if they can and wish to work. Higher employment promotes social inclusion and reduces poverty risks; it can contribute to improved mental health or faster recovery; it lowers public spending on disability benefits; and it helps to secure labour supply and thereby raise the prospect of higher longer-term economic output. The latter is also important in consideration of rapid population ageing and the likely stagnation or fall in labour supply in most OECD countries in the coming decades. People with disability will be among the groups of the population that need to be mobilised for the workforce, in addition to women and older workers.

This is why policy objectives are shifting in most OECD countries in the search for a new balance between the two potentially conflicting goals of disability policy: i) to provide an adequate and secure income for those who cannot work and their families; while ii) providing good incentives and supports to work for those who can. Until the mid 1990s, but still in many cases today, policies were biased towards generous and easily accessible disability benefits with little or no emphasis on the latter goal. This is neither in the interest of the worker nor of the society at large.

Recent reforms have not gone far enough in most cases

Rising concerns about the rapidly growing disability rolls have led to changes in policy settings over the past two decades. For instance, disability policy packages now contain a broader range of employment and rehabilitation measures in most OECD countries. Among the most important changes are attempts to improve the quality of supports, broaden access to available services, link better the provision of services and benefits, profile the needs of clients earlier, and case-manage clients through the system. At the same time, a few countries have also tightened up gate-keeping to limit access to long-term sickness and disability benefits.

Despite such changes, the shift in policy orientation was generally not strong enough and investment in employment and rehabilitation supports insufficient to increase the rate of employment of people with health problems. The composition of disability spending is still biased towards passive benefits, which make up 95% and more of total spending in most countries; only a few countries, Germany, Norway, the Netherlands and Denmark, spend over 10% on active labour market programmes for persons with disability. The take-up of employment measures continues to be very low and most people entering disability benefit have never participated in any such measure. In particular, beneficiaries are in many cases still not identified and supported early enough before their health problems become chronic.

However, evidence of changing disability outcomes in a few countries that reformed their systems radically suggests that policy does matter. Reform packages which include not only improvements in employment supports but also, and perhaps more importantly, tighter access to disability benefits through stronger work incentives for workers and financial obligations for employers, seem to have a great potential in changing labour supply and labour demand. The annual number of disability benefit claims responds swiftly to comprehensive system change, as seen from reform in countries such as Hungary, Italy, the Netherlands and Poland. Moreover, it appears that roughly half of those no longer coming onto the disability benefit rolls stay in work even without, or with only very limited, employment support. This is encouraging although it will be important to understand better what is happening to the other half, many of who will probably have moved onto other inactive benefits.

In conclusion, there was considerable disability reform activity in the past two decades in a large number of countries. Where reforms have included changes in gate-keeping, they have generally been quite successful in curbing inflows into the disability benefit system. However, much remains to be done to help longer-term disability beneficiaries off benefit into work and more generally to raise employment opportunities and labour force participation of workers with chronic health problems or disability.

What remains to be done: policy conclusions

The single most important element for a far-reaching change in disability policy and the key to success is to strengthen the financial incentives of all actors involved to promote the same objective: increase employment opportunities for individuals with disability.

- For sick workers and disability beneficiaries, it must pay to remain in work, seek work or increase work effort;
- For employers, it must pay to retain sick workers and help them back quickly into their job or to find another job, and there may need to be subsidies for hiring workers with health problems;
- For benefit authorities, it must pay to assess people's work capacity rigorously and avoid the granting of a benefit just because this seems easiest;
- For service providers, it must pay to reintegrate their clients into the regular labour market at a sustainable level.

Better financial incentives for each stakeholder will have to be matched by, first, stronger employment expectations on the part of both workers with health problems and those helping them into work; secondly, corresponding mutual responsibilities especially for workers and employers; and thirdly, better supports so that every stakeholder can fulfil the strengthened requirements. Stronger employment expectations and corresponding responsibilities and supports are equally important for two other stakeholders: Doctors, who have to make more efforts to keep sickness absence periods as short as possible and refocus sick workers on re-employment early on, and employment service caseworkers, who have to profile the client carefully and make every effort to bring the person closer to the labour market.

The required policy changes will depend on each country's starting position, the setup of the system, the weaknesses and missing links, and to some extent the policy priorities. However, looking across a range of OECD countries, a number of general key policy challenges emerge.

Transforming disability benefits into an employment instrument

Disability benefits too often provide cash only although many of the current and potential beneficiaries have partial work capacity and need support to find work in line with their abilities. Current systems still predominantly support people in being out of work with a strong focus on a person's disability. People claiming a disability benefit have no participation requirements and limited attention is paid in most systems to the work incentives/disincentives arising from granting an often generous and in most cases permanent benefit. Many countries have started to change the approach for those with partial work capacity. The following are key elements for any such shift in policy.

Assess work capacity, not disability. Traditionally, disability benefit systems were built on the principle of providing benefits for people who cannot be expected to work. Accordingly, entitlement was related to the existence of a disability and proving the inability to work. Conversely, to avoid unnecessary benefit claims and make the best use of people's remaining work capacities, disability systems should start with an assessment of the *remaining work capacity* of a person applying for a benefit and provide adequate employment supports to try to maintain the claimant in contact with the labour market. The assessment and corresponding supports should be done quickly so as to avoid claimants being inactive for too long and losing contact with the labour market.

Move to an activation stance. Disability benefits like unemployment benefits target jobless people who are, in many cases, able to work at least partially. However, the operation of a disability benefit scheme differs drastically from that of an unemployment benefit scheme, with strict participation requirements in the latter but not in the former. This difference is justified for people who are unable to work but not for the much larger number of those who have partial work capacity, in part explaining the low take-up of potentially effective services. The logic to make every effort to activate an unemployment benefit recipient should also be applied to the disability benefit system; for instance, benefit payments should be linked to the willingness of the beneficiary to co-operate with the responsible authority and engage in employability-enhancing and, where appropriate, job-search activities. Some countries use a *rehabilitation-before-benefit* principle and countries such as Switzerland are recently trying to tighten this by moving towards a rehabilitation-instead-of-benefits principle.

Make disability benefit a transitory payment. Except for a few people with severe health problems, disability benefit, like other working-age benefits, should be a temporary payment with entitlement being reassessed at periodic intervals. Such practice is being adopted in an increasing number of countries including Austria, Germany and Poland. This is of particular importance for younger people who would otherwise stay on disability benefit for a long time, with little hope for better social and economic integration. Such change may raise difficult questions with respect to current beneficiaries, whose entitlements would have to be reassessed on the grounds of *new and often tighter* eligibility criteria following comprehensive reform. This is not seen as a problem in some countries, for example the Netherlands, but it is politically not possible in others.

Make work pay. A big challenge facing governments is how best to reform tax and benefit systems for persons with disability with a view to providing appropriate financial incentives to take up jobs, remain in work and increase work effort. This issue has not received enough attention so far, although some countries have recently started to address it, *e.g.* with in-work payments in the United Kingdom and Ireland and a benefit which depends on the individual's work effort in the Netherlands. Disability benefit should not be more attractive than other working-age benefits; payments should be phased out gradually to make sure that every extra hour worked, pays; and extras or secondary benefits paid to compensate for additional costs associated with the disability should be paid irrespective of beneficiary or labour market status. Ways to implement these principles will differ across countries depending on whether a system provides earnings-related, flat-rate or means-tested benefits.

Activating employers and medical professionals

Employers are key players in the disability benefit system, even if they are not always recognised as such. Too often they are outside the policy process, being viewed as part of the problem, not part of the solution. In particular, sickness absence is a period during which much more could be done in most countries to monitor the health status of workers and manage their return to work. Today, too often sickness and disability benefit schemes are being used as camouflage behind which employers can downsize their workforce. Not only employers, but also administrations, workers' representatives and doctors, seem to lack sufficient knowledge about such workers in order to prevent them from gradually sliding into sickness and, later, disability benefits. To make employers part of the solution will require a number of key changes.

Strengthen the role and incentives for employers. First of all, employers need to be given a much more prominent role in sickness monitoring and sickness management. They are in a good position to judge what work their employees can still do and what work or workplace adjustments might be needed to accommodate the health problem that has arisen. In co-operation with the workers' representatives, employers are well placed to prevent chronic problems, ideally with the support of an employment-oriented occupational health service, which is most developed in Finland, and to intervene early, where necessary. This advantage and the employers' knowledge about the worker's abilities should be used systematically, as in the Netherlands where employers, together with their employees, are now obliged to develop, follow and update a reintegration plan, with a number of markers along the way. Employer responsibility can be strengthened with corresponding financial incentives in the form of sickness benefit co-payment, as is common in several OECD countries, or experience-rated premiums to the disability benefit system as in Finland and the Netherlands – to ensure employers do their utmost to help the worker return to their job, or adjust the job as quickly as possible.

Provide better supports for employers. Employers also need better supports to fulfil their obligations. For instance, advice on appropriate workplace adjustment and corresponding financial supports should be available easily because employers understandably shy away from cumbersome administrative procedures and contacts. In Norway, for example, each employer has a personal contact with specialised knowledge in the nearby public employment office. In order to stimulate more hiring of people with health problems or disability, and to avoid that strengthened job-retention obligations and incentives lead to falling recruitment of people with weaker health, employers need compensation of some form (including through wage subsidies) for reduced work capacity or productivity of their workers. These subsidies, common especially in the Nordic countries, should be well targeted to the capacity of the worker but might be needed for a long period (even a permanent subsidy might be justified in some cases) and should include ongoing coaching where needed. Care should be taken to address moral hazard, especially where a system allows the transformation of an existing into a subsidised job.

Engage different actors in a joint process. Employers will not be able to fulfil their role without complementary changes for other actors involved early on. In particular, it is essential to better direct the actions of general practitioners by emphasising the value and possibility of work at an early stage, and then to keep the sickness absence period as short as possible. Medical guidelines for doctors on the necessary duration of a sickness absence for the most frequent illnesses recently developed in Sweden are a promising step in this direction. More control of sickness certificates, common in countries like Austria, France and Spain, would also be necessary in many cases. Public authorities also have an important role in monitoring sickness, as recognised for instance in Denmark. In particular, they have to take on the sickness-monitoring and sickness-management role for those people who do not or no longer have an employer and workers' representative – unemployed and inactives, a large and in some countries increasing group among disability benefit claimants.

Getting the right services to the right people at the right time

More people with disability could work if they were given the right supports at the right time. Take-up of employment supports is low although there is a great need to improve the employability of people with disability who often lack the necessary labour market qualifications and recent work experience. Low take-up of services is partly related to the way these services are provided. Currently, in many countries too many actors and agencies are involved in benefit and service provision; they do not co-operate effectively; they do not have sufficient incentives to promote the new employment focus of policy; and they lack the tools and resources to provide timely services and in the mix needed by the client. Countries are investing more into rehabilitation and employment measures than they used to, but, despite pro-work rhetoric, they are generally not investing enough: Most countries only spend 0.1-0.2% of their GDP on rehabilitation and employment programmes for people with disability. Much could be gained from improvements in three areas.

Improve cross-agency co-ordination and co-operation. Much better co-operation is needed in most countries between the benefit authority and the public employment service, and between the different agencies involved in providing services. Better co-operation can be achieved in different ways, ranging from (at one extreme) merging entities as was done in the Netherlands, New Zealand, Norway and the United Kingdom, to having various agencies work together in shared premises, to linking agencies better by systematic exchange of information and cross-subsidising of services, as in Sweden. The purpose in all cases is to identify the right role for the right agency and to match resources and funding responsibilities accordingly. Benefit systems and/or employment support systems should also be streamlined in some countries; system fragmentation bears the risk that outcomes depend on the pathway into the system chosen by, or imposed on, the individual.

Engage with clients systematically and in a tailored way. Ideally, countries would move their systems towards a one-stop-shop; all people who experience difficulties on the labour market would then enter the system through the same gate and be led through the same process. The process should include a *systematic profiling* of clients, as in Australia and Norway, a *comprehensive assessment of their work capacity* and, if needed, a *swift referral to the most appropriate service.* The whole process should be driven by the needs of the client, not the interests of the agencies involved. Access to supports should be broadened so that those with partial work capacity could also benefit and only depend on need, not on entitlement to particular benefits, for instance – a principle increasingly common across the OECD. Services need to be adjusted flexibly to changing needs, and could include work-first and train-first elements.

Address incentives for authorities and service providers. It is important for public authorities to have sufficient financial incentives to invest in active labour market strategies with clients who will often need special support and more time, rather than doing what seems to be easiest, *i.e.* to grant them a benefit. This requires good monitoring of the actions taken at regional and local level in the first place, and sharing of outcomes across local entities with the objective to stimulate a situation whereby each locality aims at being a good performer, as recently done in Denmark and Switzerland. The next step would be direct financial incentives for public entities to raise their accountability, again most developed in Denmark through much higher reimbursement from national budgets for municipalities (which run the entire system in this country) for any employment-near measure provided. Equally important is to improve the quality and effectiveness of employment services by a change in the funding mechanism, from block or output funding to funding based on actual employment outcomes, as done in Australia and the United Kingdom. Such change is presumably easier in connexion with a (partial) privatisation of services but outcome-based funding approaches can also be introduced for public employment services.

Conclusion: critical policy choices

Tightening inflows or raising outflows

Shall policy makers focus on reducing new disability benefit claims or raising the outflow from such benefits into work? For a lasting change in outcomes, more can be gained from limiting the inflow to what has become a quasi-permanent benefit in most countries. Many countries have indeed chosen this route and have only changed the approach for those applying for a disability benefit, while at the same time explicitly grandfathering those already on benefit at the time of reform. In some countries this policy choice reflects a strategy to win stakeholders over to support the reform; in others, it is legally impossible to expose current recipients to new eligibility criteria. However, changes in inflows will translate only slowly into changes in the total benefit caseload. There is a case for introducing change for current beneficiaries also, especially those who are younger and who can expect to remain on benefits for decades. The choice of policies for this group will depend on the country context. In countries where retesting beneficiaries according to new criteria is not possible, even with better supports offered, it might be the best and only viable political solution to draw a line and treat current beneficiaries differently altogether, as is done in Sweden: Rather than retesting them, promote their seeking work by a full right to return to benefit at any time in the future.

Promote job retention or new hiring

Related to the question of focussing on either benefit inflow or outflow is the issue whether policy should focus on keeping workers in work, building on the existing employer-employee relationship, or bringing inactives into the labour force. Policy will have to be very different for the two cases. For better job retention of workers, the main focus will be on the sickness absence phase, while to promote hiring of new workers, especially those without work experience, employer subsidies and the like play a crucial role. There is an inherent dilemma: Strengthened retention requirements and financial incentives for employers can quickly turn into an obstacle against hiring jobseekers. In fact, most policies for persons with disability, including mandatory employment quotas and anti-discrimination legislation, are subject to this dilemma. Evidence from the country reviews suggests that for all those policies, those in work gain and those without a job find it even more difficult to access the labour market, with the net employment effect often being negative. This is the usual insider/outsider problem of labour market policy and labour market regulation. The Dutch approach of using experience-rating for disability insurance premiums is a good example: It is an effective tool for lowering sickness absence and disability benefit entries, but potentially hinders employment of people who are judged by employers to be susceptible to sickness or disability in the future. This is why the Netherlands has introduced additional mechanisms to stimulate labour demand.

Moving to a single working-age benefit

Much of the widespread and increased use of disability benefit systems over the past two decades is related to the large and, in many cases, increasing difference between disability benefits and other working-age benefits; in particular differences in benefit generosity, participation and job-search requirements and the way in which beneficiaries are reactivated and supported into work. In many countries, the end result is that people are being shifted around between different benefits and agencies and not supported in the best possible way. Giving all people access to mainstream employment services has been one response but this does not remove the benefit-related differences nor does it automatically secure better-targeted supports for people with disability. An alternative approach is to simplify benefits and systems, with the ultimate objective to abolish the strict differentiation between different contingencies and to replace the array of available working-age benefits by just one such payment.

This radical approach has not yet been tried in any OECD country and is unlikely to be so in the near future. However, it is a promising concept and several countries have made steps in this direction. For people with partial work capacity, the new Employment and Support Allowance in the United Kingdom (which replaces Incapacity Benefit) works in a similar way to the country's unemployment benefit. Germany has recently introduced a single benefit for all employable people of working age, but has chosen to keep disability benefit separate. The new Work Assessment Allowance in Norway merges together different types of rehabilitation and time-limited disability benefits. New Zealand was the first country to consider the introduction of a true single working-age benefit, but the process was halted for political reasons. The main advantages of a single benefit would be the possibility to, first, stop the frequent transfers of jobless people across different income-support schemes and, secondly, apply the very same process to *all* jobless people of working age – including early identification, profiling, capacity assessment, assessment of support needs and, if needed, referral to the most appropriate service. In exceptional cases, a single working-age benefit could be a permanent payment, but in principle it would provide temporary income support in a situation of need, together with a strong and well-targeted activation regime. There may also be a case for certain benefit top-ups to compensate for extra costs arising for an individual, but these should not be related to the person's labour force status.

Policy success requires a better evidence base

Rigorous evaluation of particular programmes, especially employment and rehabilitation measures, and policy components is scarce all over the OECD. This lack of evidence is a major bottleneck for identifying what works, and for whom, for people with health problems or disability. In a first step, it will be important for all countries to invest more in collecting data and evaluating outcomes to understand which programmes are effective. For instance, better data are needed to understand pathways into and through the system and conditions for and factors behind off-flow from benefits; differences in inflow and outflow dynamics depending on a number of determinants such as the disabling health condition; long-term employment and earnings patterns of both those coming into the benefit system and those moving out of it; the impact on off-benefit transitions and employment uptake of particular employment and vocational rehabilitation programmes, and how this impact varies for different risk or target groups; and the impact of particular policy components such as temporary benefit payment or entitlement reassessment. In a second step, it will be important to share evidence *across* countries and identify good practices. As all OECD countries face much of the same problems, despite using different schemes and approaches, there is much to learn from what is done elsewhere.

The political economy of disability reform is key

The discrepancy in many countries between the big change in policy rhetoric and objectives on the one hand and the slow pace of actual change and poor employment opportunities for people with health problems on the other, suggests that partly the problem is one of political constraints. This is largely explained by the fact that disability systems have to support people who cannot be expected to work as well as others with considerable work capacity. As a result, cutting benefit entitlements for people who are already suffering from ill-health and forcing them to undergo training or even seek work is both highly unpopular and not fair for some groups. However, the observed very slow-moving reform approach is not good enough for those people who can and want to work and who are too often excluded and living in poverty. This approach is also very expensive for the public purse and, thus, not only inequitable but also highly inefficient for the society at large. Taking also into account the rapidly ageing population in many OECD countries and the associated need to promote an effective labour supply to sustain economic growth and the wellbeing of society, it becomes unavoidable to address some of the more complex and more controversial disability policy challenges. Succeeding in implementing what are often perceived as unpopular reforms will require a strong political will and close collaboration of government, social partners and civil society.

Chapter 1

The Economic Context for Disability Policy

Despite the recent economic downturn, globalization, together with demographic and technology transitions, remain powerful forces of change in the labour markets of OECD countries. This chapter argues that integrating more fully into the labour market people with disability is essential in meeting economic and social challenges arising from these broad drivers of change. The recent economic downturn is further reinforcing this urgent need, as people with disability have been hard hit by job losses and the reduction in job vacancies. This may push them to the margin of the labour market, raising the risk of further structural increases in the disability beneficiary caseload.

Disability policy is an important factor in responding to the short and long-term economic challenges facing many OECD countries. In the long run, the participation of individuals with chronic health problems or disability is essential to address the decline in the effective labour supply associated with population ageing and thus help secure the economic wellbeing of many OECD countries. Disability is not a marginal phenomenon: Across the OECD, one in seven people of working age regard themselves as having a chronic health problem or disability which hampers their daily life, rising to more than one in five in some countries (Figure 1.1).

Figure 1.1. Disability prevalence at working age is high in most OECD countries

Self-assessed disability prevalence, as a percentage of the population aged 20-64, late 2000s

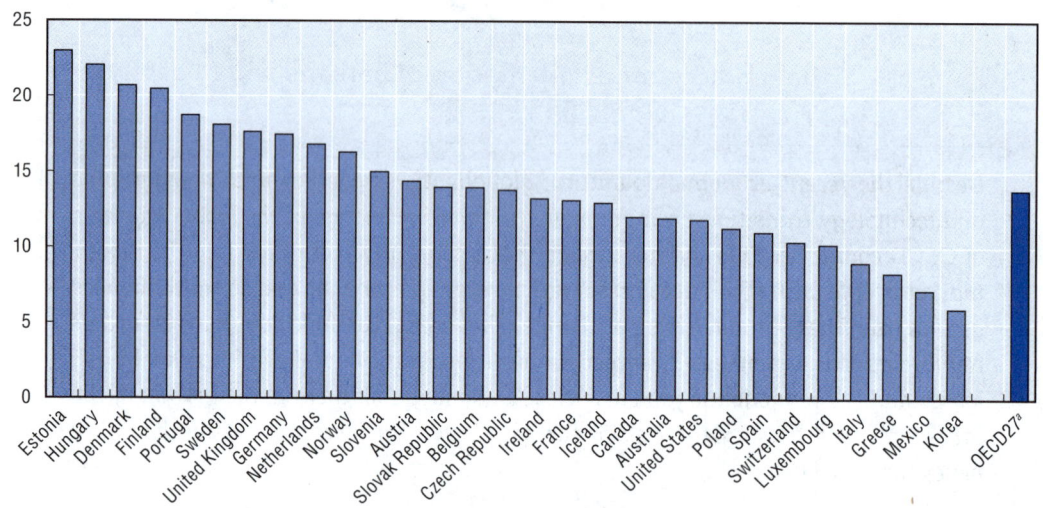

a) OECD27 is an unweighted average for 27 countries. Estonia and Slovenia are not included in the OECD average. See Annex 1.A1 on definitions and measurement of disability.

Definitions and sources: Chronic health problem for at least six months limiting daily activities from EU-SILC (Income, Social Inclusion and Living Conditions) 2007 (wave 4), except: Australia: profound/severe or moderate/mild core activity restriction, from SDAC (Survey of Disability and Carers) 2003; Canada: persons with health and activity limitation (from mild to very severe), from PALS (Participation and Activity Limitation Survey) 2006; Denmark, Norway: persons with a long-standing health problem or disability, from LFS (Labour Force Survey) 2005; Korea: persons registered to the local government with their type of disability and level of severity as assessed by a medical doctor, from National Survey on Persons with Disabilities 2005; Mexico: permanent or temporary disability, from ENESS (National Survey of Employment) 2004; Netherlands: suffering from a long-lasting complaint, illness or disability which impedes carrying out or obtaining a paid job (work disabled), from LFS 2006; Poland: persons declaring they are legally disabled, from LFS 2004; Switzerland: persons with reduced capacity due to a long-lasting health problem of more than a year, from LFS 2008; United Kingdom: persons with reduced capacity due to a long-lasting health problem of more than a year, from LFS 2006; United States: work-limiting physical or mental condition from SIPP (Survey of Income and Program Participation) 2008.

This chapter begins by providing the rationale for disability policy as an essential economic objective. It then reviews how developments in the socio-economic context over the past decade have led to deteriorating employment prospects of workers with disability.

In particular, in light of the changing labour market conditions, the chapter investigates the impact of the economic downturn on workers with disability. The final section looks at the impact of other factors, in particular ongoing ageing of the working-age population.

1.1. The importance of workers with disability to the economy and society

Social and economic inclusion of people with disability

The integration of individuals with disability[1] in the OECD labour markets was difficult even before the onset of the global economic crisis, when for about a decade economic growth was rather strong in many OECD countries and employment rose quite significantly.

Low levels of employment and high rates of unemployment and inactivity reflect the huge labour market disadvantage of people with disability (Figure 1.2). In the late 2000s, just before the onset of the recent economic downturn, their employment rate was only slightly over half and their unemployment rate nearly twice the OECD average for people without disability. Closely related to these poor labour market outcomes, people with disability also experienced poverty more intensely than their peers without disability (see Chapter 2 for more details on outcomes).

Figure 1.2. **Social and economic integration of persons with disability is lagging behind**

Key labour market indicators,[a] by disability status, OECD average,[b] late 2000s and mid-1990s, percentages

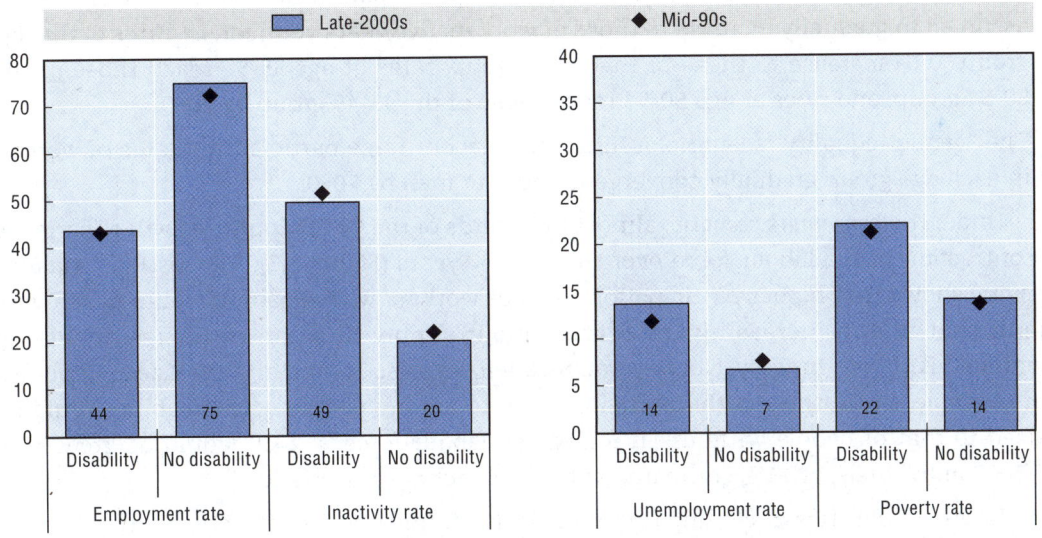

a) Employment rate: employment as a percentage of working-age population; Inactivity rate: inactive population as a percentage of working-age population; Unemployment rate: unemployed as a percentage of the labour force; working-age population; Poverty rate: percentage of people with disability in households with less than 60% of the median adjusted disposable income.
b) The OECD average is an unweighted average across 27 OECD countries (excluding Japan, New Zealand and Turkey).

Source: See Figure 2.1 except for poverty rate, see Figure 2.6.

Coping with demographic challenges and future labour supply shortages

The difficult labour market integration of people with disability will create bigger problems in the future for many OECD countries given their rapidly changing demographics. Over the next 50 years, all countries will experience a steep increase in the share of retirees and a large decline in the share of the population of prime-age workers. For example, by 2050, more than one-third of the population is projected to be over age 65 in Italy, Japan, Korea and Spain (OECD, 2006). These developments are likely to lead to a sharp drop in the labour force and consequently could result in slower economic growth.

Population ageing provides a solid argument for enhancing the efforts to mobilise the under-utilised labour potential among workers with disability. This can contribute to raising the productive capacity of the economy and reduce the costs associated with disability benefit programmes. The potential contribution of higher participation rates among workers with disability to offset the negative impact of ageing on the future size of the labour force can be illustrated by comparing a scenario where participation rates by age and gender remain unchanged at their current levels (the "benchmark" scenario) with an another scenario where participation rates for workers with disability gradually increase. The results are compared with alternative scenarios that assume participation rates to increase further among older workers and women, respectively.[2] The following assumptions are used in constructing the scenarios:

- In the "benchmark" scenario, labour force participation rates by age and gender in each disability group are assumed to remain constant at their 2007 levels.

- In the "disability equality" scenario, labour force participation rates for people with disability are gradually raised to the level of those without disability, assuming that the disability gap in participation rates is closed by 2050.

- In the "later retirement" scenario, labour force participation rates of older workers are assumed to gradually increase to those of workers five years younger; i.e. rates of the age group 60-64 increase to those of the 55-59 group, rates at age 55-59 reach those of the 50-54 group, and rates at age 50-54 reach those of the 45-49 group by 2050.

- The "gender equality" scenario assumes that labour force participation rates of women in each age group gradually converge to those of men by 2050.

Under the benchmark scenario, almost two-thirds of the OECD countries will experience a contraction in the labour force over the next 40 years (Figure 1.3). The disability equality scenario shows that higher participation rates of workers with disability could play a very significant role in increasing the future labour supply in some countries, including Denmark, Finland, Hungary, Norway and Sweden, but also Poland and the Czech Republic. For example, in Hungary, if the participation rate among people with disability could be raised to that of people without disability, the labour force in 2050 would be greater by 350 000 individuals, or 11%, compared with the benchmark scenario.

In other countries, including Australia, Iceland, Ireland, Netherlands, Portugal, Spain and the United Kingdom, raising participation rates for workers with disability has just as much impact on future labour supply as changing rates for other underrepresented groups. For instance, in the Netherlands, the impact of raising participation rates for either people with disability or women (gender equality scenarios) could increase the labour force in 2050 by around 7% compared with the benchmark scenario. The later retirement scenario leads to labour force growth similar to the disability equality scenario in most countries, with the exception of those countries in which early retirement is still especially widespread, e.g. Austria, France and Italy.

Figure 1.3. **Higher participation rates for people with disability can help prevent future labour force declines**

Projected labour force according to four different scenarios on age, gender and disability-specific participation rates, 23 OECD countries, 1980-2050 (in thousands)

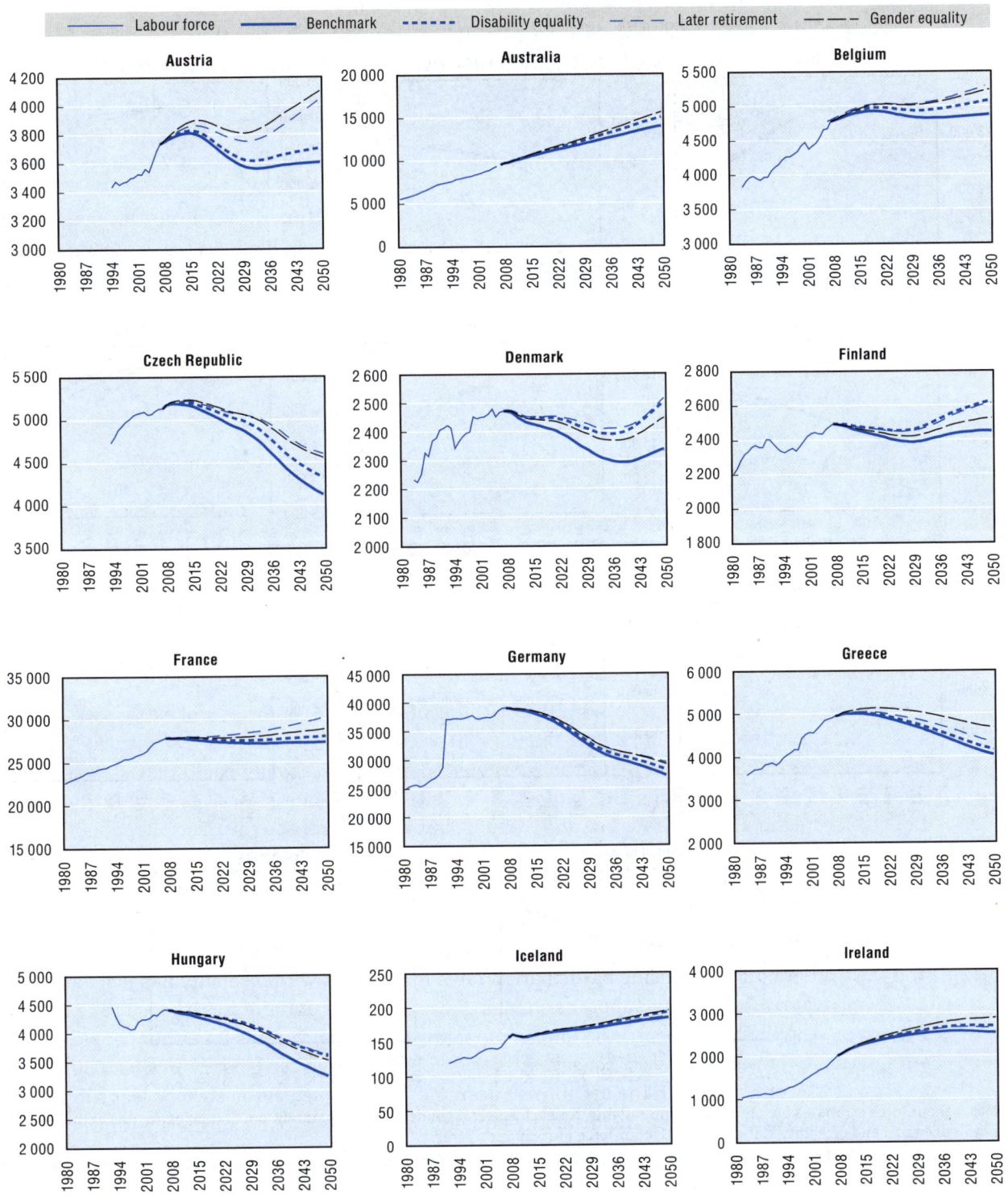

Figure 1.3. **Higher participation rates for people with disability can help prevent future labour force declines** (cont.)

Projected labour force according to four different scenarios on age, gender and disability-specific participation rates, 23 OECD countries, 1980-2050 (in thousands)

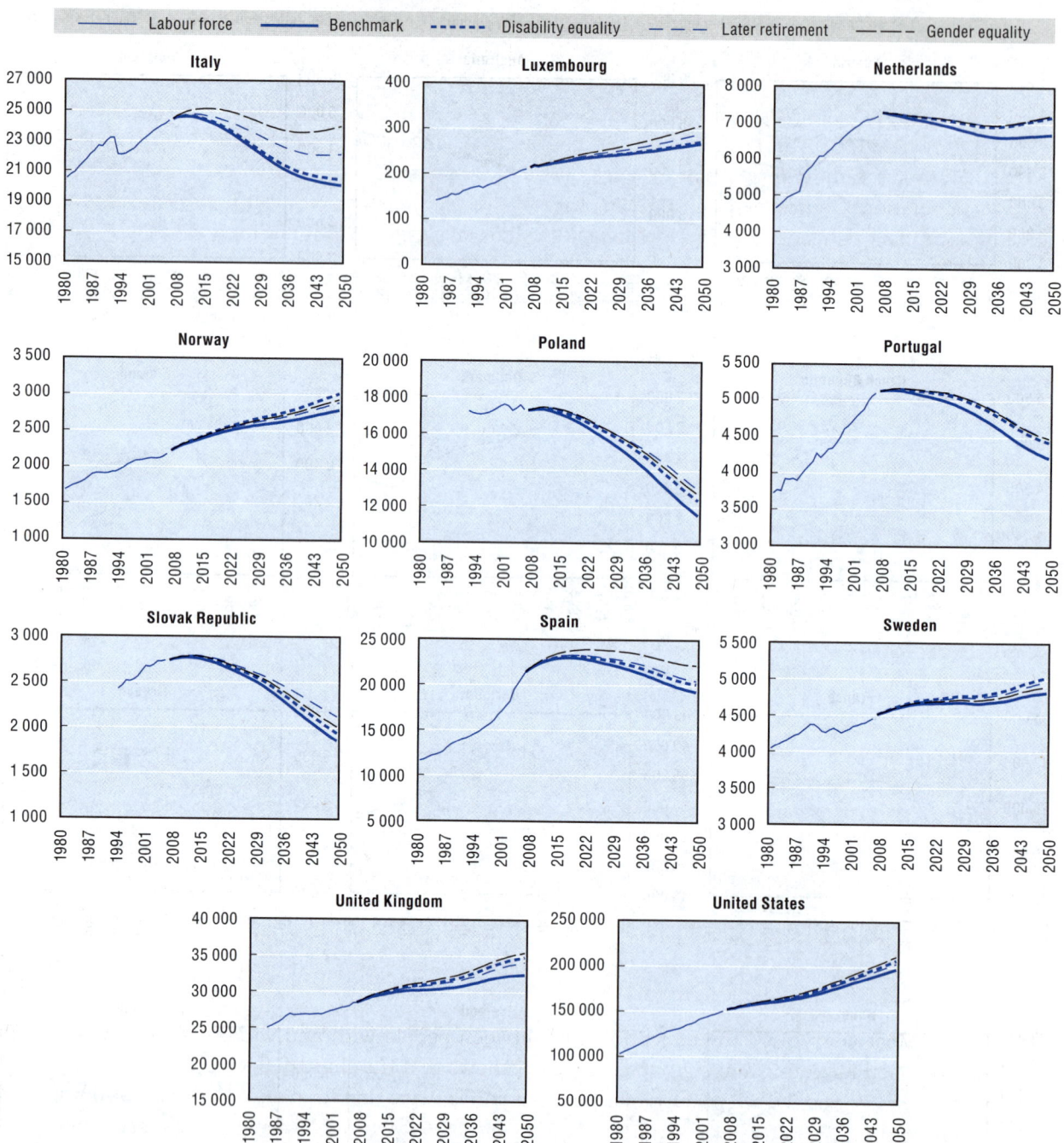

Note: Labour force estimates are obtained by multiplying, for each age and gender group separately, population estimates with disability prevalence rates and disability status-specific labour force participation rates.

Source: OECD *Population Projections Database* for population figures; Figure 1.1 for disability prevalence rates and Figure 1.2 for labour force participation rates.

1.2. Workers with disability face greater barriers in the labour market

The changing labour market context

The large systemic changes that have affected the OECD labour markets over the past decades have often created new challenges for workers with disability. In particular, skill-biased technological changes, together with the emergence of new major trade partners in the global economy and the associated shifts in low-skilled activities away from the OECD countries, have had a negative effect on the employment opportunities of low-skilled workers (OECD, 2007). These developments have disadvantaged people with disability more since they have lower average levels of education compared with the rest of the population. On average, in 2007, the share of persons with disability with less than upper secondary education was almost twice the share of those without disability (Figure 1.4).

Figure 1.4. **People with disability have significantly lower levels of education**

Share of the working-age population with low education level,[a] by disability status,[b] late 2000s

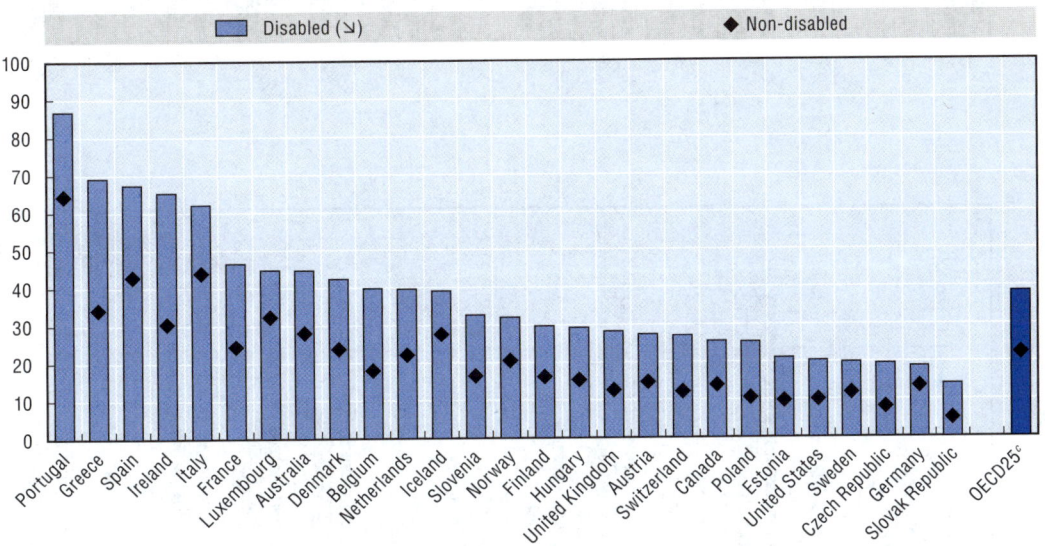

Note: Throughout, (↘) in the legend indicates the variable according to which countries are ranked, in decreasing order.

a) A low education level corresponds to an educational attainment of less than upper secondary (ISCED 0-2).

b) See definitions of self-assessed disability in Figure 1.1.

c) OECD25 refers to an unweighted average for 25 countries. Estonia and Slovenia are not included in the OECD average.

Source: See Figure 1.1.

Most worryingly, the education gap between people with and without disability has worsened for younger age groups. Figure 1.5 shows that the share of people with disability in their 20s and 30s with a low level of education is twice that for people without disability while the gap is smaller between the 50-59 and 60-64 year-olds, relative to the same age groups for people without disability. Only in a few countries, including in particular the United States, has the trend been in the opposite direction and in several countries, *e.g.* Ireland, Poland and the Slovak Republic, the education gap grew much faster.

As a response to greater competition and more rapid technological changes, working conditions have been changing in OECD countries, with less job security for the growing number of workers on temporary or atypical contracts, heavier workloads and increased

Figure 1.5. **The education gap between people with and without disability has increased over cohorts**

People with disability[a] with low education level,[b] relative to their peers without disability, by age cohort, late 2000s

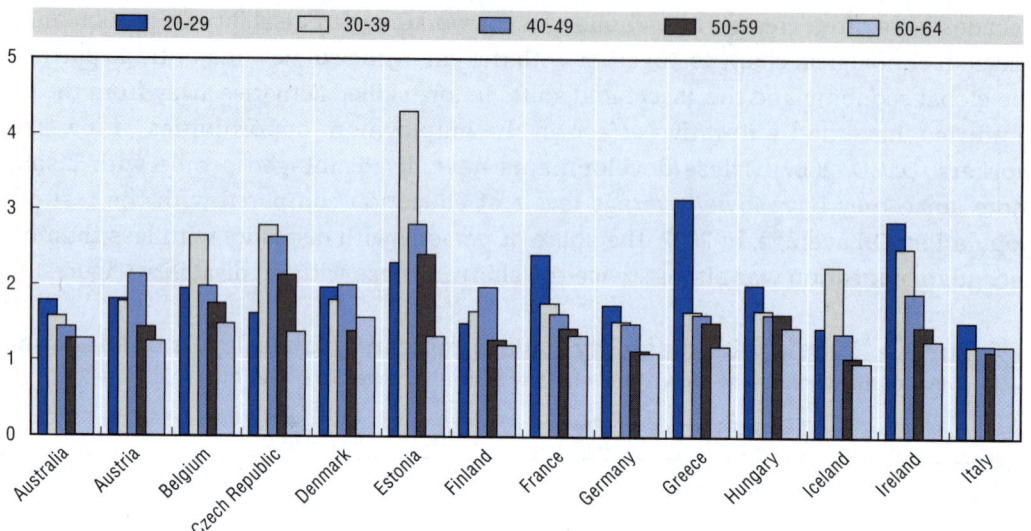

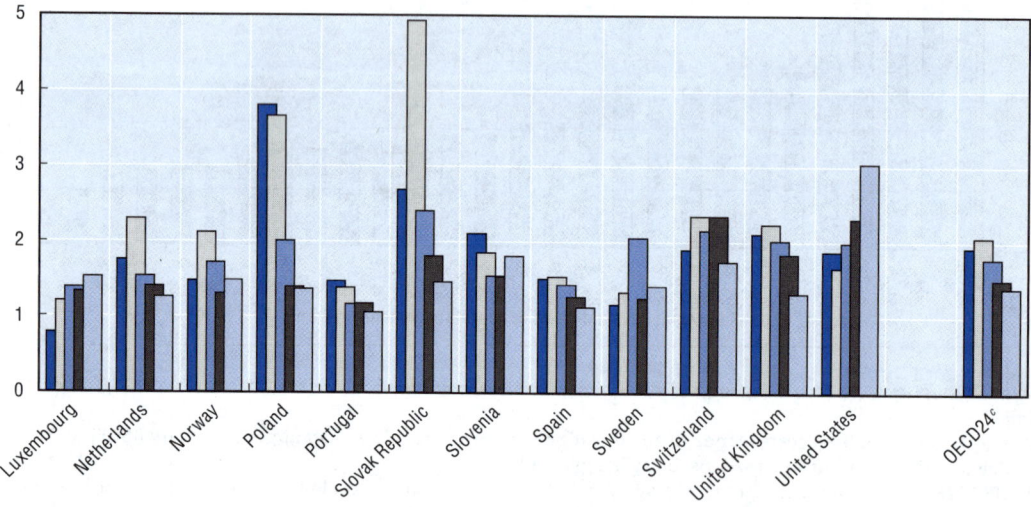

a) See definitions of self-assessed disability in Figure 1.1.
b) A low education level corresponds to an educational attainment of less than upper secondary (ISCED 0-2).
c) OECD24 refers to an unweighted average for 24 countries. Estonia and Slovenia are not included in the OECD average.
Source: See Figure 1.1.

work pressure. These patterns have made access to jobs by individuals with disability more difficult. Figure 1.6 summarises some of these indicators of labour market conditions in the OECD countries. There has been an increase in the share of temporary jobs and more workers have job tenure of less than one year, while average job tenure (now around ten years) has also increased. These indicators suggest a further dichotomisation of labour markets in many OECD countries, with declining job security, more frequent job changes and reduced attachment to a specific employer and the labour market for some groups. At the same time, however, the increase in so-called "non-standard" forms of employment including part-time work may provide more work opportunities for workers with disability.

Figure 1.6. **Trends in labour market and working condition indicators are inconclusive**

Percentage-point change in a range of labour market and working condition indicators, 1995-2008
Unweighted average of a selected set of OECD countries

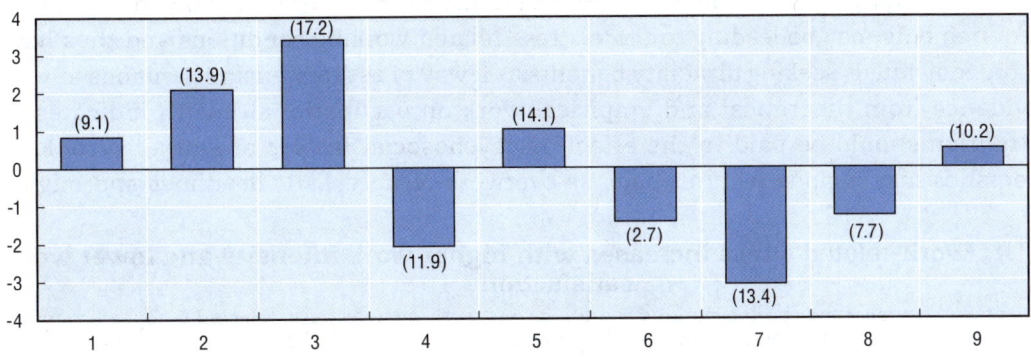

Panel A. **Change in employment by occupation in Europe**[a, b]

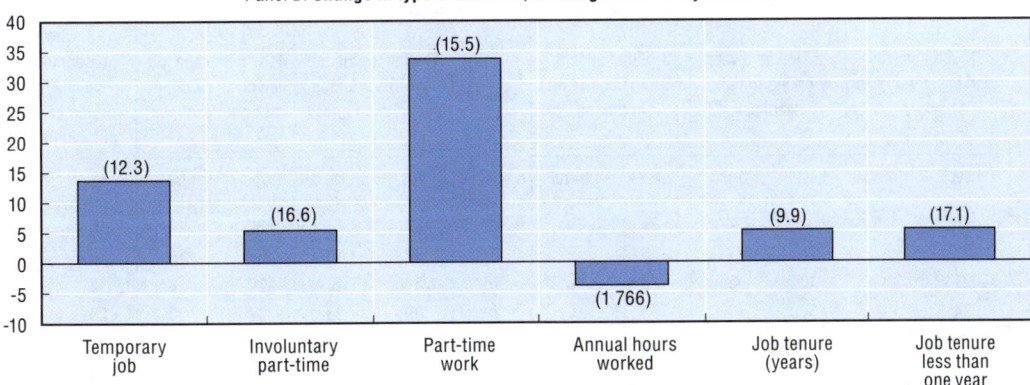

Panel B. **Change in type of contract, working hours**[c] **and job tenure**

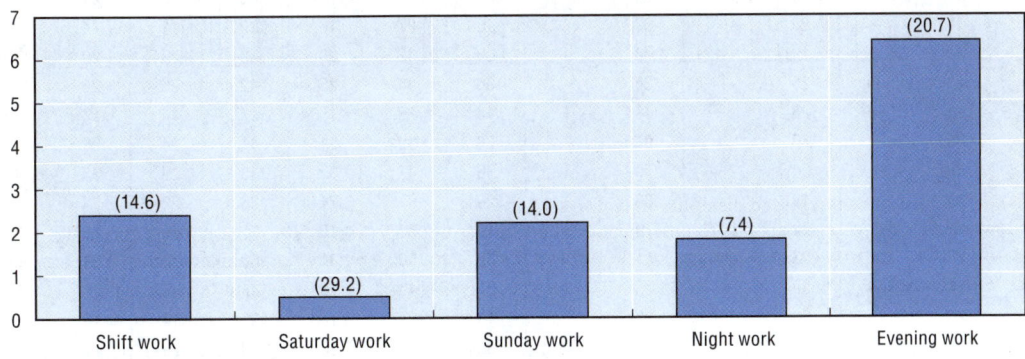

Panel C. **Change in unsocial working hour arrangements in Europe**

Note: Values within parenthesis are the OECD average in the last year.

a) Occupation based on ISCO-88, one-digit occupations: 1: Legislators, Senior Officials and Managers; 2: Professionals; 3: Technicians and Associate Professionals; 4: Clerks; 5: Service Workers and Shop and Market Sales Workers; 6: Skilled Agricultural and Fishery Workers; 7: Craft and Related Trades Workers; 8: Plant and Machine Operators and Assemblers; 9: Elementary Occupations.

b) Data refer to EU15 excluding Finland and Sweden.

c) Percentage change for average annual hours worked.

Source: Panels A and C, European Labour Force Survey (EULFS); Panel B, OECD *Database on Labour Force Statistics.*

Workplace changes and mental health

The self-reported exposure of European workers to a number of working conditions suggests a trend increase in work intensity in the majority of countries (Table 1.1, columns 1-4). This finding is important insofar as work intensity appears to be one of the key factors for perceived stress at work (Table 1.1, columns 8-11). Such, demanding work requirements may be leading to more stress-related working conditions and thus having more individuals seeking disability benefits as a way of escaping rising demands at work.[3] Evidence from theoretical and empirical work on occupational health indicates that attention should be paid to the effect of psychosocial factors at work. Psychological demands may include features such as overwork or unrealistic deadlines and might be

Table 1.1. Work-related stress increases with higher work intensity and lower work satisfaction

Percentage of workers reporting specific working conditions and work-related stress, selected European countries, levels in 2005 and trends (percentage changes) 1995-2005

	Panel A. Percentage of employed persons reporting specific working conditions, 2005 and changes since 1995[a]							Panel B. Share of respondents reporting stress at work, according to various working conditions, 2005[b]					
	1. Job involves working at very high speed		2. Job involves working to tight deadlines		3. Satisfied with working conditions in the job		Overall	1. whether the job involves working at very high speed		2. whether the job involves working to tight deadlines		3. whether respondent is satisfied with working conditions in main paid job	
	Level	Trend	Level	Trend	Level	Trend		Yes	No	Yes	No	Yes	No
Austria	36	+++	32	---	89	=	21	31	14	36	14	16	49
Belgium	22	+	25	+++	88	=	22	34	18	37	16	16	59
Czech Rep.	21	+++	43	+++	79	=	16	27	12	20	8	12	23
Denmark	34	+++	35	+++	93	=	29	39	23	34	25	25	68
Finland	36	+	36	=	85	–	25	32	20	34	18	20	48
France	23	=	28	+	81	=	20	33	16	28	15	14	45
Germany	32	+++	27	=	88	=	16	28	10	29	11	12	40
Greece	37	+++	34	+++	57	–	58	67	52	68	54	46	73
Hungary	33	+	35	+++	74	–	26	44	16	36	19	21	40
Ireland	15	–	28	=	87	–	18	27	16	29	11	14	40
Italy	24	+	19	+	76	–	26	42	20	39	23	20	43
Luxembourg	23	+++	25	+++	86	–	30	44	25	42	25	25	60
Netherlands	19	---	25	–	88	=	18	29	15	27	14	12	56
Norway	36		30		93		28	39	21	41	24	26	49
Poland	19	---	24	+++	79	+	36	47	32	48	29	33	45
Portugal	15	---	19	+	85	=	26	31	24	36	22	23	41
Slovakia	21	---	22	+++	79	+	19	33	15	31	15	16	31
Spain	23	+	23	+++	81	=	39	56	31	60	32	34	68
Sweden	34	+++	30	+	85	–	32	49	26	48	26	26	51
Switzerland	25		25		92		18	27	15	31	14	15	52
Turkey	39		41		56		35	41	30	40	29	22	49
United Kingdom	19	–	36	–	92	+	12	18	10	20	6	9	44
OECD22	27		29		82		26	37	21	37	20	21	49
OECD19	26	+	29	+	83	=							

a) "+++" denotes an increase of more than 20%; "+" 5-20% increase; "=" changes between –5% and +5%; "–" more than 5% decrease; "---" more than 20% decrease. For Czech Republic, Hungary, Poland and Slovak Republic trends refer to the period 2000-05; the interpretation of +/– signs is adjusted accordingly ("+++" denotes an increase of more than 10%).

b) Don't knows/refusal are omitted from calculations. Figures shown are the percentage reporting stress at work of those with (yes) or without (no) demanding or satisfying working conditions.

Source: OECD calculations based on various waves of the European Working Conditions Survey from the European Foundation for the Improvement of Living and Working Conditions.

aggravated by job insecurity because uncertainty about the stability of one's job is also associated with stress (Ferrie *et al.*, 2002, 2005; *Siegrist, 1996*).

Indeed, one major explanation for the increasing number of inflows into disability benefits on grounds of mental health conditions can be attributed to changes in the workplace that have increased the prevalence of work-related stress. For example, recent longitudinal evidence for selected countries presented in OECD (2008) shows that employees, who change from standard to "non-standard" employment – measured by the type of contract or working hours – generally experience a decline in their mental well-being. However, the same study also shows that employees are better off in terms of mental health than inactives and unemployed: Mental health tends to deteriorate significantly when people leave employment and improve again when people move back into employment (see Annex Figures 1.A2.1 and 1.A2.2).[4]

The impact of the economy on labour market outcomes for people with disability

The role of the business cycle

The recent deep recession and its associated and still ongoing jobs crisis are likely to worsen labour market opportunities for people with disability. Evidence suggests that their employment rates are more adversely affected during economic downturns. Results from country-specific analysis show that a recession hits people with disability harder than people without disability. Burkhauser *et al.* (2001), for example, examined the relative outcomes of workers with disability over the business cycles of the 1980s and the 1990s in the United States and concluded that employment fell more for people with disability than for those without disability. Similarly, for the United Kingdom, Balloch *et al.* (1985) showed that employment opportunities for people with disability decreased during the recession of the 1980s.

Calculations by the OECD Secretariat, based on data for Europe for the period 1994-2001,[5] suggest that, while having a disability reduces the employment chances significantly at any phase of the business cycle (by 19% for men and by 12% for women, Table 1.2, first row), a larger output gap further contributes to lower employment opportunities for individuals with disability than for those without (see Box 1.1 for technical details, including on the definition of the output gap). Indeed, when economic output falls, for men in general the

Table 1.2. **The impact of the business cycle on employment of people with disability is small compared with the effect of disability itself**

Regression results: impact of a 1 percentage-point increase in the output gap on employment levels in general and the additional disadvantage for people with disability, percentages

	Employment effect	
	Men	Women
Effect of having a disability	−19.03	−11.94
	(0.000)***	(0.000)***
Overall impact of the output gap change on people with disability	−1.12	−2.01
Of which:		
Impact of output gap change on all individuals	−0.72	−1.15
	(0.000)***	(0.000)***
Additional impact of the output gap change on those with disability	−0.39	−0.86
	(0.001)***	(0.000)***

*** Significant at 1% level. The output gap is the percentage difference between potential and actual output.

Source: OECD calculations based on ECHP 1994-2001.

probability of being employed decreases by 0.7% for each percentage-point increase in the output gap, plus another 0.4% if it is a worker with a disability. The overall impact of the economic cycle on the employment rate of men with disability would, therefore, be 1.1% (Table 1.2, second row). This is a relatively small effect compared with the 19% impact on the employment rate stemming from having a disability. The impact of the economic cycle on women with disability is roughly twice as much as for their male counterparts.

Box 1.1. How labour market outcomes of workers with disability are affected by the economic cycle

The following model has been estimated pooling all the countries' observations together to assess the potential impact of economic conditions on labour market outcomes of people with disability;

$$Pr(e_{ijt} = 1 | X_{ijt}) = \Phi (X_{ijt}\alpha + gap_{jt}\beta + disab_{ijt}\lambda + gap_{jt}{}^*disab_{ijt}\delta + country)_j + \varepsilon_{ijt}$$

where i, j, and t are the respective individual's, time and country's notations; e is a dummy variable coded as one if the person is employed (the same equation is used if the individual is unemployed). This implies that the probability of being employed or unemployed is a function of a set of controls X (including demographic variables and educational attainment) and of the output gap of the country interacted with a disability variable. The latter is set at 1 if the person reports having any chronic physical or mental health problem, illness or disability, and 0 otherwise. The output gap, or GDP gap, is defined as the percentage difference between potential output or GDP and actual output or GDP (a positive output gap indicates a situation where the growth of *aggregate demand* is outpacing the growth of *aggregated supply*).

The parameter δ captures the additional effect of the economic cycle on the employment (unemployment) probability of persons with disability as compared with those without disability. Countries fixed effects have been included in order to exclude country-specific effects (*e.g.* institutional factors and other unobservable variables). The parameters have been estimated using the full ECHP sample for the 1994-2001 period.

Policy lessons from past crises

The pressures to mitigate the short-run labour market effects of the crisis increase the risk that governments might repeat the policy mistakes of the past. Indeed, past episodes of recessions point to several useful insights. Figure 1.7 shows the trends in disability benefit and unemployment rates and the peak recession years in selected OECD countries. Three main conclusions can be drawn from these charts.

At the onset of a recession, disability beneficiary rates tend to increase.... Virtually all recessions were initially associated with increases in both unemployment and – typically with some time lag – disability beneficiary rates. Compared to the cyclical fluctuations of the unemployment rate, there is very little cyclical movement in disability beneficiary rates in all countries. In some countries, including Australia and the United Kingdom, the recession of the 1980s had a very significant impact on the disability beneficiary rate.[6]

... but even when economic growth resumes, many people do not move off disability benefit rolls. Disability beneficiary rates did not drop again during the subsequent economic expansion, when job growth was substantial and unemployment was falling rapidly. With fewer job opportunities, more people are likely to resort to disability benefits in economic downturns, while the low exit rates from those benefits induce "ratchet" effects by which benefit rolls remain at a higher structural level after each period of high inflows resulting from an economic downturn.

Figure 1.7. Following the peak of a recession, disability benefit recipiency rates tend to increase

Long-run trends in unemployment and disability recipiency rates in 11 OECD countries, 1970-2008

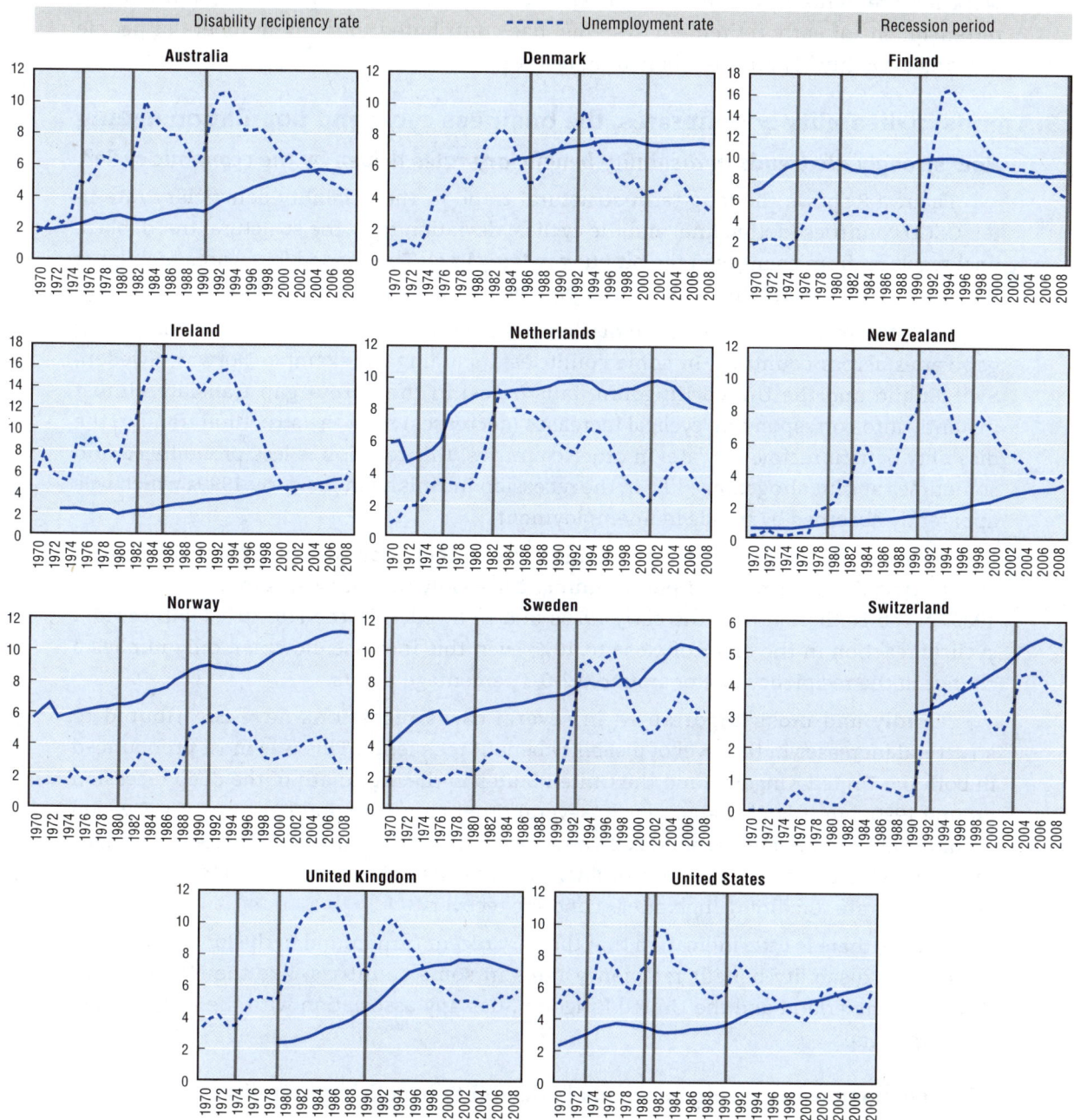

Source: OECD calculations based on data provided by national authorities and *OECD Economic Outlook 2009.*

Disability can become a substitute to persistent long-term unemployment. When the economy picked up again and unemployment fell, many countries have seen a simultaneous rise in disability recipiency rates. It appears that in the past decades in many OECD countries labour market problems have gradually been shifted from unemployment to sickness and disability.[7] This can be explained to a certain extent by the inability of some of the long-term unemployed and discouraged inactives to find employment when the economy is in boom, thus, to some extent reflecting "substitution" between benefit schemes. The relative generosity of disability programmes, as well as increasingly stricter work requirements in unemployment and social assistance programmes, and gradual retrenchment of early retirement systems, has contributed to rising numbers of people drawing disability benefits as a benefit of last resort.[8]

1.3. Trends in disability benefit rates, the business cycle and population ageing

How strongly are trends in disability beneficiary rates driven by the economic cycle?

Figure 1.8 shows the long-term structural trend of the disability beneficiary rate in ten OECD countries (dotted line) and the cyclical deviation from the structural trend (black line) resulting from changes in the output gap (grey line). The shaded (blue) area highlights the duration of a recession (peak-to-trough). The following findings emerge.

First, the responsiveness of the disability rate with respect to changes in the output gap varies across countries. In some countries, including for example Norway, Sweden, Switzerland and the United Kingdom, falls (rises) in the output gap translate almost instantly into corresponding cyclical increases (decreases) from the structural trend in the disability benefit recipiency rate. In other countries, this reaction is less pronounced and sometimes absent altogether – like in the recession in Finland in the early 1990s which was apparently absorbed by trends in unemployment.

Secondly, the impact of the economic cycle in most episodes and countries is very small, typically in the range of plus or minus 2-5%. Only the recessions in Ireland in 1979/1980, in the Netherlands in the early 1970s and in Sweden in the late 1970s witnessed a cyclical reaction in the order of close to 10%; even this increase, however, only implies a change in the recipiency rate of around 0.2-0.3 percentage points.

Thirdly and most importantly, in several cases recessions have contributed to structural increases in the level of disability benefit recipiency. This was most pronounced in both the United Kingdom and the United States in the aftermath of the deep recession around 1990, but it is also apparent in several other countries and episodes, *e.g.* Sweden around 2001, Switzerland around 2002 and New Zealand around 1998. Hence, recessions often translated into a structural problem for the disability benefits system, with the beneficiary rate remaining high after economic recovery.

Finally, there is little indication that the very recent turnaround in the long-term trend increase in disability benefit recipiency rates in some countries, like the Netherlands, Sweden, Switzerland and the United Kingdom, has any association with the variations in the output gap.

Effects of population ageing on trends in disability beneficiary numbers

Given that the business cycle explains so little of the overall trend, what else drives the trends in disability beneficiary rates? One other argument sometimes brought forward to explain the increasing number of people on disability benefits is population ageing. As

Figure 1.8. **The economic cycle is only one and often not the main factor explaining fluctuations in the disability beneficiary rate**

Structural trend increase in disability recipiency rates and cyclical deviations from the trend caused by output gap changes, 1970-2008

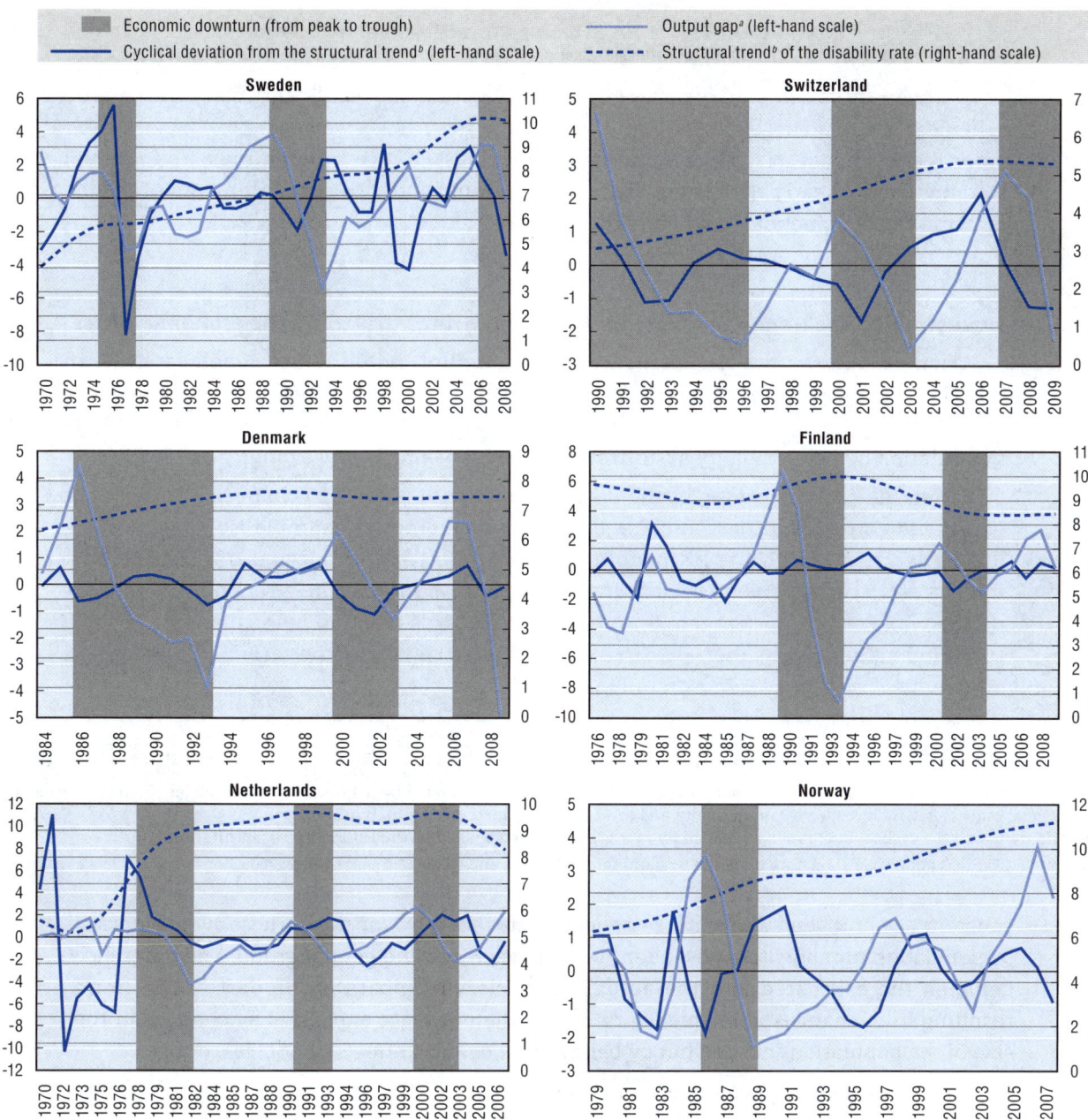

shown below, in all OECD countries disability prevalence increases strongly with age: People aged 50-64 years have more than twice the probability of reporting a chronic health problem or disability than the total working-age population (Figure 1.9). Other things being equal, a higher share of people over age 50 among the working-age population should therefore translate into higher disability beneficiary rates.

The "pure" effect of ageing is explored by comparing actual beneficiary trends with an estimated historical beneficiary series for each country, which is obtained by multiplying

Figure 1.8. **The economic cycle is only one and often not the main factor explaining fluctuations in the disability beneficiary rate** (*cont.*)

Structural trend increase in disability recipiency rates and cyclical deviations from the trend caused by output gap changes, 1970-2008

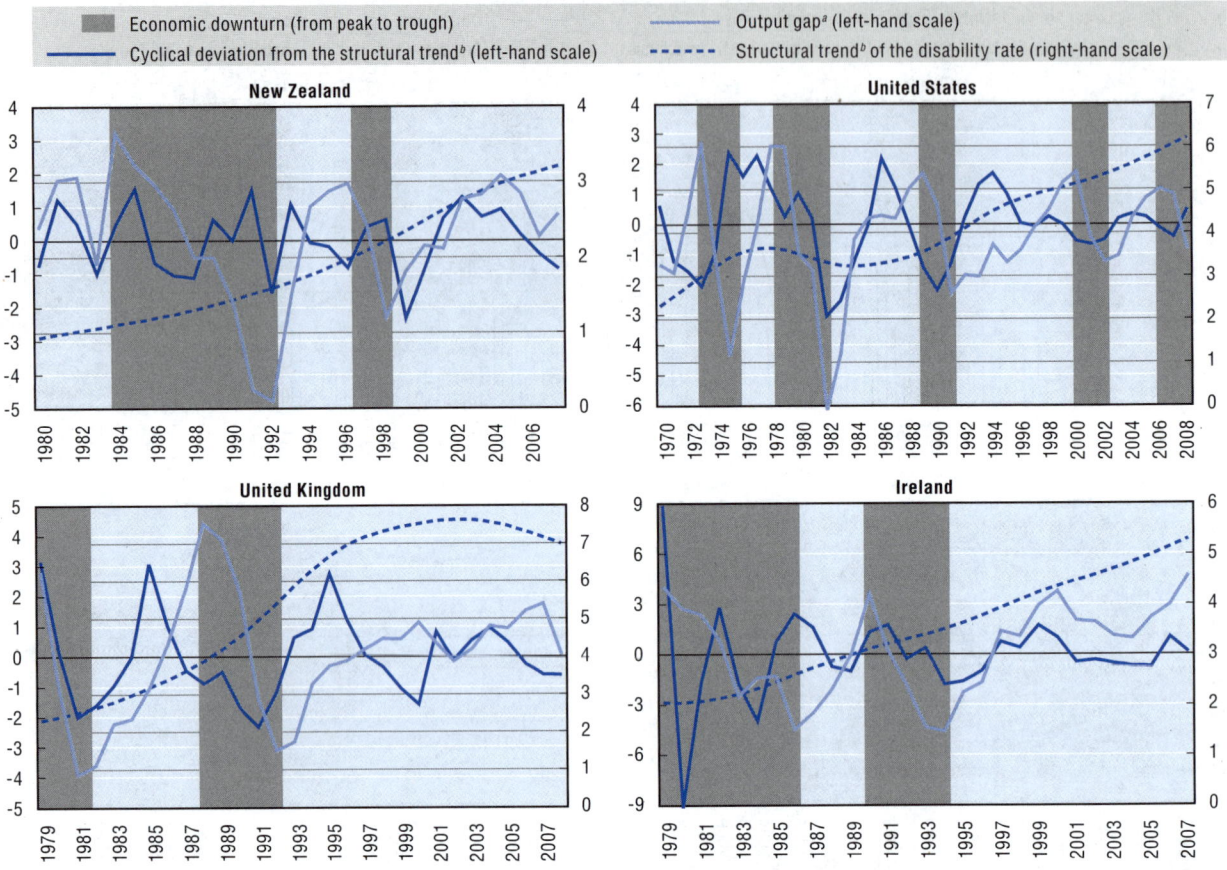

a) The gap is expressed as a percentage of potential output. This latter is calculated by means of a Cobb-Douglas production function, with labour, capital, their respective productivity and total factor productivity as function's inputs.

b) The trend and the cyclical fluctuations of disability rate have been established by the Hodrick-Prescott filter.

Source: OECD calculations based on data provided by national authorities and *OECD Economic Outlook 2009.*

constant age and gender-specific beneficiary rates for 1990 (or the earliest available year) by population numbers for subsequent years in each age and gender group. The difference between the estimated and the actual beneficiary numbers is the part of the trend resulting from changes in recipiency rates and therefore not explained by changes in the size of the population "at risk" but by behavioural change, effects of policies, or both.

In half of the OECD countries, only a small part of the strong increase in disability beneficiaries in the past decades can be explained by changes in the population age structure (Figure 1.10, Panel A). The annual average growth rate of disability beneficiaries was typically three times higher than the growth in the size of the population at risk, caused by the relatively larger increase in the number of older workers with a higher risk of becoming disabled.

In the other half of the countries, actual beneficiary trends diverged very sharply from the continuously increasing disability beneficiary trends projected for the past one to two decades by demographic change alone (Figure 1.10, Panel B). In most of these countries, beneficiary numbers are now lower – sometimes much lower – than could have

Figure 1.9. **Disability prevalence increases sharply with age which is critical in view of population ageing**

Self-assessed disability[a] prevalence, as a percentage of the population, by age group, late-2000s

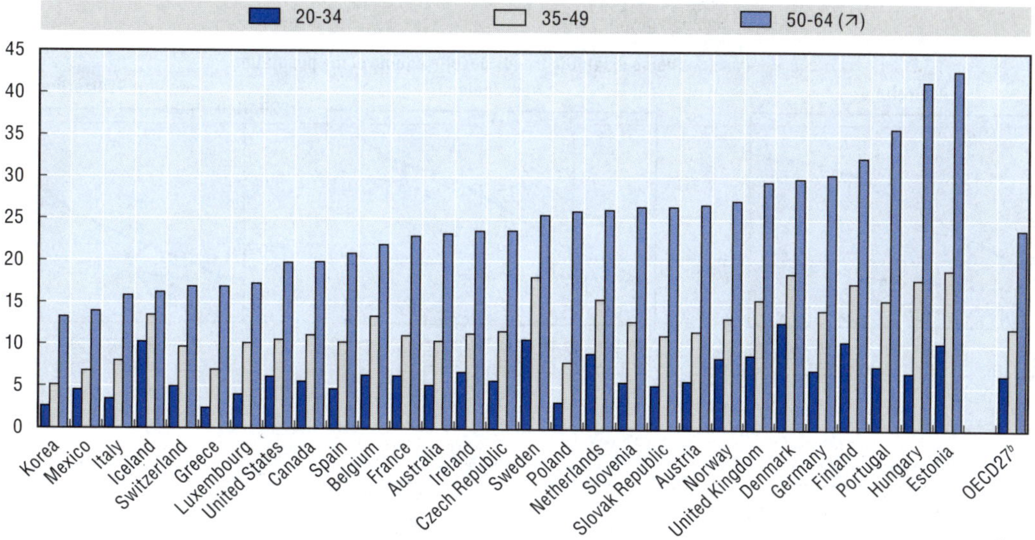

a) See definitions of self-assessed disability in Figure 1.1.

b) OECD27 refers to an unweighted average for 27 countries. Estonia and Slovenia are not included in the OECD average.

Source: See Figure 1.1.

expected otherwise. In several cases, including Finland, Luxembourg, the Netherlands, Poland, Portugal and the United Kingdom, increases in beneficiary numbers went hand-in-hand with population trends for a while before falling sharply, in response to policy reform. In some countries, such as Canada, Mexico and Spain, observed trends were consistently flatter than projected by ageing of the working-age population.

1.4. Conclusion

The economic and social context in which disability policy operates has evolved rapidly during the past decade. These changes are creating both opportunities and challenges for people with disability across OECD countries. The argument is twofold. On the one hand, the shrinking and ageing populations projected for most OECD countries over the coming decades mean that increasing labour force participation rates among people with disability will be important in securing future labour supply. On the other hand, changes in technology and globalisation may have affected labour markets in ways that are further deteriorating the employment prospects for people with disability and contributing to the high disability beneficiary caseloads in OECD countries.

At the same time, it appears that both the business cycle and population ageing can only explain a small part of observed trends in beneficiary numbers. In most countries, changes in labour supply and labour demand factors dominated. Nevertheless, employment opportunities for people with disability tend to drop significantly during economic downturns and do not recover in the subsequent recoveries. These findings highlight the importance of reforms aimed at promoting the participation of people with disability in the labour market. The remainder of this report addresses the policy reforms needed to achieve this.

Figure 1.10. **Demography explains only some of the change in disability beneficiary trends**

Disability beneficiaries, actual and estimated numbers, 1990-2008 (index: earliest year = 100)

Estimated numbers are based on constant age and gender-specific beneficiary rates[a] in each country

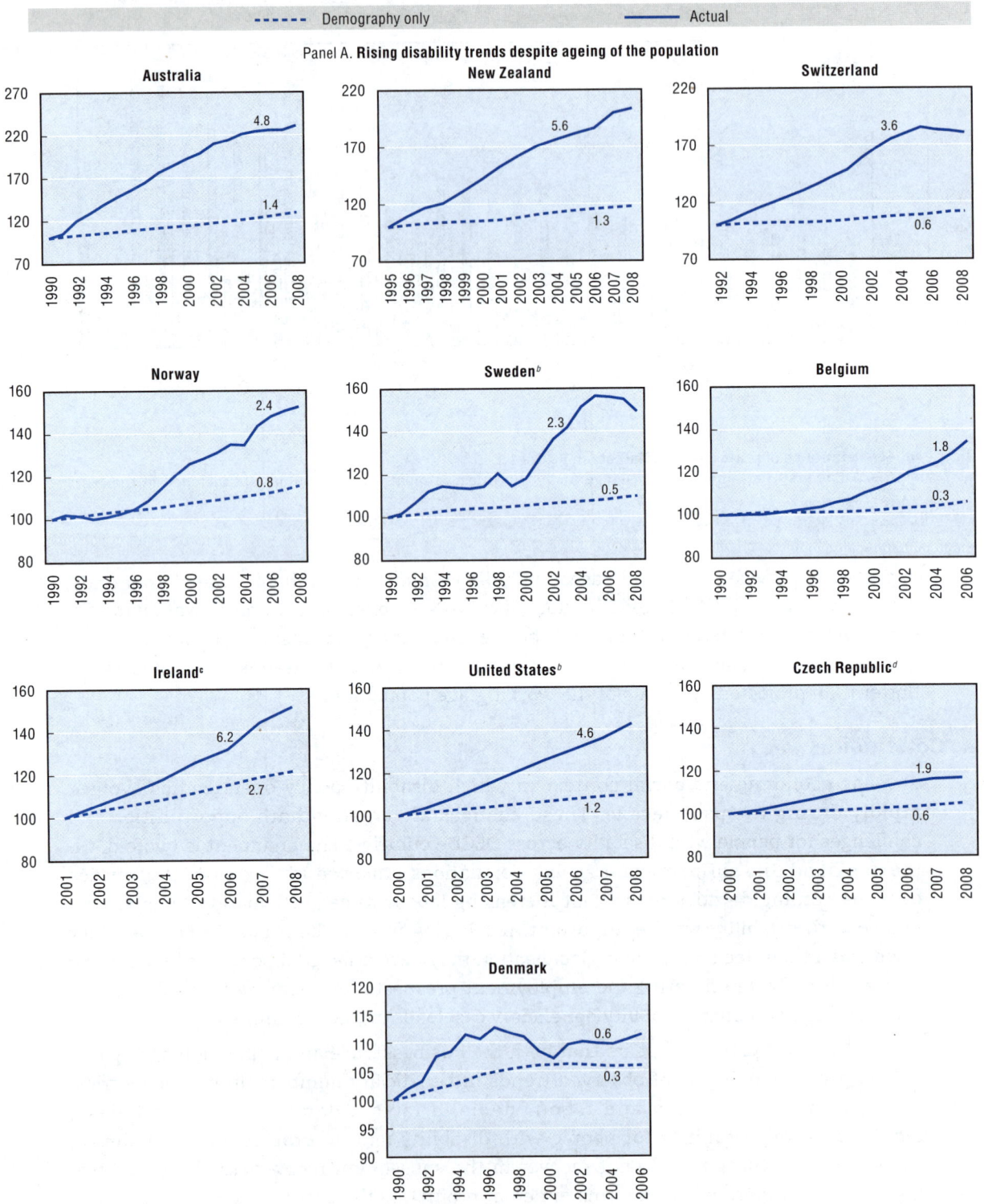

Figure 1.10. **Demography explains only some of the change in disability beneficiary trends** (*cont.*)

Disability beneficiaries, actual and estimated numbers, 1990-2008 (index: earliest year = 100)

Estimated numbers are based on constant age and gender-specific beneficiary rates^a in each country

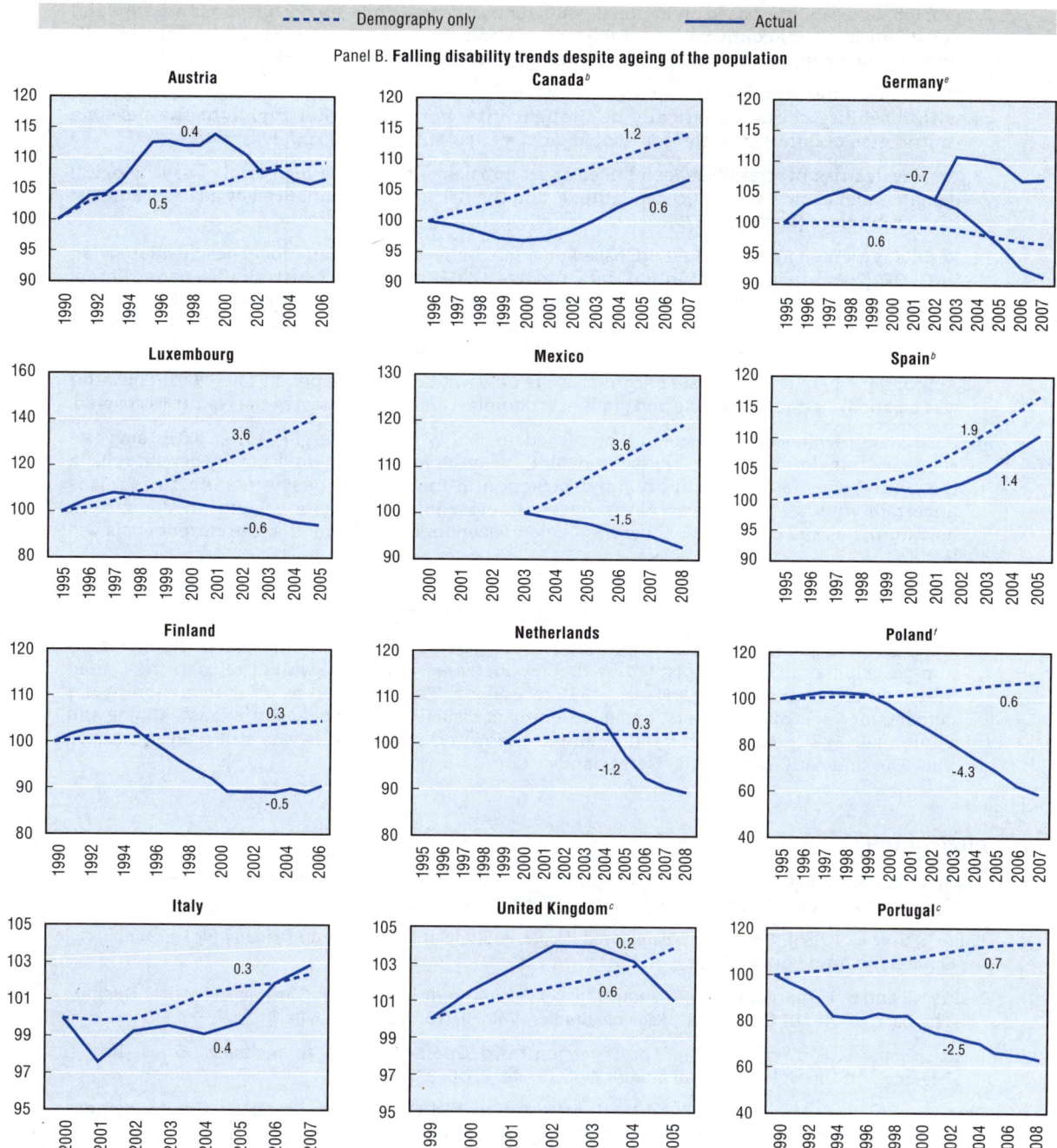

Note: The numbers shown in the charts give the average annual growth rates over the period in question.

a) The dotted lines labelled "demography only" show estimated numbers of beneficiaries under the assumption of constant age- and gender-specific beneficiary rates; the solid lines show the actual number of beneficiaries. Data refer to the age group 20-64, with the exception of Denmark which covers ages 18-64.

b) Contributory pension only for Canada (with a shift during this period from contributory to non-contributory benefits), Spain, Sweden and the United States.

c) Both contributory and non-contributory pensions for Ireland, Portugal and the United Kingdom.

d) The Czech Republic includes both full and partial pensions.

e) German projections are based on total population and not by gender. The thin black line excludes social assistance for persons with reduced earning capacity (GRUSI).

f) Poland covers the FUS scheme only.

Source: OECD Population Database and beneficiary data from National Insurance Administrations.

Notes

1. The population with disability – disability prevalence – is identified through *self-assessment* (people reporting that their activities of daily living are hampered by a long-standing or chronic health problem or disability), based on national population surveys. While survey questions are similar if not identical, cross-country comparability is restricted due to the subjective element of self-reporting and cultural differences in the interpretation of the questions (see Annex 1.A1).

2. These illustrative scenarios do not argue for what proportion of women, older workers and people with disability could realistically be brought into work but rather highlight the possible contribution of different underrepresented groups to potential labour supply growth.

3. An elevated risk of stress has been linked to an imbalance between a high level of psychological demands and a low level of decision latitude, and the risk is further enhanced by a lack of support in the workplace (Karasek, 1979).

4. Results presented in Annex 1.A2 are based on a fixed-effects regression model described in detail in OECD (2008) using longitudinal data for five OECD countries (Australia, Canada, Korea, Switzerland and the United Kingdom). Controlling for individual factors, the analysis finds strong similarity in outcomes across countries in terms of the mental-health improving effect of employment. In all countries, effects are larger for men than for women.

5. Appropriate data for a larger set of countries are only available for the period 1994-2001. The latter was a period of relatively strong and gradual economic expansion in most of the countries covered.

6. Case study evidence, such as that presented in Beatty and Fothergill (1996, 2005), suggests economic transformation is a key factor behind the observed increase in disability benefit rolls in the United Kingdom, particularly job destruction in mining and heavy manufacturing. It is uncertain whether job destruction in heavy industry is as important a factor in the current downturn; it is still too early to know what kind of economic transformation the current crisis will lead to.

7. Norwegian researchers estimated that enterprise closures and downsizing account for some 30% of the total inflow into permanent disability benefits (Rege *et al.*, 2009; Bratsberg, *et al.*, 2010).

8. Autor and Duggan (2003), for example, argue that increased flows onto disability, and increased non-participation, can be explained by the low increases in unemployment rates in the United States during and after the 1980 and 1991 recessions. This followed a "clear reduction in the demand for low-skilled workers, and a loosening of disability insurance restrictions". Kooing and Vuuren (2006) suggest that hidden unemployment in disability rolls was still relevant during the 1990s and early 2000s in the Netherlands.

Bibliography

Autor, D. and M. Duggan (2003), "The Rise in the Disability Rolls and the Decline in Unemployment", *Quarterly Journal of Economics*, Vol. 118, No. 1, February, pp. 157-206.

Balloch, S. *et al.* (1985), *Caring for Unemployed People. A Study of the Impact on Demand for Personal Social Services*, Bedford Square Press, London.

Beatty, C. and S. Fothergill (1996), "Labour Market Adjustment in Areas of Chronic Industrial Decline: The Case of the UK Coalfields", *Regional Studies*, Vol. 30, No. 7, pp. 627-640.

Beatty, C. and S. Fothergill (2005), "The Diversion from 'Unemployment' to 'Sickness' Across British Regions and Districts", *Regional Studies*, Vol. 39, No. 7, pp. 837-854.

Bratsberg, B., E. Fevang and K. Røed (2010), "Disability and the Welfare State: An Unemployment Problem in Disguise?", *IZA Discussion Paper*, No. 4897, Institute for the Study of Labour, Bonn.

Burkhauser, R., M. Daly, A. Houtenville and N. Nargis (2001), "The Employment of Working-Age people with Disabilities in the 1980s and 1990s: What current data can and cannot tell us", *Working Paper in Applied Economic Theory*, No. 2001-20, Federal Reserve Bank of San Francisco.

Ferrie, J.E., M.J. Shipley, S. Stansfeld and M. Marmot (2002), "Effects of Chronic Job Insecurity and Change in Job Security on Self-reported Health, Minor Psychiatric Morbidity, Physiological Measures and Health-related Behaviours in British Civil Servants: The Whitehall II Study", *Epidemiology and Community Health*, Vol. 56, No. 6, pp. 450-454.

Ferrie, J.E., M.J. Shipley, K. Newman, S.A. Stansfeld and M. Marmot (2005), "Self-reported Job Insecurity and Health in the Whitehall II Study: Potential Explanations of the Relationship", *Social Science and Medicine,* Vol. 60, No. 7, pp. 1593-1602.

Johansson, P. and P. Skedinger (2005), "Are Objective, Official Measures of Disability Reliable?", *IFAU Working Paper*, No. 2005-14, Institute for Labour Market Policy Evaluation, Uppsala.

Karasek, R. (1979), "Job Demands, Job Decision Latitude and Mental Strain: Implications for Job Redesign", *Administrative Science Quarterly*, Vol. 24, pp. 285-306.

Kooing, P. and D. Vuuren (2006), *Disability and Unemployment Insurance as substitute pathways*, An empirical analysis based on Employer Data, Netherlands Bureau for Economic Policy Analysis.

OECD (2006), *Ageing and Employment policies: Live Longer, Work Longer*, OECD Publishing, Paris.

OECD (2007), *OECD Employment Outlook,* Chapter 3, OECD Publishing, Paris.

OECD (2008), *OECD Employment Outlook,* Chapter 4, OECD Publishing, Paris.

Rege, M., K. Telle and M. Votruba (2009), "The Effect of Plant Downsizing on Disability Pension Utilisation", *Journal of the European Economic Association*, Vol. 7, No. 5, pp. 754-785.

Siegrist, J. (1996), "Adverse Health Effects of High-effort/Low-reward Conditions", *Journal of Occupational Health Psychology,* Vol. 1, pp. 27-41.

ANNEX 1.A1

Defining and Measuring Disability

Identifying disability is not straightforward. In contrast to the contingency "unemployment", for instance (which is defined as "not having a job but searching and being available for work"), disability status is rarely dichotomous and much more a matter of degree. Much like the concept of social exclusion, disability is understood as a multidimensional and dynamic phenomenon, including the person's physical and/or mental impairments, the functional limitations arising from them and the interaction with the society and the environment – as reflected in WHO's International Classification of Functioning and Disability (ICF). Distinguishing the four layers of this classification – impairment, functional limitation, resulting handicap and, lastly, supportive and protective factors – is not easy and not always possible. Definitions of disability often mix these concepts in different ways.

Disability can be defined or measured in two different ways: as a *self-assessed* status or a *legal* status based on administrative definitions, *e.g.* benefit eligibility. Often, and perhaps inaccurately so, these two definitions are referred to as "subjective" *versus* "objective" disability. Both subjective and objective disability may be reported in error. This is plausible in the case of self-assessed disability: Responses may, *inter alia*, depend on employment or benefit outcomes one wishes to explain. However, administrative records may also be reported with bias – as has, for example, been shown for Sweden by Johansson and Skedinger (2005), who find systematic over-reporting of disability in administrative data, explained by incentives for caseworkers to inflate their placement success.

No one of the above disability definitions and measures is "superior" to the others; their use depends on the topic being investigated (*e.g.* benefit expenditures *versus* income adequacy), but occasionally also on data availability. Throughout the report, several of the measures are analysed. In general, when mention is made of "disability prevalence", this refers to self-reported disability status, while "disability benefit recipiency" (or new disability benefit claims) is calculated from administrative records. Other legal definitions – such as those used in several countries to determine eligibility for certain types of in-kind benefits, including to count for the mandatory disability employment quota – are not used.

Self-assessed disability status is measured via household surveys. Assessment is generally based on answers to questions concerning the "existence of long-lasting health problems or disability which limits daily life activities", thus, largely following the functional impairment level of the ICF classification. The exact formulation of the question used in different countries and surveys, however, will often vary. "Long-lasting", for instance, is usually defined as a problem lasting at least 12 months, but in some cases six months are used as a threshold.

Benefit recipiency status is usually measured through administrative records but in some cases also through population surveys. The latter estimates are used for linking benefit information with labour force and income information. Results between the two sources are likely to differ, for at least two main reasons: Administrative records typically count *cases* rather than *persons*, which in a situation of multiple benefits can lead to double counting. On the other hand, surveys are based on responses on benefit status, which some people may not wish to reveal.

Benefit recipiency status is a stricter definition than disability prevalence, because it goes beyond a person's functional limitation. It also takes some of the social and environmental context into account, as it is generally based on the reduction in a person's work or earnings ability. As such, it aims but often fails to take into account that the same degree of "biological" difference does not necessarily imply the same degree of disability or disadvantage or work capacity reduction.

Disability benefit recipiency figures in this report reflect the aggregate of all disability benefits granted under contributory and non-contributory schemes (with Belgium, Canada, France, Germany, Greece, Ireland, Japan, Korea, Poland, Portugal, Spain, the United Kingdom and the United States having both types of schemes), full and partial disability benefits, as well as early retirement schemes specific to disability or reduced work capacity (the latter exist in Austria, Denmark, Finland and Germany). Non-contributory schemes also include regular social assistance schemes provided these schemes have a specific disability component (as is the case, for instance, in Canada and the United Kingdom). To improve comparability across countries, persons receiving sickness benefits for more than two years are also counted towards disability benefit recipiency (which matters for Ireland, New Zealand and Sweden). Where persons can receive more than one disability benefit, the overlap has been taken into account where possible.

Not included in the disability benefit recipiency figures used in this report, largely due to data limitations, are recipients of *i)* workers' compensation schemes; *ii)* private disability insurance benefits; and *iii)* special disability benefit systems for civil servants (which exist *e.g.* in Austria, Belgium, France and Germany). The varying importance across countries of these types of benefits poses some limitations on the comparability of the resulting beneficiary figures.

ANNEX 1.A2

Additional Supporting Evidence

Figure 1.A2.1. **Leaving employment leads to higher mental distress...**

Fixed-effects regressions[a, b]

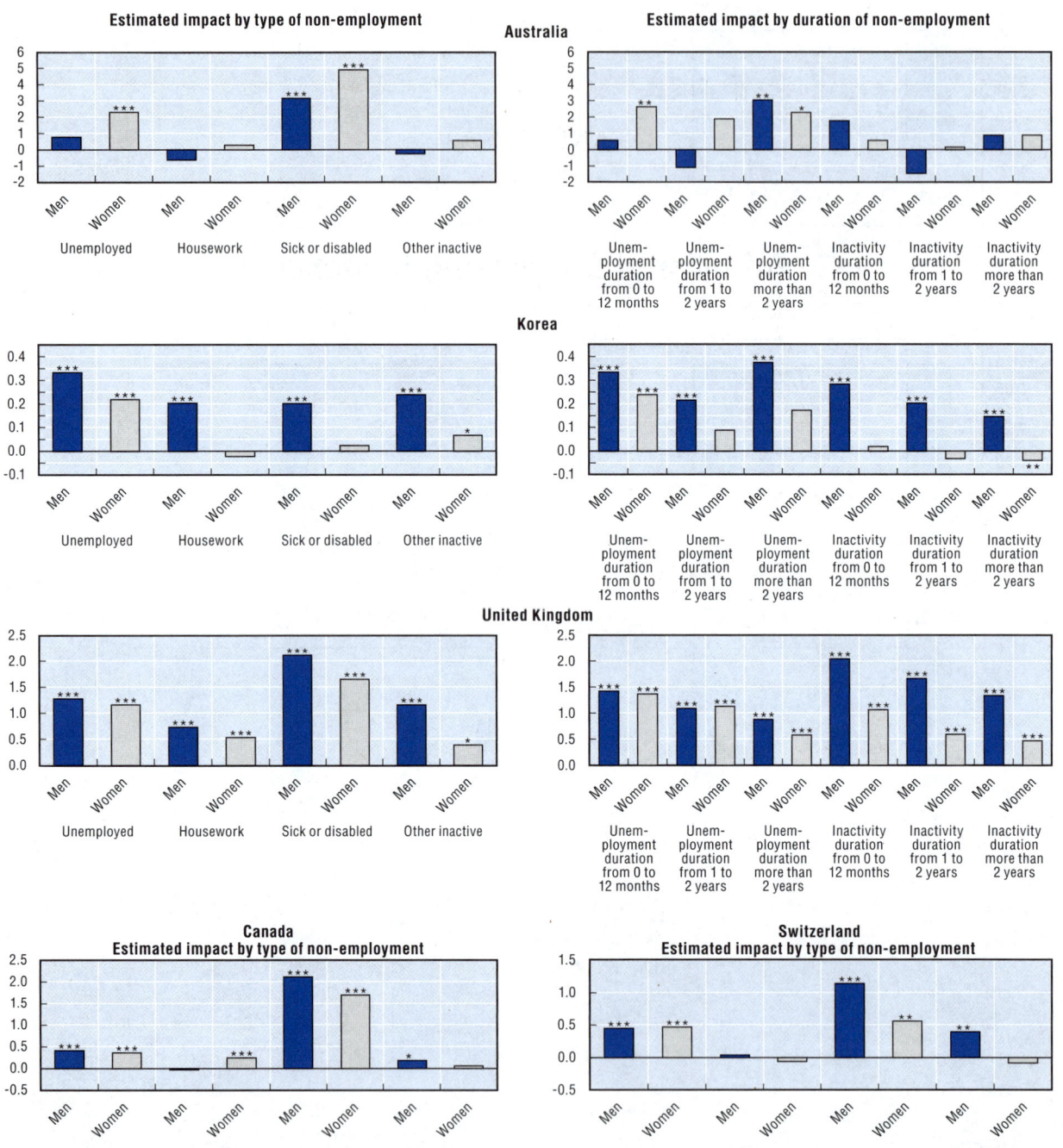

*, **, *** statistically significant at the 10%, 5%, and 1% level, respectively.

a) Sample includes persons aged 15-64 who are never enrolled in school or retired during the period analysed of the survey.

b) Regressions including controls for life events except for Korea.

Source: OECD estimates based on the HILDA for Australia; the NPHS for Canada; the KLIPS for Korea; the SHP for Switzerland; and the BHPS for the United Kingdom. See *OECD Employment Outlook 2008* for details on the dependent and control variables.

Figure 1.A2.2. **... while finding a job results in improved mental health**

Fixed-effects regressions[a, b]

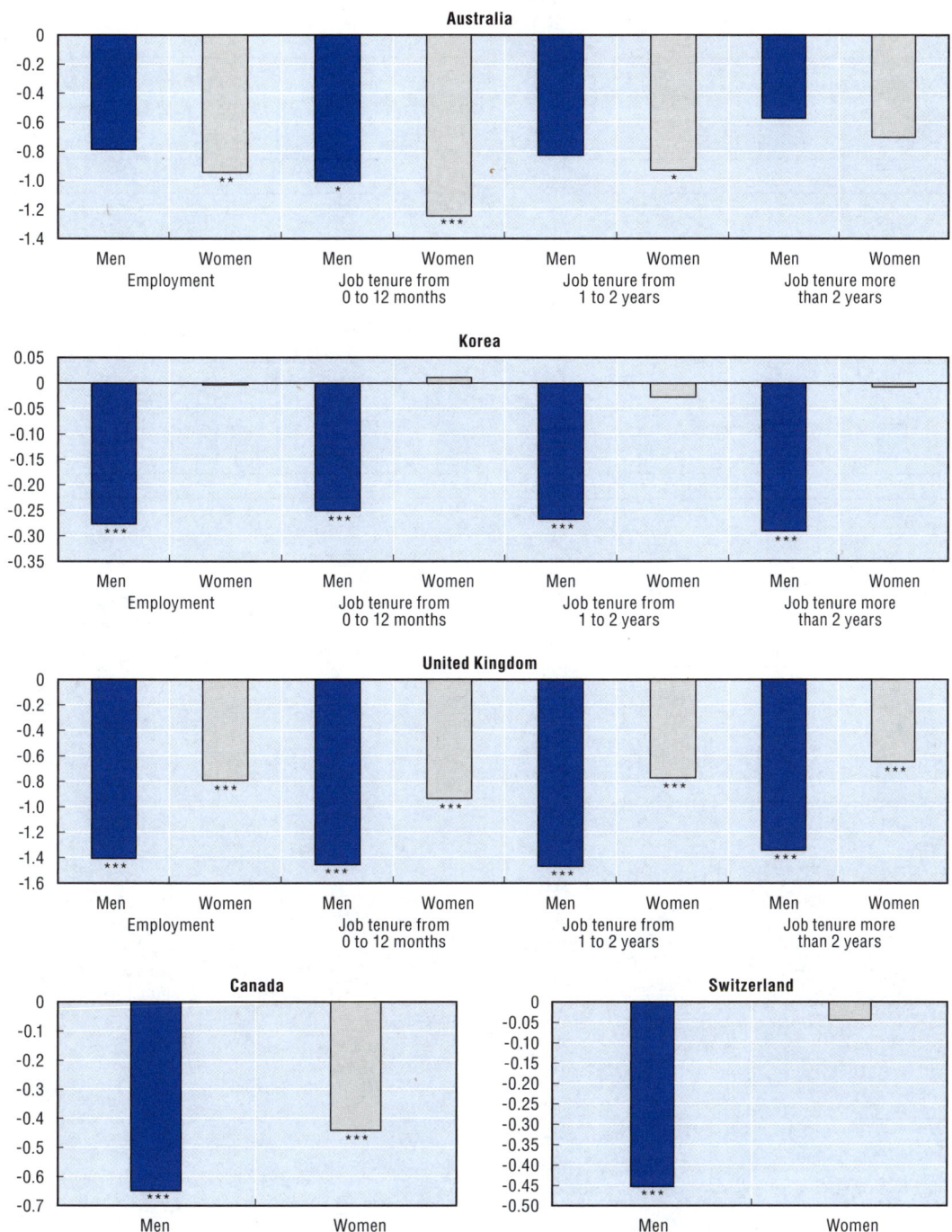

*, **, *** statistically significant at the 10%, 5%, and 1% level, respectively.

a) Sample includes persons aged 15-64 who are never enrolled in school or retired during the period analysed of the survey.

b) Regressions including controls for life events except for Korea.

Source: OECD estimates based on the HILDA for Australia; the NPHS for Canada; the KLIPS for Korea; the SHP for Switzerland; and the BHPS for the United Kingdom. See *OECD Employment Outlook 2008* for details on the dependent and control variables.

Chapter 2

Key Trends and Outcomes in Sickness and Disability

What are the main challenges policy makers across the OECD will need to address in the future? This chapter highlights the key outcomes and trends in the field of sickness and disability during the past 10-15 years, focusing on four areas: labour market integration of people with disability and workers with reduced work capacity; financial resources of those people; costs of sickness and disability benefits schemes; and beneficiary dynamics. It concludes that despite reforms and good economic conditions until recently, employment, unemployment, income and poverty outcomes have not improved for people with disability. Disability benefits have become the main working-age benefit in most countries and their role as a benefit of last resort is still increasing in many cases. However, outcomes also suggest that policy can have a large influence on beneficiary developments: Several countries have recently seen a promising turnaround in beneficiary trends.

This chapter provides a summary of key sickness and disability trends across the OECD to illustrate the main challenges countries face in this area. Data in most countries refer to years prior to or at the very beginning of the recent economic downturn, which poses special challenges over and above those outlined below. Several of the outcomes are likely to worsen in the course of the crisis, at least temporarily, and – similar to what has happened in previous crises (see Chapter 1) – in some cases there is a risk for worsening outcomes in the short run to turn into longer-term structural problems. The key outcomes in the sickness and disability field include:

● the insufficient labour market integration of persons with disability;

● the poor financial resources of households with persons with disability;

● the high costs of sickness and disability benefit schemes to the public finances;

● the unfavourable dynamics lying behind high disability beneficiary numbers.

2.1. Insufficient labour market integration of people with disability

Lower employment

Having a job is fundamental to social inclusion, but employment opportunities of people with health problems or disability are limited. In the late-2000s, on average across the OECD their employment rates were just over 40% compared with 75% for people without disability (Figure 2.1). Employment rates of people with disability were highest in the Nordic countries, Mexico and Switzerland. Relative to their peers without disability, these rates were also comparatively high in Germany and Luxembourg. At the other end of the spectrum are Hungary, Ireland and Poland, with the lowest employment rates of people with disability in both absolute and relative terms.

Higher employment rates of people with disability are not systematically associated with a particular set of employment policies. For instance, higher rates are found in countries with a strong focus on vocational rehabilitation, with a mandatory employment quota, with other employer obligations and incentives or with widespread subsidised employment, but also where none of these provisions are in place.

Despite increased efforts to develop and expand employment integration measures, employment levels of people with disability have not improved. Relative to their peers without disability, on average employment rates of people with disability have even fallen below 60% since before the turn of the century. In other words, in most OECD countries individuals with health problems have not benefited to the same extent from increased growth and employment opportunities in the past decade. This is of great concern in view of the current jobs crisis which is likely to hit already vulnerable groups such as people with disability hardest.

Employment rates of people with mental illness are particularly low: By and large, only about one in four individuals reporting a mental health problem is in employment. In most countries this corresponds to around 40-70% of the rates for people with other health

Figure 2.1. Employment rates of people with disability are low and have been falling in many countries

Employment rates by disability status in the late-2000s (left axis) and trends in relative employment rates since the mid-1990s (people with disability over those without, right axis)

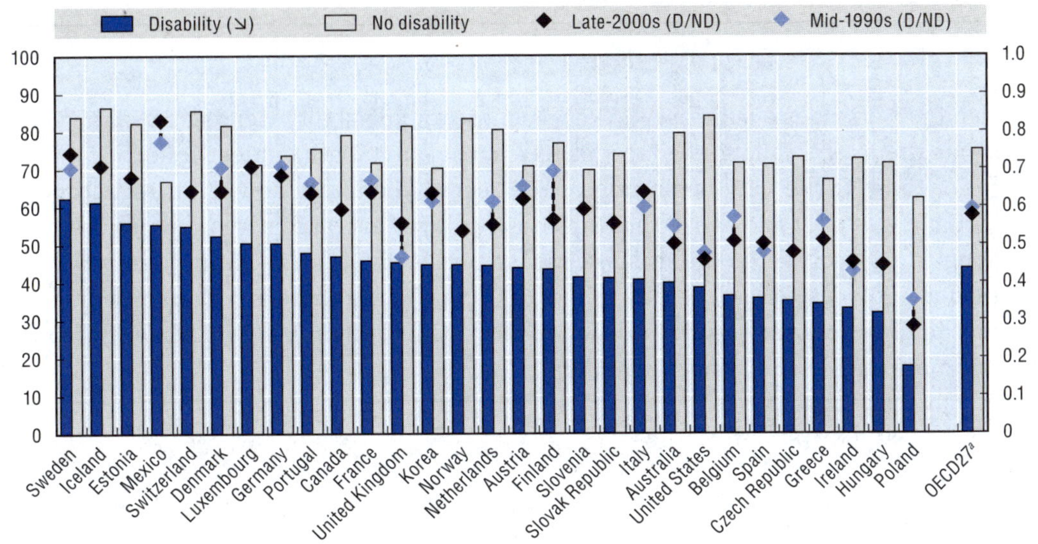

Note: Throughout (↘) in the legend indicates the variable according to which countries are ranked, in decreasing order. D/ND refers to the employment rate of people with disability relative to the employment rate of those without disability.

a) OECD27 refers to an unweighted average for 27 countries for employment rates and 19 countries for trends over roughly the past decade in relative employment rates. Estonia and Slovenia are not included in the OECD averages.

Source: EU-SILC 2007 (Wave 4) and ECHP 1995 (Wave 2), except: Australia: SDAC (Survey of Disability and Carers) 2003 and 1998; Canada: PALS (Participation and Activity Limitation Survey) 2006; Denmark: LFS 2005 and 1995; Finland: ECHP 1996; Korea: National Survey on Persons with Disabilities, 2005 and 1995; Mexico: ENESS (National Survey of Employment), 2004 and 1996; Netherlands: LFS 2006 and 1995; Norway: LFS 2005; Poland: LFS 2004 and 1996; Sweden: ECHP 1997; Switzerland: LFS 2008; United Kingdom: LFS 2006 and 1998; United States: SIPP (Survey of Income and Program Participation) 2008 and 1996.

conditions (Figure 2.2). This is striking in view of the large and increasing number of mild and moderate mental health problems which have become one of the biggest challenges for workplaces today.

Higher share of part-time work

Employment characteristics generally differ little by disability status over and above what could be expected from the lower average level of educational attainment of those with disability (see Chapter 1). For instance, people with disability seem to be represented relatively equally across industries as well as in the public sector; they tend to be self-employed to a similar degree; and they work in temporary jobs as frequently as people without disability.[1] However, in most OECD countries people with health problems are significantly more likely to work part-time (Figure 2.3). On average, almost one in four people do so compared with one in six or seven among those without disability. In Poland and Sweden, people with disability are even three times more likely to hold a part-time job. In a few countries, on the contrary, including e.g. Austria, Germany, Italy and Spain, the difference in part-time employment shares between people with and without disability is small.

Figure 2.2. **Employment rates of people with mental health conditions are particularly low**

Employment rates by health condition, as a ratio of the employment rate of all people with disability, 2002

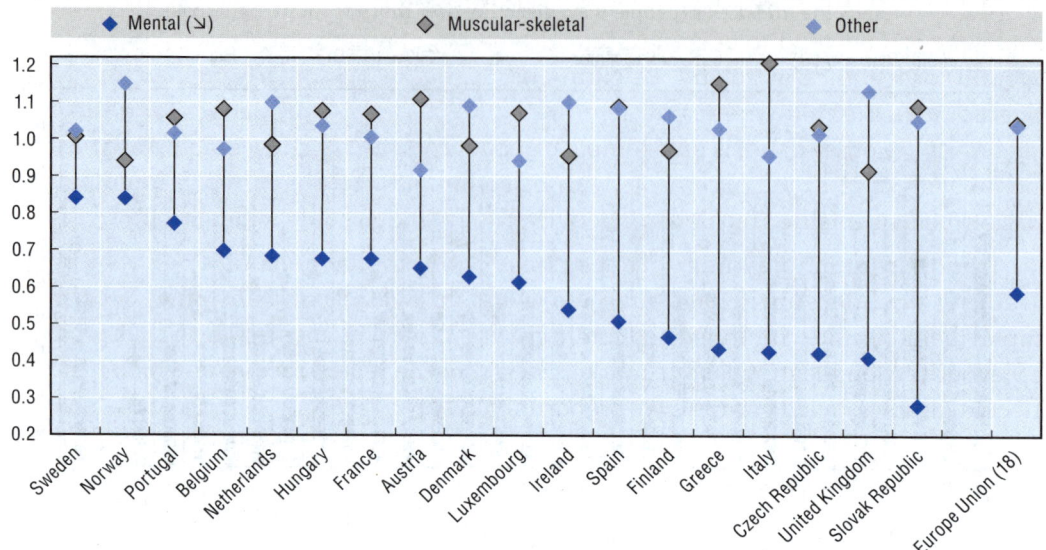

Source: European Labour Force Survey (2002), Ad-hoc module on employment of people with disability.

Figure 2.3. **When employed, people with disability work part-time more often than others**

Share of part-time employment^a in total employment by disability status in the late 2000s

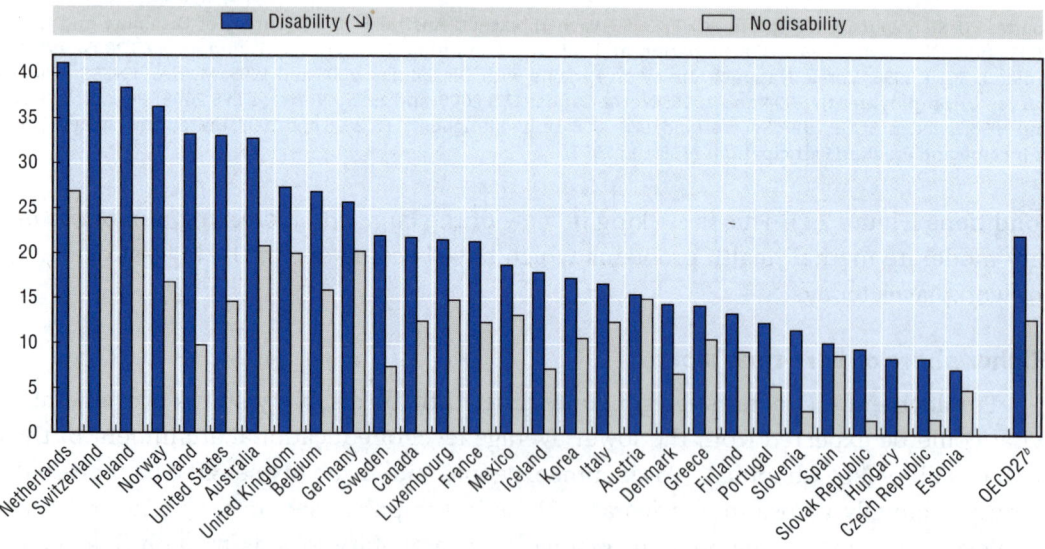

a) Part-time employment refers to persons who usually work less than 30 hours per week in their main job, except for the United States where it refers to persons who worked less than 35 hours all weeks in the previous month.
b) OECD27 refers to an unweighted average for 27 countries. Estonia and Slovenia are not included in the OECD average.

Source: EU-SILC 2007 (Wave 4), except: Australia: SDAC (Survey of Disability and Carers) 2003; Canada: PALS (Participation and Activity Limitation Survey) 2006; Korea: National Survey on Persons with Disabilities, 2005; Mexico: ENESS (National Survey of Employment), 2004; Norway: LFS 2005; Poland: LFS 2004; Switzerland: LFS 2008; United Kingdom: LFS 2006; United States: SIPP (Survey of Income and Program Participation) 2008.

Higher level of unemployment

At an OECD average of 14% in the mid-2000s, unemployment is typically twice as high for people with disability as for those without (Figure 2.4). Across countries, lower employment rates tend to be associated with higher unemployment risks. Such a pattern is found for instance in Poland, Belgium and Spain, while similarly Iceland and Mexico have both high employment and low unemployment rates of people with disability. Ireland, on the other hand, is an example of a country with both low employment and low unemployment rates among people with disability prior to the current economic crisis, possibly being explained by higher inactivity rates among people with disability.

Trends in unemployment are not steady: Unemployment rates of people with disability declined until 2000 but then went up again, hand-in-hand with falling employment, despite continued economic growth in most countries. This is not promising in view of the long-lasting labour-market impact of the recent recession which has so far affected disadvantaged groups over-proportionally.

Figure 2.4. **People with disability are twice as likely to be unemployed, even in good times**

Unemployment rates by disability status (left axis) and relative unemployment rates (people with disability over those without, right axis) in the late 2000s

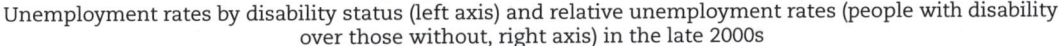

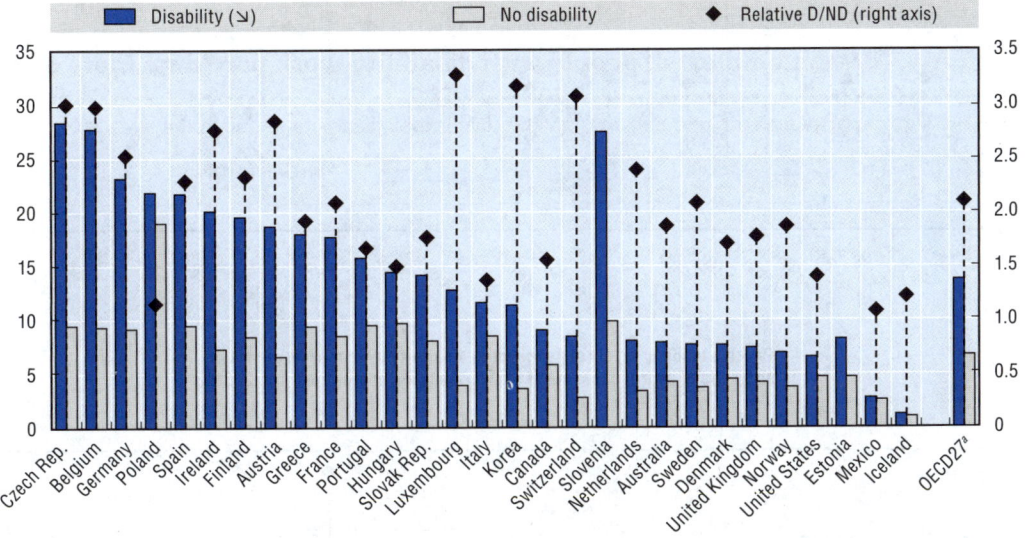

a) OECD refers to an unweighted average for 27 countries. Estonia and Slovenia are not included in the average.

Source: See sources for the mid-2000s in Figure 2.1.

2.2. Poor financial resources of people with disability

Lower disposable income

In most countries, people with health problems or disability have less financial resources. On average across the OECD, the income of people with disability is some 15% lower than the national average and as much as 20-30% in some countries (Figure 2.5, Panel A).[2] People with disability are in a particularly weak income position in English-speaking countries while in Nordic countries relative income differences are narrow (below 10%).

Figure 2.5. **Incomes of people with disability are relatively low, unless they are highly educated and have a job**

Panel A. **Trends in income^a levels of people with disability, as a ratio of average income of the working-age population**

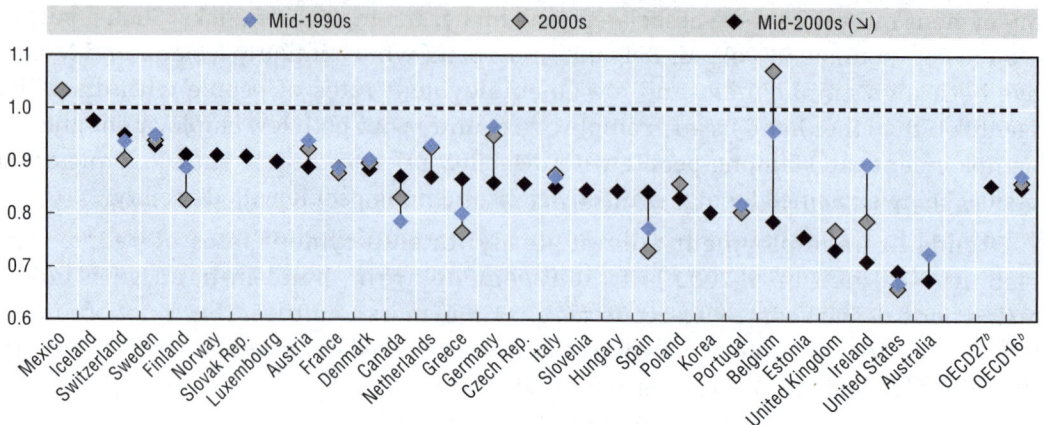

Panel B. **Income^a levels of people with disability by educational attainment, as a ratio of average income of the working-age population, mid-2000s**

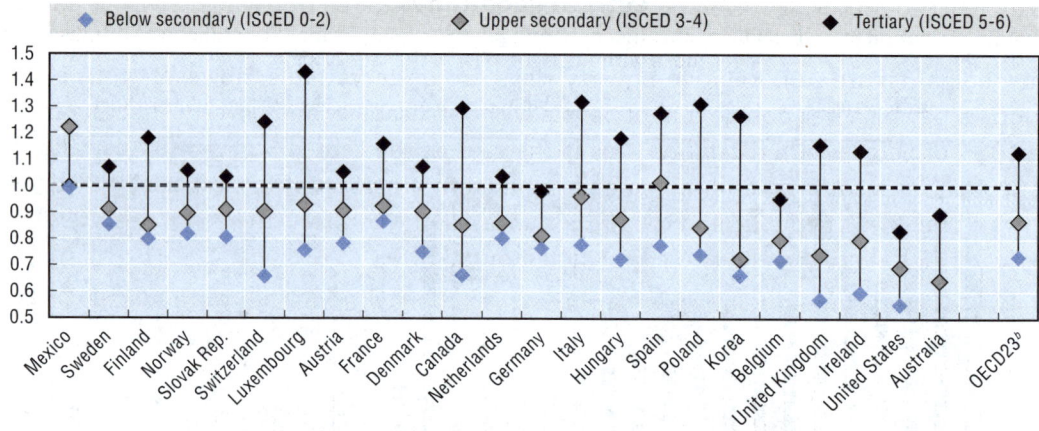

Panel C. **Income^a levels of people with disability by labour force status, as a ratio of average income of the working-age population, mid-2000s**

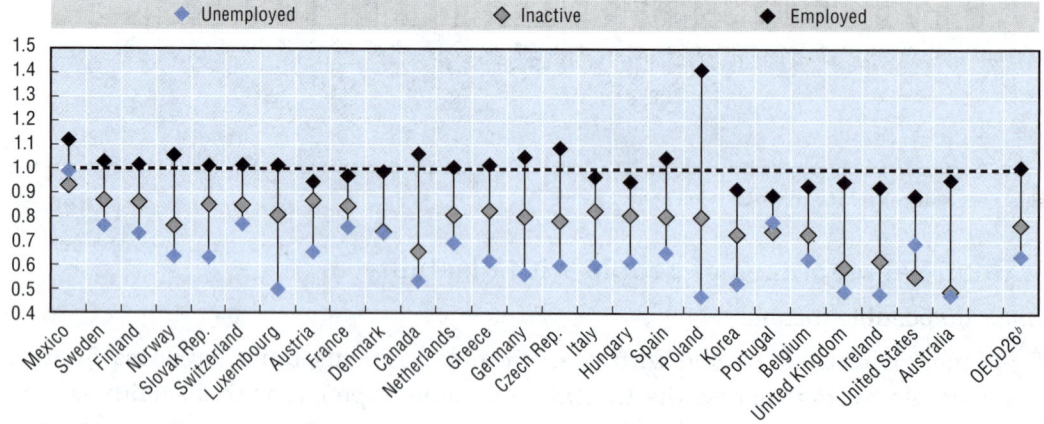

a) Income refers to household-size equivalised disposable income per person.
b) OECD refers to unweighted averages of countries for which data are available. Estonia and Slovenia are not included in the OECD average.

Source: See source in Figure 2.6.

Income levels of people with disability are much higher than this, however, when they have a higher educational attainment or are employed (Figure 2.5, Panels B and C). Employed persons with disability have an income which is around the average of the total working-age population. In Poland, employment is even associated with an income 40% higher than the country-specific average. Similarly, in many OECD countries tertiary education is associated with a relative income among people with disability 10-20% above the country average. In contrast, relative incomes of unemployed people with disability can be as low as 50% of the income of the entire working-age population.

Over the past ten years, the relative financial situation of people with disability has deteriorated in more than half of the countries for which trends can be observed. On average, relative incomes have declined from 88% in the mid-1990s to 85% in the mid-2000s and decreases in relative incomes have even reached 20% in some cases.

Higher poverty risk

In turn, compared with the population without disability, working-age households with a person with disability are at a significantly higher risk of *relative* income poverty in most OECD countries. On average across the OECD, 22% of all households with a person with disability live below the poverty threshold, compared with 14% for the other households (Figure 2.6). Relative poverty risks are quite variable, however, with some countries having a risk double that of people without disability and poverty affecting more than 30% of people with disability: This is the case in the United States and Australia, in particular, but also in Ireland, Korea and Canada. In other countries, especially Sweden, Norway, the Slovak Republic and the Netherlands, on the contrary, there is little difference in poverty risks between the two population groups.

Trends over time in relative poverty risks of people with disability are mixed. Of the 15 countries for which trend data are available, seven have seen an increase in the poverty risk for people with disability relative to the rest of the working-age population; this was particular pronounced in Finland, Germany and Ireland. In three countries, relative poverty risks remained unchanged. And in the remaining five countries, the relative poverty risk of household with people with disability has fallen, especially so in Canada and Greece.

Neither employed nor receiving a benefit

Cross-country differences in equivalised disposable incomes and income poverty are linked to the variation in employment rates and otherwise partly explained by differences in the structure of the benefit system and the level of benefits paid. Systems in some countries offer higher income-replacement rates because benefits are earnings-related rather than flat-rate or means-tested, for example. Population coverage rates and benefit eligibility criteria can be more or less inclusive. As a result, the shares of people with a disability receiving a disability benefit, receiving any other public benefit or not receiving any benefit, despite not being employed, can vary considerably.

Figure 2.7 compares different estimates of *benefit inclusion*, or *exclusion*. On average, one in four people with disability receive a disability benefit (*i.e.* 75% do not), but this share can be as low as 10-15% in Portugal and Germany or as high as one-third in Norway, Poland and the United States. In most countries, the number of people with disability receiving a disability benefit is lower than the number receiving another working-age benefit. The proportion of people with disability not receiving any public benefit is as low as 10-25% in most countries. Only in some English-speaking and Mediterranean countries is this proportion higher,

Figure 2.6. **People with disability are at greater risk of living in or near poverty**

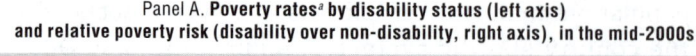

Panel A. **Poverty rates**[a] **by disability status (left axis) and relative poverty risk (disability over non-disability, right axis), in the mid-2000s**

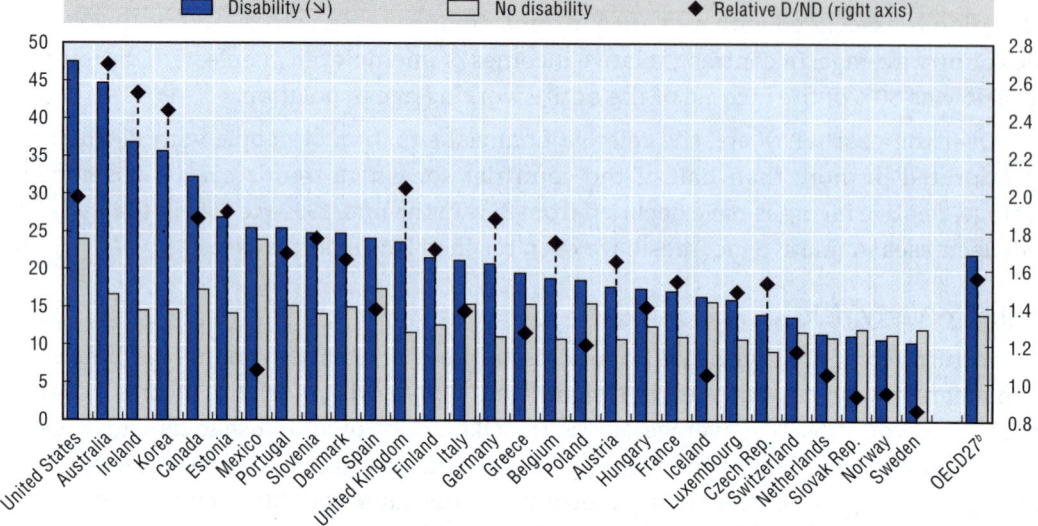

Panel B. **Trends in poverty rates**[a] **of people with disability, in percentage of poverty rates of the working-age population, mid-1990s and mid-2000s**

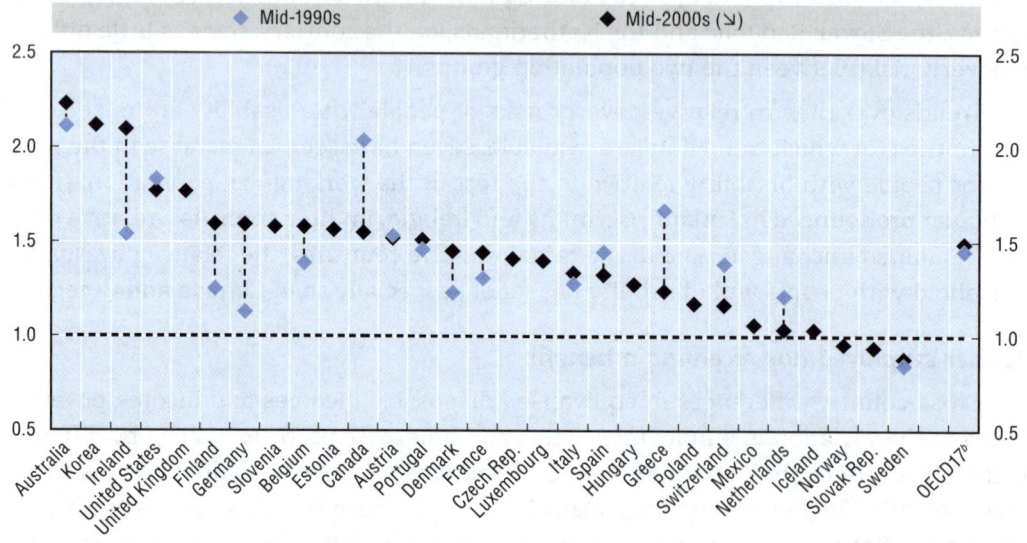

a) Poverty rates: percentages of people with disability in households with less than 60% of the median adjusted disposable income.

b) OECD refers to unweighted averages of countries for which data are available. Estonia and Slovenia are not included in the OECD average.

Source: EU-SILC 2005 (Wave 2) and ECHP 2000, 1995 (Waves 7, 2), except: Australia: SDAC (Survey of Disability and Carers) 2003 and 1998; Canada: SLID (Survey of Labour and Income Dynamics) 2005, 2000 and 1995; Denmark: SFI database 2005, 2002, 1995; Finland: IDS database 2005, 2000, 1995; Korea: Korean Welfare Panel Study, 2006; Mexico: ENESS (National Survey of Employment), 2004, 2000, 1996; Norway: EU-SILC 2004; Poland: HBS (Household Budget Survey) 2004, 2000; Sweden: ECHP 1997; Switzerland: SHS (Swiss Health Survey) 2002, 1997; United Kingdom: FRS (Family Resource Survey) 2004, 2002; United States: SIPP (Survey of Income and Program Participation) 2004, 2001, 1996.

Figure 2.7. **Many non-employed persons with disability are not eligible for or do not receive public benefits in Mediterranean countries and North America**

Different estimates of benefit inclusion or exclusion around 2005 (percentages)[a]

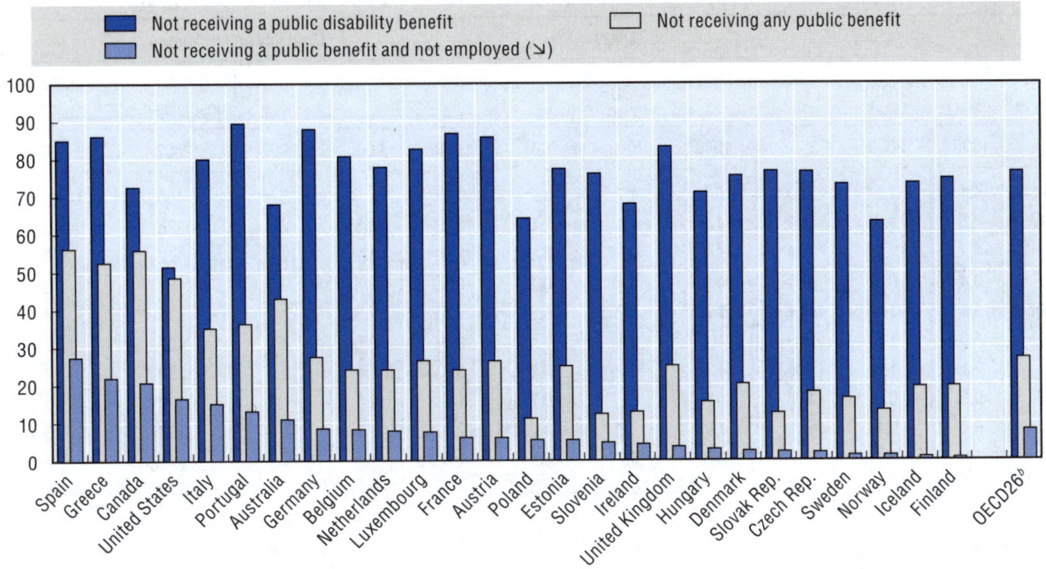

a) The category "disability benefit" includes contributory and non-contributory disability benefits (including equivalent benefits paid through the social assistance scheme); the category "any public benefit" includes disability benefits and other public benefits, such as unemployment benefits and social assistance payments, but excludes workers' compensation payments, family and housing benefits. Countries in which private benefits (which are not covered in these estimates) play a larger role will appear to exclude more people with disability from benefits.

b) OECD26 refers to an unweighted average for 26 countries.

Source: EU-SILC 2005, except: Australia: SDAC 2003; Canada: PALS 2006; United States: SIPP 2008.

typically around 50%. As a result, in those countries some 10-20% of all people with disability have no own income, be it income from work or a public benefit. In all other countries, this share is significantly below 10% and in many cases below 5% or close to nil. These rough inclusion/exclusion estimates suggest that benefit systems are by and large quite successful in providing income support to people with disability who are not employed.

2.3. High costs of sickness and disability benefit schemes

High public spending

Sickness and disability generate considerable public finance costs to society. On average, OECD countries spend 1.2% of GDP on disability benefits alone and this figure reaches 2% when including sickness benefits (Table 2.1). Prior to the recent jobs crisis, this was almost 3 times as much as what was spent on unemployment benefits. In some countries, however, *e.g.* the Netherlands, Norway and Sweden, expenditures are much higher, exceeding 3.5% of GDP.

Disability benefit expenditures for the OECD in total have remained quite stable over the past 15 years. However, several countries have seen increases (see Annex Figure 2.A1.1 for more details on the trend in benefit spending in the period 1990-2005). In some cases, this increase has been compensated in part by a decrease in sickness-related expenditures. Even so, the very high incapacity-related costs are a large commitment of resources. Measured as a percentage of total public social spending, the cost of disability is around 10% on average across the OECD, and even up to 20-25% in some countries (Table 2.1, last column).

Table 2.1. **Incapacity-related spending is much higher than unemployment-related spending**

Trends in expenditure on disability and sickness programmes, in percentage of GDP, 1990, 2000 and 2007, and in percentage of unemployment benefit spending and total public social spending, 2007

	Disability			Sickness			Disability and sickness				
	% GDP			% GDP			% GDP			% unemployment	% public social spending
	1990	2000	2007	1990	2000	2007	1990	2000	2007	2007	2007
Australia[a]	1.1	1.2	1.2	0.4	1.7	1.2	1.5	2.9	2.4	450	15
Austria	2.0	1.3	1.4	1.3	1.1	1.0	3.3	2.5	2.4	278	9
Belgium	1.4	1.2	1.3	1.4	0.7	0.8	2.8	1.9	2.1	77	8
Canada[b]	0.4	0.4	0.4	0.1	0.1	0.1	0.5	0.5	0.5	81	3
Czech Republic	1.2	1.1	1.2	1.0	1.2	0.9	2.3	2.3	2.2	371	12
Denmark	1.6	1.5	1.8	1.4	1.1	1.4	2.9	2.6	3.1	455	12
Finland	2.1	1.9	1.8	1.5	1.2	1.2	3.7	3.0	2.9	250	12
France	0.9	0.8	0.7	0.6	0.7	0.7	1.6	1.5	1.4	109	5
Germany	0.7	0.1	0.1	1.7	1.6	1.3	2.5	1.7	1.4	103	5
Greece	1.0	0.7	0.7	0.8	0.7	0.5	1.9	1.4	1.2	272	6
Hungary	..	0.2	1.3	..	0.7	0.6	..	1.0	1.9	315	8
Iceland	0.9	1.7	2.1	1.5	1.4	1.5	2.3	3.1	3.6	1 895	24
Ireland	0.5	0.6	0.8	0.8	0.6	0.8	1.3	1.1	1.6	163	10
Italy	1.2	0.9	0.7	0.9	0.7	0.5	2.1	1.6	1.2	351	5
Japan	0.3	0.3	0.4	0.1	0.1	0.1	0.4	0.4	0.4	141	2
Korea	0.1	0.2	0.2	0.1	0.1	0.1	0.2	0.3	0.3	101	3
Luxembourg	2.0	1.7	1.0	0.6	0.6	0.8	2.6	2.3	1.8	269	9
Mexico	0.0	0.0	0.0	0.0	0.0	0.0	0.0	0.0	0.0	..	..
Netherlands	4.7	2.7	2.1	2.9	2.2	1.6	7.6	4.9	3.7	324	18
New Zealand	0.6	0.9	0.9	0.3	0.3	0.3	0.9	1.2	1.3	553	7
Norway	2.5	2.3	2.5	2.6	2.7	2.3	5.1	5.1	4.8	2 403	23
Poland	2.1	2.0	1.2	0.7	0.7	0.6	2.8	2.7	1.8	993	9
Portugal	1.7	1.7	1.7	0.0	0.0	0.0	1.7	1.7	1.7	172	8
Slovak Republic	..	0.9	0.8	..	1.0	0.3	..	1.9	1.2	1 087	7
Spain	1.2	1.2	1.2	1.0	1.0	1.1	2.2	2.2	2.3	107	10
Sweden	1.9	2.0	2.2	3.1	2.0	1.4	5.0	4.1	3.6	545	13
Switzerland	1.0	1.8	1.9	1.2	1.1	1.0	2.2	2.8	2.9	462	16
Turkey	0.1	0.1	0.1	0.0	0.0	0.0	0.1	0.2	0.1	..	1
United Kingdom	1.6	2.0	1.9	0.6	0.7	0.4	2.2	2.8	2.3	1 126	11
United States	0.7	0.9	1.0	0.8	0.6	0.7	1.5	1.5	1.7	516	385
OECD	1.3	1.2	1.2	1.0	0.9	0.8	2.3	2.0	1.9	284	10

Note:

. .: Data not available. Disability refers to public and private disability pensions; sickness refers to public and private paid sick leave programmes (occcupational injury and other sickness daily allowances).

a) 2005 instead of 2007.

b) Data for Canada do not include spending on provincial social assistance payments with a disability designation (which would roughly double the spending figure), nor spending on voluntary private long-term disability plans.

Source: OECD Social Expenditure Database (www.oecd.org/els/social/expenditure).

Still and despite recent shifts in policy orientation, disability-related spending is largely limited to passive benefit payment. Except for a few countries, the share of spending on vocational rehabilitation and employment programmes is less than 8%, and in most cases less than 4%, of total disability-related spending (Figure 2.8). Exceptions are Germany, Norway, Denmark and the Netherlands although in the latter country much of this is used for sheltered employment.

Figure 2.8. **Limited disability-related resources go to employment and rehabilitation programmes**

Active labour market spending on employment programmes and vocational rehabilitation, 2007[a, b]

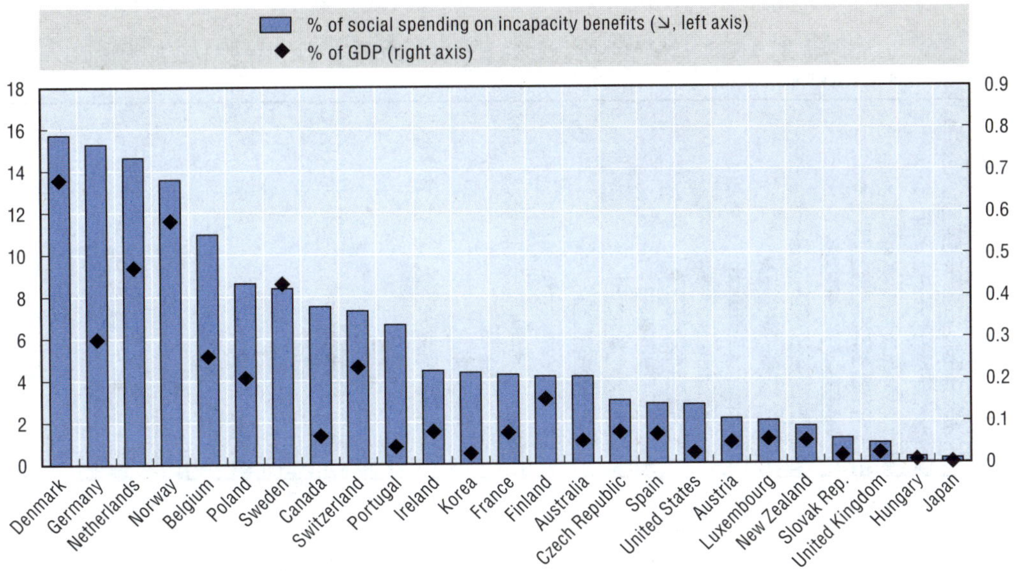

a) 2004 for Spain; 2005 for Korea; 2006 for Australia, Belgium, Canada, the Czech Republic, Denmark, Finland, Germany and Switzerland. Spending on incapacity benefits: 2005 for Japan and the Netherlands; 2006 for New Zealand and the United States.
b) Incapacity benefit spending includes spending on both sickness and disability benefits.
Source: OECD ALMP Database, OECD SOCX Database and data provided by national authorities.

High and increasing benefit recipiency

High public spending is a direct consequence of very high disability beneficiary numbers. On average, about 6% of the OECD working-age population received a disability benefit in 2007; a figure of a similar magnitude to the average OECD unemployment rate at that time (Figure 2.9). In some countries, Hungary, Norway and Sweden, disability recipiency rates at around 10% far exceeded unemployment rates. In the non-European non-English-speaking countries of the OECD, Japan, Korea and Mexico, on the contrary, these rates are at or below 2%.

On average over the past 10-15 years, disability recipiency rates have increased only slightly across the OECD but this masks substantial differences across countries. More than half of the countries, including all English-speaking countries (except Canada), have seen a substantial growth in disability beneficiary rates (Figure 2.10). These rates have declined significantly in a few countries, especially Poland, Portugal, Luxembourg and the Netherlands, following policy changes which tightened access to disability benefits. The beginning of a turnaround in the increasing beneficiary trend is also visible more recently in several other countries, including Sweden, Switzerland and the United Kingdom, though the levels in 2008 were still much higher than 10-15 years before.

Shifting composition of beneficiaries

The *age gradient* in disability prevalence is reflected in the use of disability benefits. Among the 20-34 year-olds, beneficiary rates are around 2% in most countries, up to almost 4% in both the Netherlands and the United Kingdom. For the prime-age group of

Figure 2.9. **Disability benefit recipiency rates are high and still increasing in many countries**

Disability benefit recipients in percentage of the population aged 20-64 in 28 OECD countries and three accession countries,[a] mid-1990s[b] and latest year available[c, d]

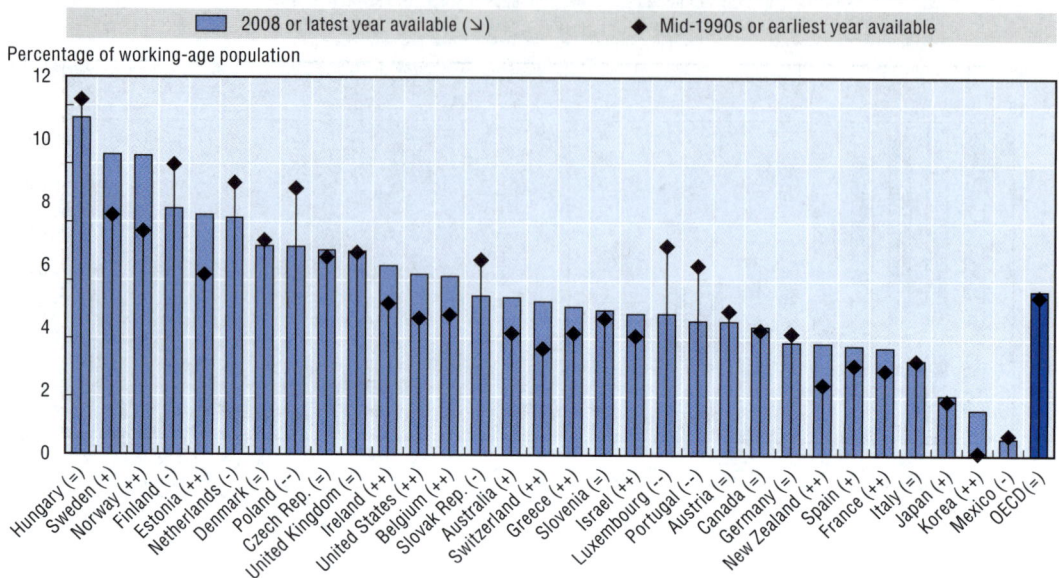

Note: (↘) in the legend relates to the variable for which countries are ranked from left to right in decreasing order.
(++)/(--) refers to a strong increase/decline of 2% or more; (+)/(–) refers to a moderate increase/decline between 0.75% and 2%; (=) refers to a rather stable trend between –0.75% and 0.75%; percentages refer to the annual average growth rate in employment rate of persons with a disability. OECD refers to the unweighted average of the 28 countries.
a) The statistical data for Israel are supplied by and under the responsibility of the relevant Israeli authorities. The use of such data by the OECD is without prejudice to the status of the Golan Heights, East Jerusalem and Israeli settlements in the West Bank under the terms of international law.
b) 1996 for Belgium and Canada; 1999 for the Netherlands; 2000 for Hungary, Italy and the Slovak Republic; 2001 for Ireland; 2003 for Japan and Mexico; 2004 for Poland.
c) 2005 for Luxembourg; 2007 for Austria, Canada, France, Israel, Italy, Poland, the Slovak Republic, Spain and the United Kingdom.
d) Data for Hungary include three different non-contributory allowances all requiring serious health impairment and aimed to promote equal opportunities.
Source: Data provided by national authorities.

35-49 year-olds, beneficiary rates fluctuate around 4-6%. For older workers aged 50-64, rates are typically 10-15%, up to over 20% in Sweden, Norway and Hungary (see Annex Figure 2.A1.2 for more details on the levels and trends in beneficiary rates by broad age group). Most countries have a similar rank among all three broad age groups, *i.e.* countries tend to have either relatively high or low beneficiary rates among all age groups. However, in some countries beneficiary rates are quite high among older workers but comparatively low among young and prime-age groups. In these countries, including Luxembourg and Austria, disability benefit partly fulfils an early-retirement function.

Reflecting the size of the three broad age groups, overall changes in beneficiary rates were predominantly driven by changes in the use of disability benefits by older workers – with upwards changes of 2-3 percentage points in several cases and significant drops in countries that reformed their systems. However, in many countries beneficiary rates have increased very substantially among young and prime-age workers. As a result, the average recipient is now in most cases younger than in the past and the average duration on benefits longer.

Figure 2.10. **Disability benefit rolls have evolved differently across the OECD, reflecting policy choices**

Number of disability benefit recipients aged 20-64 as a share of the working-age population,[a] 1990-2008

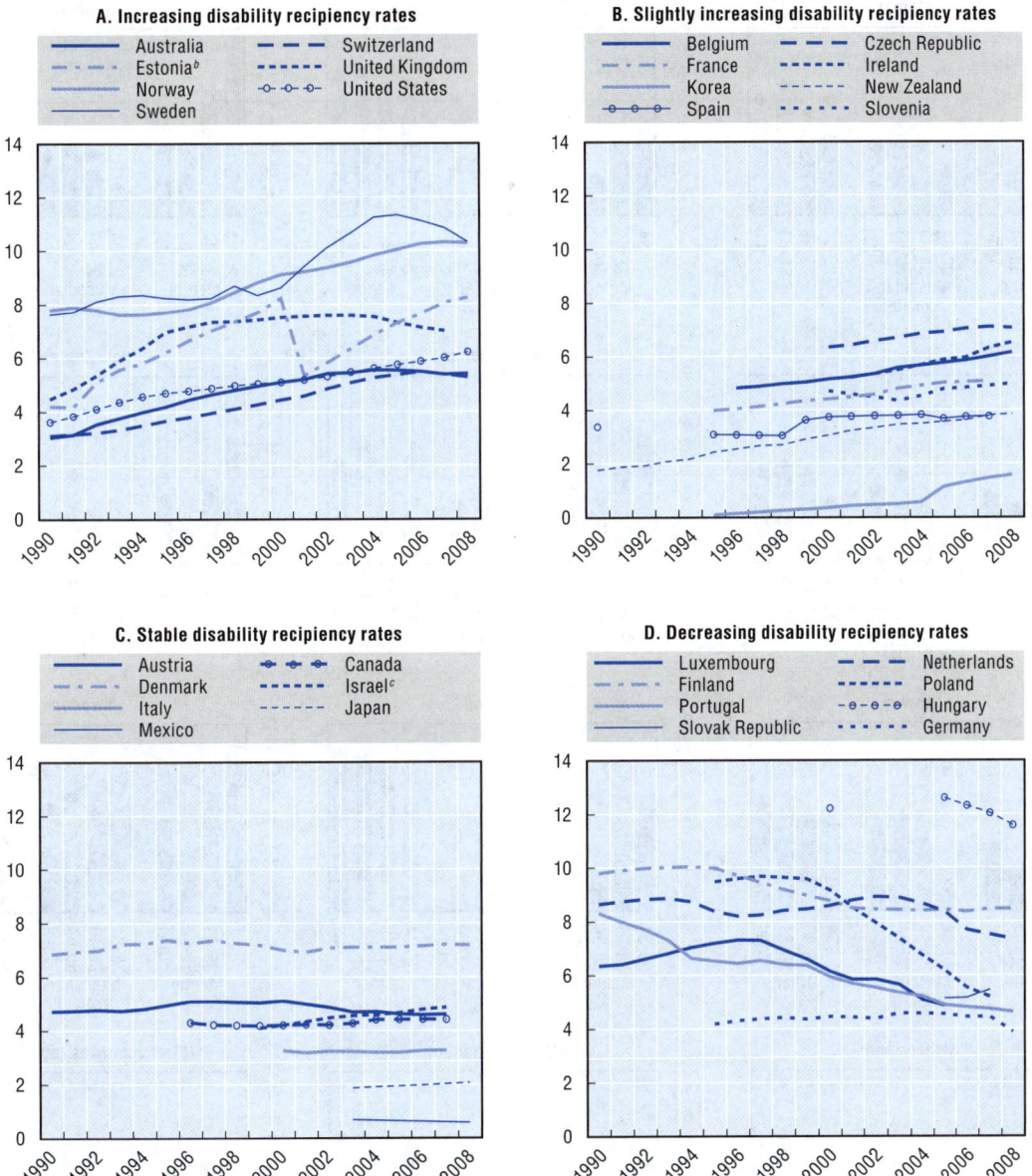

a) Data for Austria and Germany would be approximately 1 percentage point higher if civil servant schemes were included. Data for the Netherlands cover ages 15-64. Data for Poland refer to the employee contributory scheme only; were the farmers' contributory scheme and the non-contributory scheme included, the rate would be 2 percentage points higher.

b) For Estonia, as of 2001 the pension for incapacity for work has been granted instead of the former disability pension, and pensioners receiving a pension for incapacity for work were transferred to old-age pension or the national pension.

c) The statistical data for Israel are supplied by and under the responsibility of the relevant Israeli authorities. The use of such data by the OECD is without prejudice to the status of the Golan Heights, East Jerusalem and Israeli settlements in the West Bank under the terms of international law.

Source: Data provided by national authorities.

Figure 2.11. **More and more inflows into disability benefit because of mental health conditions**

New disability benefit claims by health condition as a percentage of all claims, by age group, 1995 and 2008[a, b]

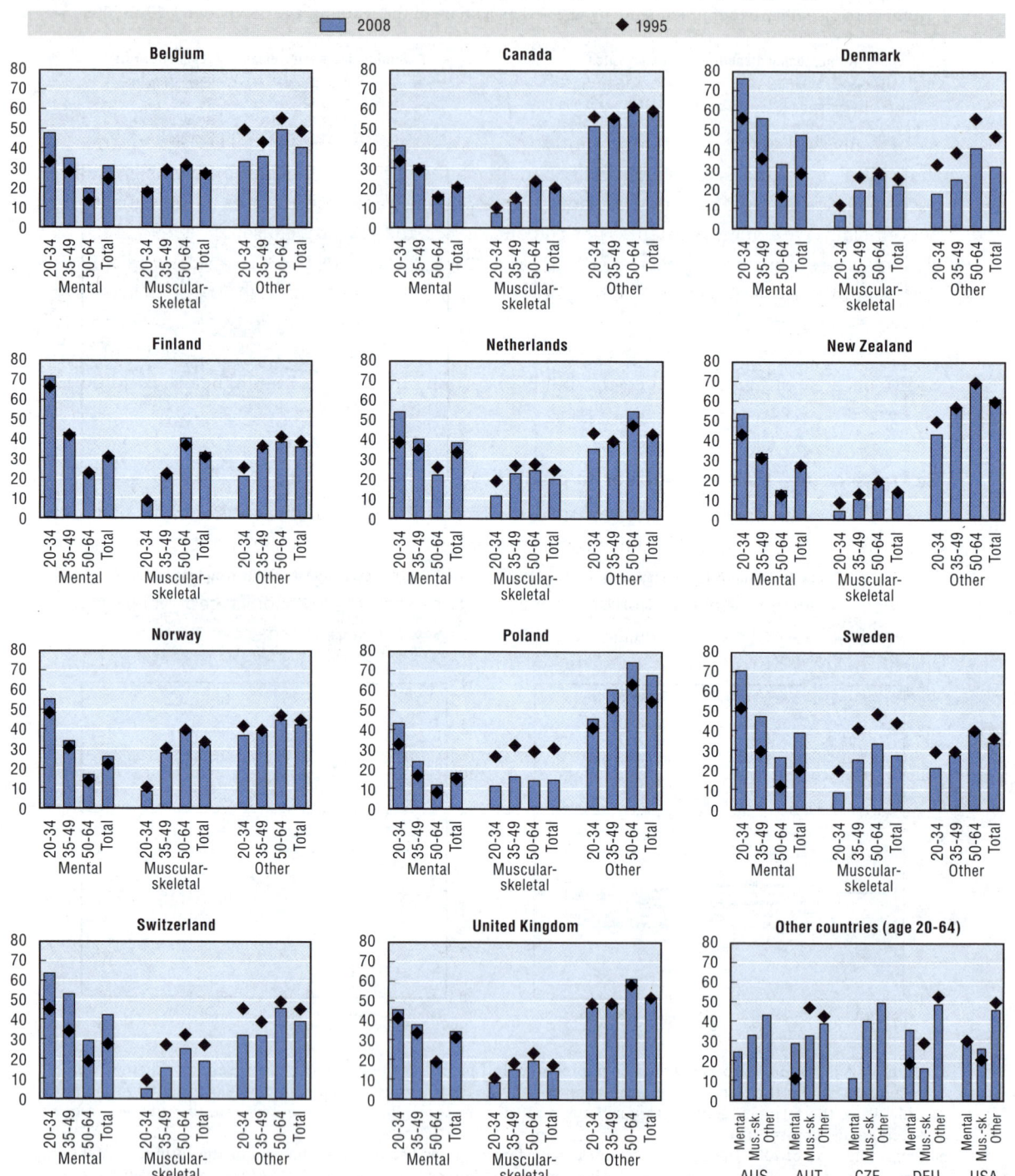

a) Data for Canada and Germany refer to the contributory benefit only; data for Poland cover the FUS scheme only; data for the United States do not account for the overlap in contributory and non-contributory benefit receipt.

b) Data for 1995 refer to: 1996 for New Zealand, 1999 for the Netherlands, 2000 for Denmark, Finland, the United Kingdom, the United States and 2001 for Canada. Data for 2008 refer to: 2005 for the United Kingdom, 2006 for Norway and 2007 for Austria, Canada and Poland.

Source: Data supplied by national authorities.

Similarly, there is a shift in many countries in the *gender* structure of disability beneficiaries. Beneficiary rates tended to increase more (or fall less) for women, so that the share of women in the total beneficiary roll has increased. The share of men is still over 50% in a majority of countries, but women dominate disability beneficiary rolls in the Nordic countries (see Annex Figure 2.A1.3 for more details on the levels and trends in beneficiary rates by gender).

Finally, and maybe most importantly, there is a big shift in virtually all OECD countries in the *medical causes* underlying a disability benefit claim, with mental health problems gradually becoming, or having become, the leading cause. On average, one-third of all new disability benefit claims are due to a mental health condition as the primary cause, rising to as high as 40% in some countries and almost 50% in Denmark (Figure 2.11). The share of new recipients with mental health problems is highest among young people, with around 70% of all claims in the 20-34 age groups. Mental health problems are also more often present in inflows to disability among women than men. These figures do not reveal the full extent of mental ill-health because of the frequent co-morbidity of certain physical and mental health conditions.

2.4. Benefit system dynamics

Sickness absence as a precursor to disability

Sickness absence levels are critical for the inflow into disability benefits. In most countries, a majority of disability benefit claimants, typically 50-90%, enter the system after a period of varying length on sickness benefit. It does not come as a surprise that absence rates are highest in many of those countries with high disability beneficiary rates, especially the Nordic countries (Figure 2.12). However, there are some countries, especially in the east of Europe, that have large numbers of people on disability benefit but comparatively low absence rates.

Figure 2.12. **Sickness absence rates are correlated with disability beneficiary rates**

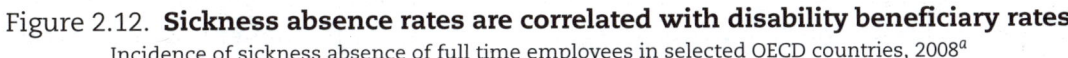

Incidence of sickness absence of full time employees in selected OECD countries, 2008[a]

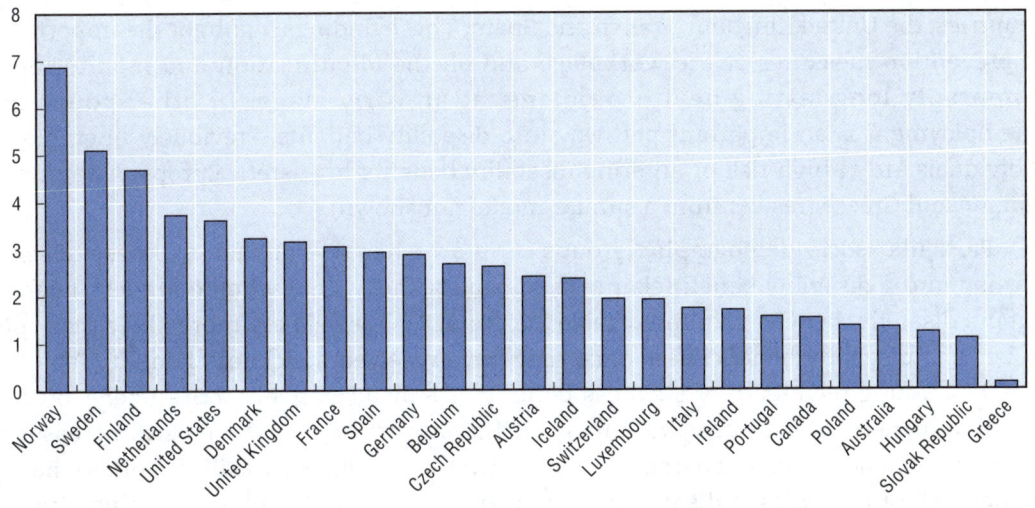

a) 2004 for Australia and 2007 for Iceland. The incidence of work absence due to sickness is defined as the share of full-time employees absent from work due to sickness and temporary disability (either one or all days of the work week). Data are annual averages of quarterly estimates. Estimates for Australia and Canada are for full-week absences only.

Source: European Union Labour Force Survey (EULFS) and national labour force surveys for Australia, Canada and the United States.

Figure 2.13. **Previous sickness benefit spells increase the probability of a disability benefit claim**

Marginal effects from a disability probability model on lagged sickness benefit[a, b, c]

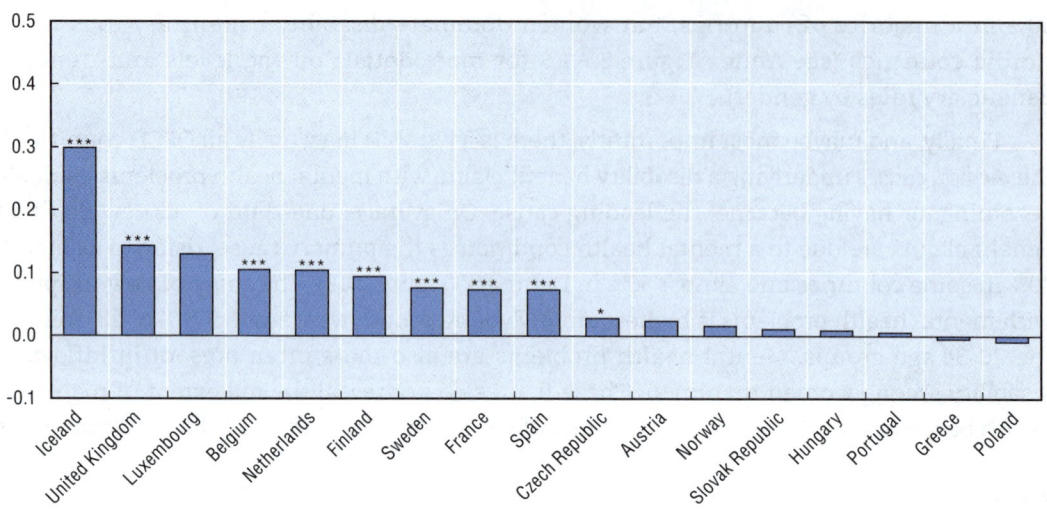

*, **, ***: statistically significant at the 10%, 5% and 1% level, respectively.

a) Marginal effects are estimated from a logit model. They capture the effect of lagged sickness benefit on the probability of receiving a disability benefit. A positive marginal effect means a higher probability of receiving a disability benefit. In the Netherlands and Sweden the effect of sickness benefit corresponds to two-period lagged spells because sickness benefits last for more than one year (in all other countries, one-period lagged spells are used).

b) Samples include persons present in at least three consecutive waves.

c) All regressions include regional dummy variables (except for Germany) and the following "initial" work characteristics: industry, occupation, type of contract, working hours, shift work, public sector and firm size.

Source: OECD estimates based on the EU-SILC longitudinal waves 2005-2006-2007.

More detailed analysis confirms that a previous sickness benefit spell greatly increases the probability of receiving a disability benefit in a majority of OECD countries (Figure 2.13). Sickness absence plays a major role as a precursor to permanent labour market detachment in the form of disability benefits in the Nordic countries, the Benelux countries, the United Kingdom, France and Spain. These findings highlight the importance of prevention measures at the workplace and on the identification and monitoring of potentially long-lasting health problems at an early stage. In other countries, unemployment is an important pathway into disability benefits. Previously unemployed individuals are at high risk of entering disability benefits in eastern European countries, Finland and Greece (results from a similar model not shown).

Particular socio-demographic groups have a higher risk of their sickness absence turning into a disability benefit claim. The analysis shows that women are less likely to enter a disability benefit than men (Table 2.2, Panel A), but they are more likely than men to become disability beneficiaries once they have received a sickness benefit (Table 2.2, Panel B). Young recipients of sickness benefits are also relatively more likely to enter disability benefits. These are two important findings in view of the recent increases in disability beneficiary rates among women and young adults. Low-skilled workers have a higher risk of becoming a disability beneficiary in general (Panel A), and this effect is reinforced for low-skilled sickness benefit recipients (Panel B). High-skilled workers, on the contrary, are generally less likely to enter disability benefits (Panel A), but their risk of sickness absence turning into a disability benefit claim is higher than for the medium-skilled (Panel B).

Table 2.2. **Probability of receiving a disability benefit after a sickness absence spell varies with personal characteristics**

Coefficients from a model estimating the likelihood of disability benefit entry (Panel A) and coefficients from a similar model conditional on a previous sickness absence spell (Panel B)[a, b, c]

	Panel A. Logit disability	Panel B. Interactions between lagged sickness benefit and personal characteristics
Lagged sickness benefit	0.029***	
Gender = female	−0.016***	0.009**
Age	0.011***	−
Age^2	0.000***	−
20-34	−	0.018*
50-64	−	0.009
Marital status		
Single	0.022***	
Separated/Divorced	0.012***	
Widowed	−0.006**	
Educational attainment		
Low-skilled	0.009***	0.157**
High-skilled	−0.020***	0.201**
Length in employment (in years)	−0.002***	
1st quintile		
2nd quintile	0.004**	−0.004
4th quintile	0.005***	0.002
5th quintile	−0.007***	0.008
1st quintile	−0.019***	0.005
Observations	128 163	

*, **, ***: statistically significant at the 10%, 5% and 1% level, respectively.

a) Samples include persons present in at least three consecutive waves.

b) Marginal effects reported (see note a in Figure 2.13).

c) All regressions include regional dummy variables (except for Germany) and the following "initial" work characteristics: industry, occupation, type of contract, working hours, shift work, public sector and firm size.

Source: OECD estimates based on the EU-SILC longitudinal waves 2005-2006-2007.

High rates of inflow into disability benefit

Recently, some OECD countries have managed to bring down the rate of inflow into disability benefits.[3] In almost all cases, such declines have either occurred hand-in-hand with, or have followed, a reduction in levels of long-term sickness absence (Figure 2.14). However, rates of inflow into disability benefit which have increased in many cases remain high in most countries – at 4-8 per thousand of the working-age population per year (Figure 2.15, Panel A). This holds in spite of relatively high rates of rejection of disability benefit claims which are around 50% in many OECD countries, except for the Nordic countries which only reject between 10-25% of all claimants (Figure 2.15, Panel B). The high rejection rates suggest that in fact a much larger group of (mostly jobless) workers is trying to get on a permanent disability benefit.

A more detailed analysis of age and gender-specific rates of new disability benefit claims suggests that, by and large, the overall trend is mirrored in each age and gender group (see Annex Figure 2.A1.4 for country-specific details). In some countries, however, significant differences arise which have contributed to the structural shift in

Figure 2.14. **Declines in sickness absence usually precede a decline in disability benefit claims**

Change in sickness absence days (1995-2008[a]) and change in new disability benefit claims[b] (2000-2008[c])

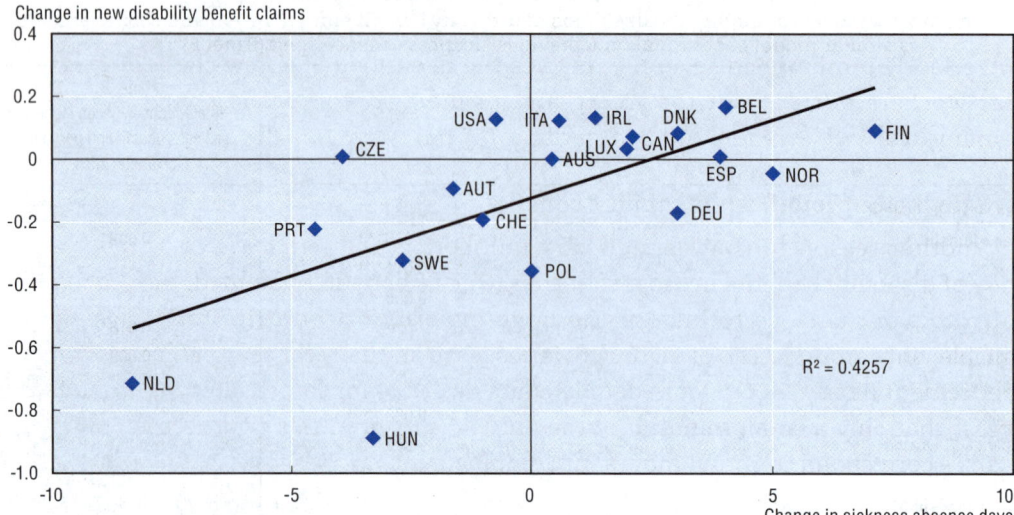

a) 1995-2004 for Australia, 1995-2007 for Iceland, 1996-2008 for Switzerland, 1997-2008 for the Czech Republic and Hungary, 1998-2008 for the Slovak Republic and the United States and 2001-08 for Poland.

b) Austria excludes civil servants. Canada refers to the contributory pension only. Germany includes civil servants and excludes the non-contributory and early retirement pension for the severely disabled. Spain covers the contributory benefit only. The United States does not take into account the overlap between the contributory and non-contributory pensions.

c) 2000-08 for Luxembourg and Spain; 2000-2007 for Austria, Belgium, Italy and Poland; 2001-06 for Ireland; 2001-07 for Canada; 2001-08 for the Czech Republic and 2006-08 for Australia.

Source: National submissions for new disability benefit claims, the European Union Labour Force Survey (EULFS) and national labour force surveys for Australia, Canada and the United States.

Figure 2.15. **Some countries have recently managed to reduce inflows into disability benefits**

New disability benefit claims per thousand of the working-age population, 2000 and 2008, and share of rejected benefit applicants, 2008

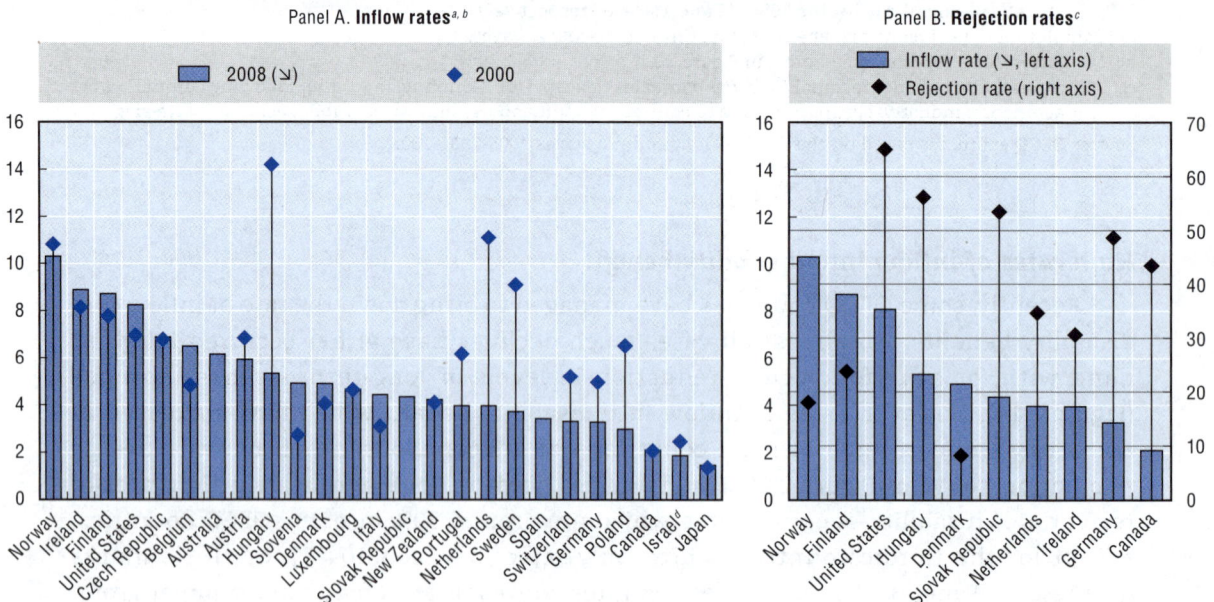

a) Data for Ireland refer to 2001 and 2006; Luxembourg to 2005; Austria, Belgium, Canada, Italy, Poland, the Slovak Republic and Spain to 2007.

b) Data for Austria exclude civil servants; those for Germany include civil servants and exclude the non-contributory and early retirement pension for the severely disabled; and those for Canada and Spain cover the contributory benefit only.

c) Data for Ireland refer to 2007 and to persons on the Illness benefit for over two years; Canada, the Slovak Republic and the United States refer to 2007 figures.

d) The statistical data for Israel are supplied by and under the responsibility of the relevant Israeli authorities. The use of such data by the OECD is without prejudice to the status of the Golan Heights, East Jerusalem and Israeli settlements in the West Bank under the terms of international law.

Source: Data provided by national authorities.

the beneficiary population to younger, female claimants. In a range of countries increases, in claim rates were higher for women than for men (*e.g.* Australia, Belgium and Slovenia) or rates fell for men but not for women (*e.g.* Germany, Israel and Switzerland). Similarly, in several countries the likelihood of a new claim decreased for older workers but did not for young and prime-age workers (*e.g.* Austria, Canada, Germany, Norway, Sweden and Switzerland).

Virtually no outflow from disability benefits

Another reason for high beneficiary numbers is the *permanent* or *quasi-permanent nature* of disability benefits in most countries. Once a benefit is awarded, the probability of return to work is close to nil. For the large majority of countries for which data are available, only around 1-2% of all beneficiaries leave annually for reasons other than death or retirement (Figure 2.16).[4] More detailed data available for some countries, *e.g.* Australia, suggest that only a small minority of the outflow shown in this figure – often only some 10-20% – correspond to actual moves into employment.

The *de facto* permanence of disability benefits suggests that policy change is likely to have more influence when oriented towards prevention of disability benefit awards in the first place. This is why reform in most OECD countries has concentrated on helping people stay in the labour force and avoid the transition into benefit dependency and long-term labour market exit (Chapter 3). However, the recent increase in outflow rates in a few countries – even if only by 1 or 2 percentage points annually – suggests that it is not impossible to bring people off benefit and back into the labour force. Consequently, more recently a few more countries are looking into ways to reduce their long-term benefit rolls.

Figure 2.16. People almost never leave a longer-term disability benefit for employment

Annual outflows from disability benefits as a share of all disability benefit recipients (percentage), 2008[a, b]

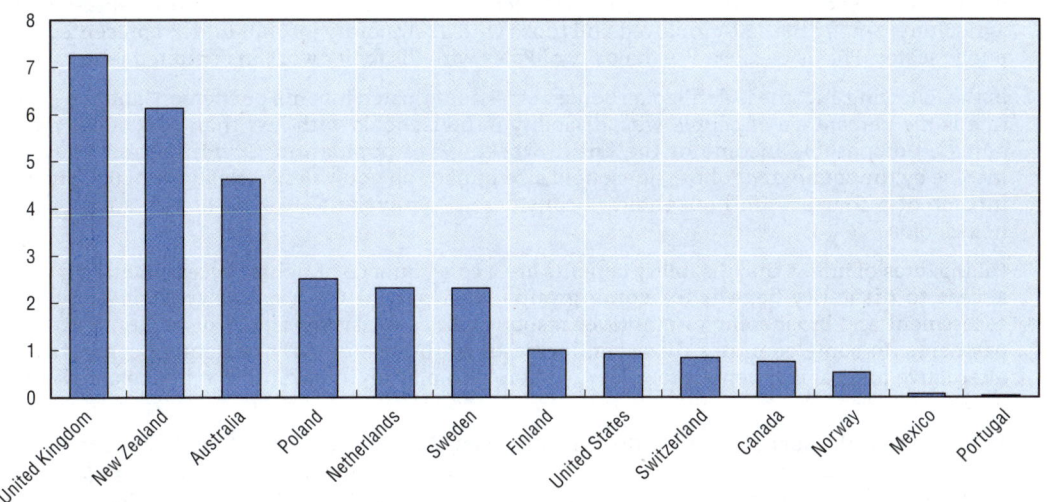

a) Outflows include moves into employment and into other inactivity as well as loss of eligibility, but exclude deaths and transfers into old-age pension.

b) Data refer to 2005 for Australia and the United Kingdom, to 2006 for Finland and to 2007 for Canada, Poland and Portugal. Data for Canada and the United States refer to contributory disability benefits only; data for Poland to the contributory farmers' scheme; and data for the United Kingdom to the long-term Incapacity Benefit.

Source: Data provided by national authorities.

2.5. Conclusion

The following facts emerge from the picture above:

- Employment outcomes for people with health problems or disability are disappointing, especially so for people with mental health issues. Good economic conditions prior to the recent recession did not help them into work in larger numbers.

- Rates of unemployment of people with disability were much higher than for other groups before the current jobs crisis. If anything, the recent deterioration of labour market opportunities will increase the disability gap in unemployment.

- Average equivalised incomes of persons with disability are much lower than for the rest of the population, and the likelihood of income poverty is much higher.

- Incapacity-related public spending is high, roughly 2.5 times the spending on unemployment benefits on average across the OECD prior to the jobs crisis.

- High incapacity-related spending is the result of a large number of people receiving disability benefit, which has become the main working-age benefit in most OECD countries.

- Most countries have seen a structural shift in the composition of disability beneficiaries, which now tend to be younger and more frequently female compared with one to two decades ago. Moreover, today the largest part of all new claims is due to mental ill-health.

- Comprehensive reforms in recent years have turned around the trend increase in a number of countries. This change was largely achieved by reforms affecting new benefit claimants.

Notes

1. Poland is an exception in this regard, with people with disability highly overrepresented in agriculture, among the self-employed and those with a temporary job, but underrepresented in the public sector. This is because the majority of Poles with disability work in sheltered jobs.

2. In the following, income is defined as household-size-adjusted income per person, and the poverty rate is the percentage of people with disability in households with less than 60% of the median adjusted disposable income of the entire working-age population. Dividing total household income by the square root of the household size implies an equivalence elasticity of 0.5. Such, the income of a four-person household is considered "equivalent" to that of two single-person households.

3. Falling rates of inflow into disability benefits are a consequence of tighter access including closing access to disability benefit for some groups with partial work capacity, stricter rules for assessment and broadening of employer responsibilities for sickness and disability matters and payments. In some countries, however, increases in the use of early retirement schemes as an alternative to disability benefit for older workers also play an important role in explaining falling inflow rates.

4. Exceptions to the low rate of outflow include New Zealand and the United Kingdom. Higher outflow rates in these two countries are to a considerable degree a result of the larger proportion of people with short-term health problems (who would be on sickness benefit in other countries) on the disability benefit rolls in the two countries.

ANNEX 2.A1

Additional Supporting Evidence

Figure 2.A1.1. **Falling trend in spending on disability benefits in the late 1990s but a slight rise lately**

Annual spending on disability and sickness benefits, percentage of GDP, 1990-2007

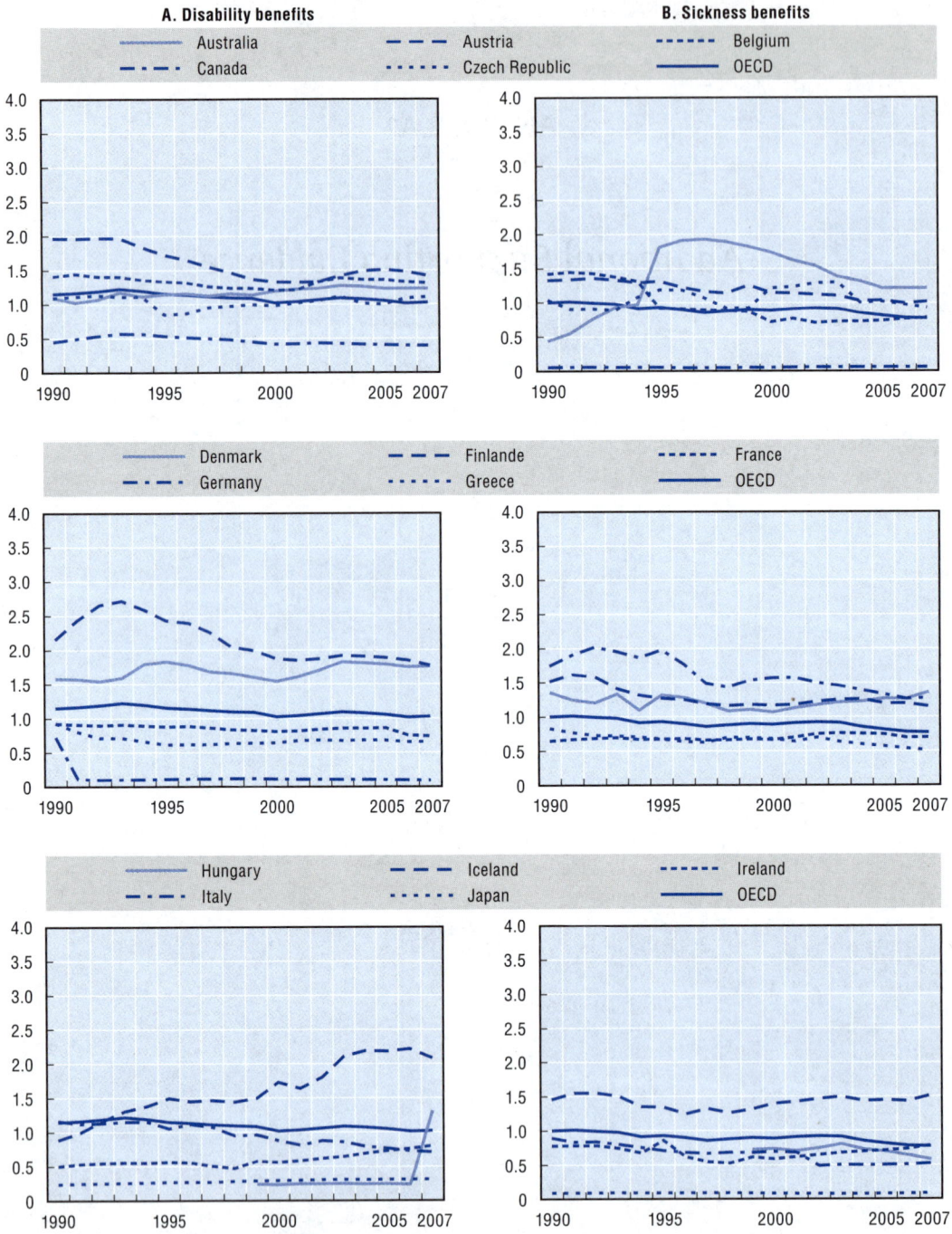

Note: Include public and private spending.

Source: OECD Social Expenditure Database and data supplied by national authorities.

Figure 2.A1.1. **Falling trend in spending on disability benefits in the late 1990s but a slight rise lately** *(cont.)*

Annual spending on disability and sickness benefits, percentage of GDP, 1990-2007

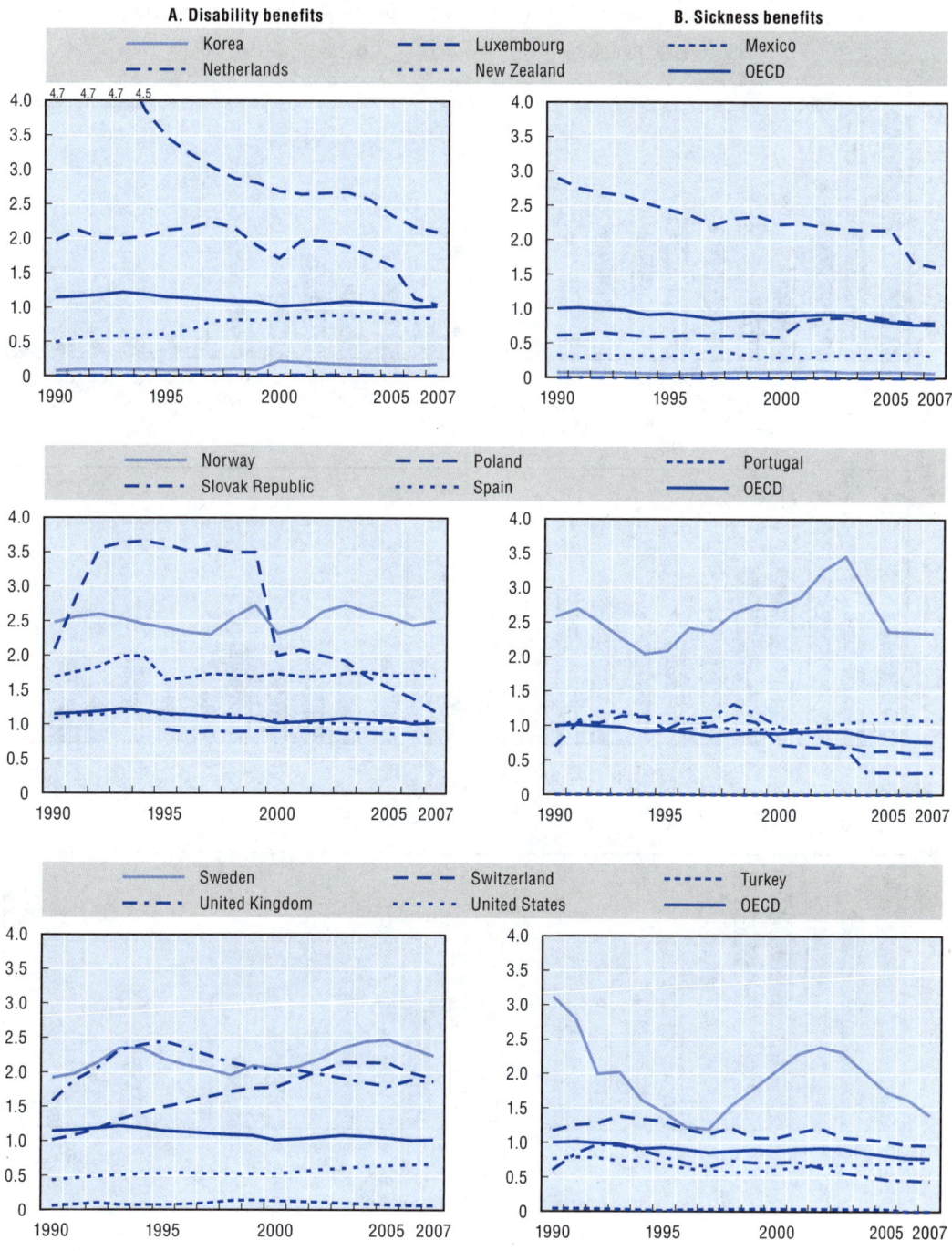

Note: Include public and private benefits.

Source: OECD Social Expenditure Database and data supplied by national authorities.

Figure 2.A1.2. **Levels and trends in disability benefit recipiency rates are dominated by 50-64 year-olds**

Disability benefit recipiency rates for three broad age groups, earliest and latest available year[a, b]

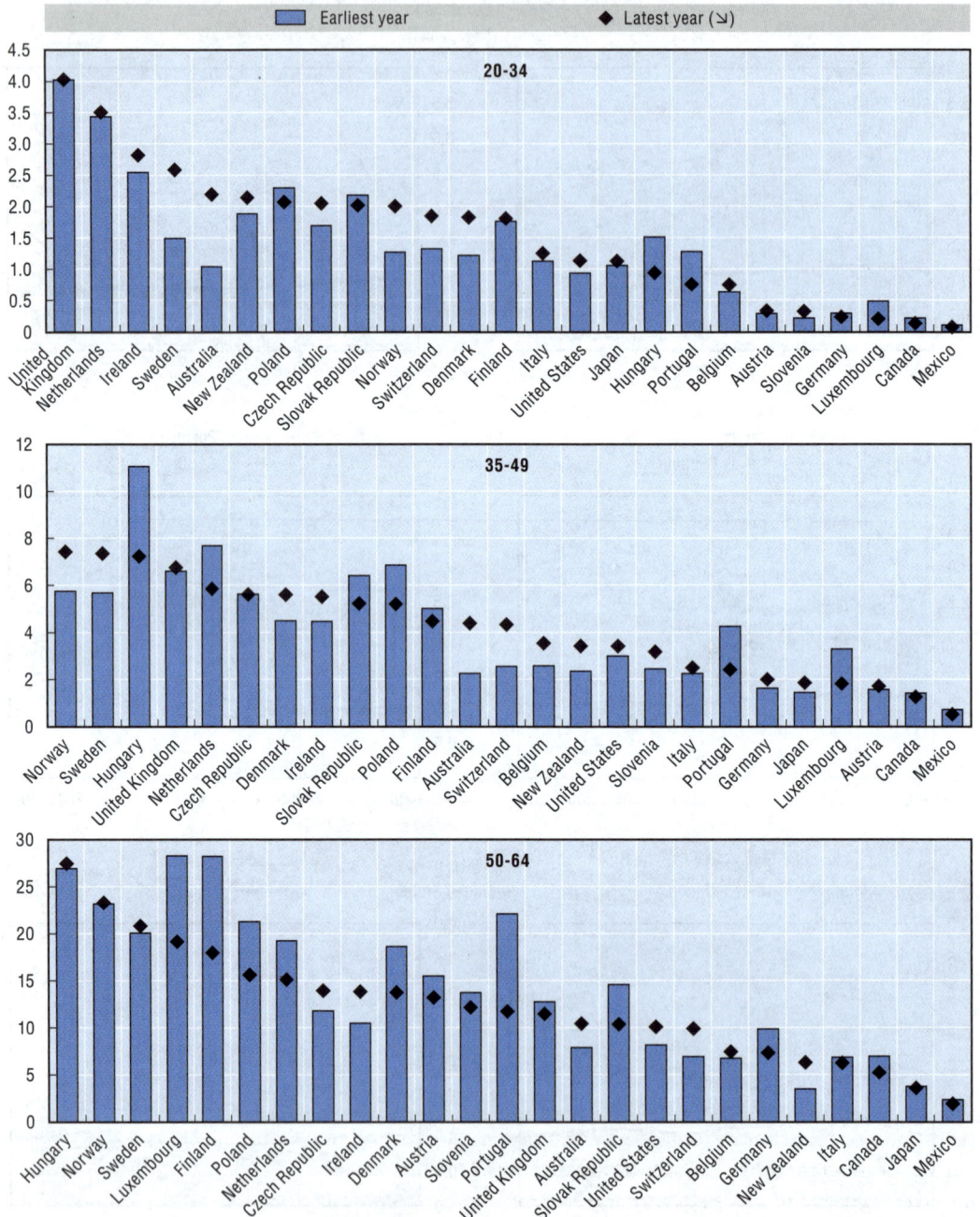

a) Years covered: 1990-2008 for Australia, Belgium, the Czech Republic, Denmark, Finland, Norway and Portugal; 1990-2007 for Austria; 1992-2008 for Switzerland; 1995-2005 for Luxembourg; 1995-2007 for the Slovak Republic; 1995-2008 for Germany, New Zealand and Sweden; 1996-2007 for Canada; 1999-2005 for the United Kingdom; 1999-2008 for the Netherlands; 2000-07 for Italy; 2000-08 for Hungary, Slovenia and the United States; 2001-08 for Ireland; 2003-07 for Japan; 2003-08 for Mexico; 2004-07 for Poland.

b) Data for Canada refer to the contributory disability benefit (Canada and Quebec Pension Plan Disability) only.

Source: Data provided by national authorities.

Figure 2.A1.3. **In some countries, women are now receiving disability benefits more often than men**

Disability benefit recipiency rates for men and women, earliest and latest available year[a],[b]

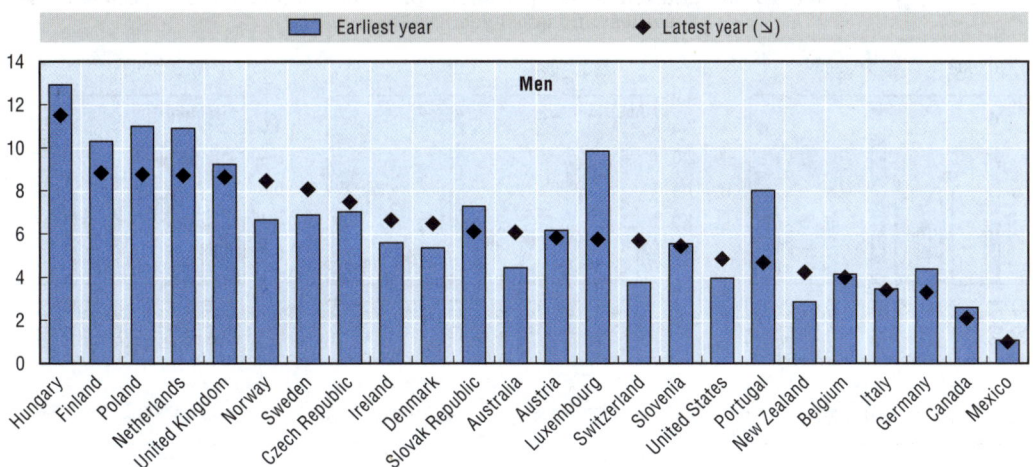

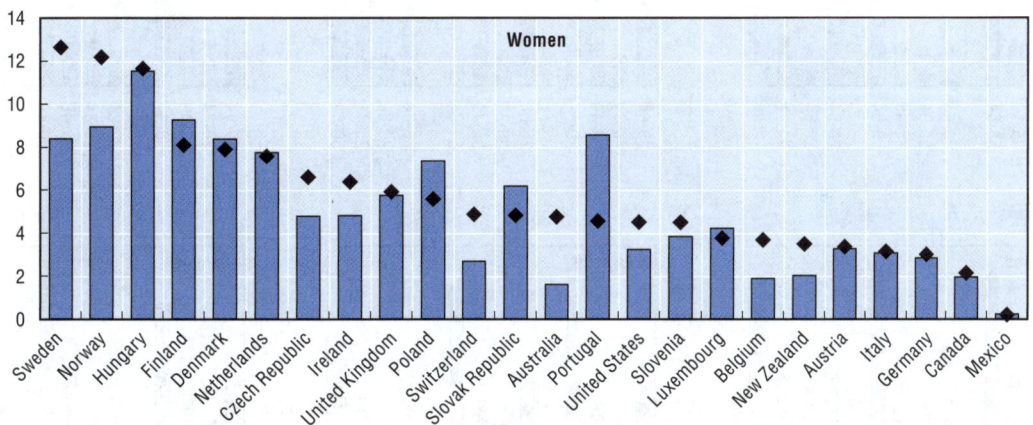

a) Years covered: 1990-2008 for Australia, the Czech Republic, Denmark, Finland, Mexico, Norway, Portugal and Sweden; 1990-2007 for Austria and Belgium; 1992-2008 for Germany and Switzerland; 1995-2005 for Luxembourg; 1995-2007 for the Slovak Republic; 1995-2008 for New Zealand and Sweden; 1996-2007 for Canada; 1999-2005 for the United Kingdom; 1999-2008 for the Netherlands; 2000-07 for Italy; 2000-08 for Hungary, Slovenia and the United States; 2001-08 for Ireland; 2003-08 for Mexico; 2004-07 for Poland.

b) Data for Canada and the United States refer to the contributory disability benefit (Canada and Quebec Pension Plan Disability and Social Security Disability Insurance) only.

Source: Data provided by national authorities.

Figure 2.A1.4. **There are large variations in the age pattern of disability benefit inflows across countries**

New disability benefit claims by age and gender as a percentage of the population in the respective age group, earliest and latest year available

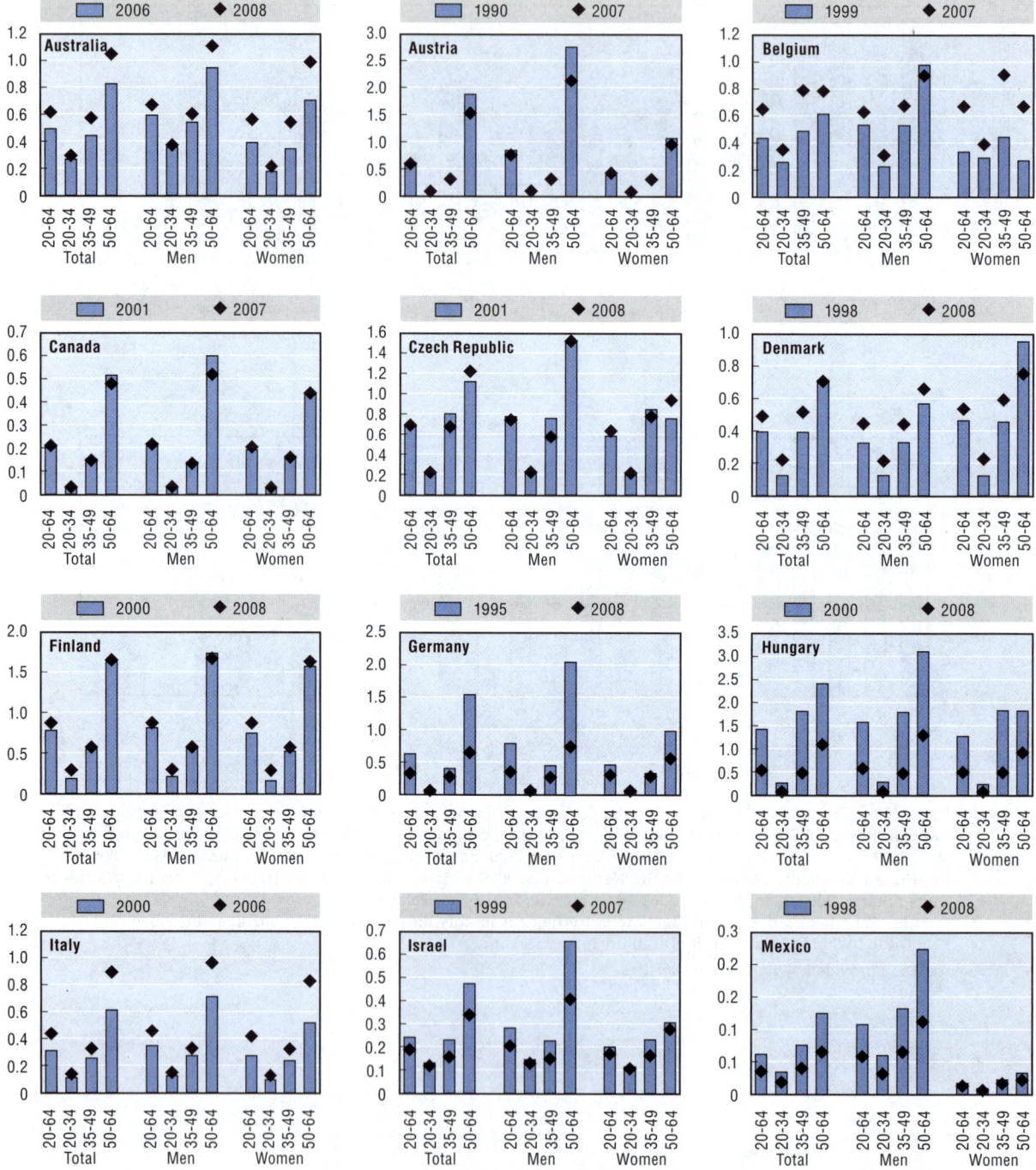

Figure 2.A1.4. **There are large variations in the age pattern of disability benefit inflows across countries** (*cont.*)

New disability benefit claims by age and gender as a percentage of the population in the respective age group, earliest and latest year available

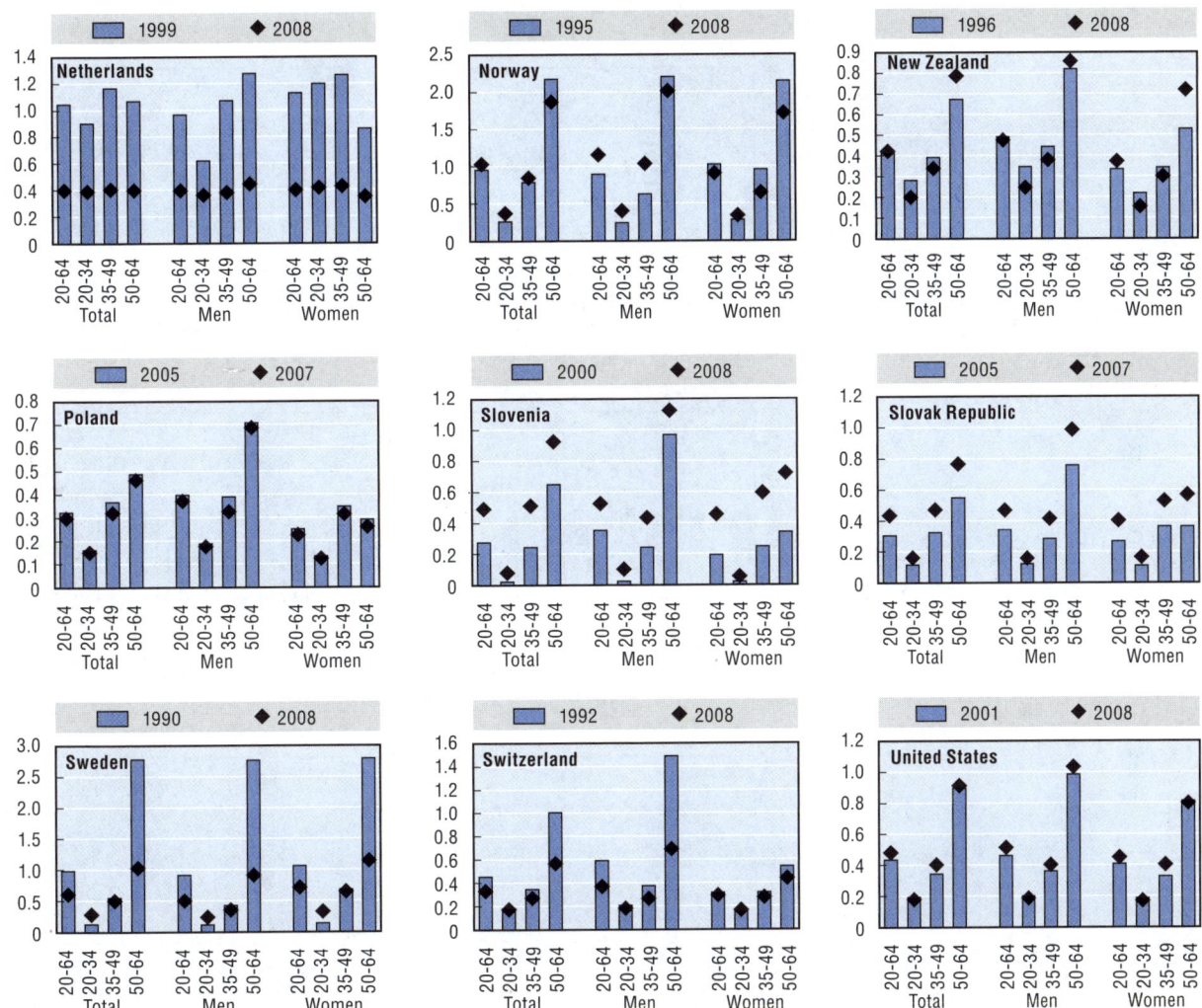

Note: For definitions, see Figure 2.15.

Source: Data provided by national authorities.

Chapter 3

The Direction of Recent Disability Policy Reforms

Sickness and disability outcomes are still disappointing in most countries, with low employment rates and high benefit dependence, calling for further often unpopular reforms. In the past 10-15 years, countries have started to shift their approach away from merely paying benefits to people with disability towards helping them stay in, or return to, work. This chapter outlines the main directions of recent reforms across the OECD and explores the question whether or not changes have gone far enough to reduce benefit dependency and increase employment rates. The chapter concludes that i) policy matters: reform has had a major impact on the observed outcomes, especially the disability beneficiary rate; and ii) policies are moving in the right direction, with considerable convergence of policies despite continued structural differences. However, in most countries more needs to be done.

In 2003, the OECD report *Transforming Disability into Ability* concluded that sickness and disability policy was in dire need of comprehensive reform, probably more than any other area of social and labour market policy. To a considerable extent this conclusion still holds today, with countries struggling to overcome the high disability beneficiary rates. This does not mean, however, that nothing has changed in the past decade. On the contrary, policy measures aimed at reaching a new balance between income security and labour market integration for people with disability have started in most OECD countries. More specifically, the focus of disability policy in many cases has recently shifted from a passive towards a more employment-orientated approach.

This chapter begins by outlining recent trends in reforms of sickness and disability policy to improve labour market inclusion for people with disability. It then explores the extent to which these reforms have sufficed to change the overall policy arrangement enough so to give the strong employment message policy makers are aiming to give. This is followed by an analysis demonstrating considerable convergence of policies across the OECD, despite continuing differences. The chapter ends with a section investigating the impact of different reforms on one key outcome, the disability beneficiary rate.

3.1. Key reform trends across the OECD

There have been many changes in policies aimed at improving employment chances for people with disability and making work a more attractive option for this group of the population. These reforms can be classified under three main broad trends, as described in the following and discussed in more detail in Chapters 4-6: an expansion of employment integration measures; an improvement of the institutional set up; and a tightening of benefit schemes.

Expanding integration policy

One development in disability policy, observed in virtually all OECD countries over the past two decades, is a gradual expansion of policy and measures aimed at helping people stay in and/or re-enter the labour market. These policies can take different forms and often include a combination of measures aimed at supporting workers and employers, coupled with stronger responsibilities for companies.

Anti-discrimination legislation

Most countries have introduced *anti-discrimination legislation* to ensure equal treatment of people with disability (and other disadvantage) in job promotion, hiring and dismissal procedures. Among the first to establish such legislation were Canada in 1985 through the Canadian Charter of Rights and Freedoms and the United States with the 1990 Americans with Disabilities Act (effective 1992). In many European countries, a ban on discrimination on the basis of disability was implemented more recently as part of the EU obligation to adopt similar legislation. In some countries, legislation was first introduced softly and then strengthened gradually in terms of scope and eligibility. In the United Kingdom, for instance, the Disability Discrimination Act was initially implemented in 1994 but the employment rights part came into force only a few years later; in another round of change, the latter was extended to cover a larger number of companies including smaller ones. Also the United States, with its latest reform, recently aims to reach a larger group of people.

Modified employment quotas

Mandatory *employment quotas* are another tool used in some OECD countries, especially in the east, west and south of Europe and in Asia, to entice employers to retain or hire people with disability or, alternatively in some of the existing regulations, subcontract with companies with a significant share of workers with disability. Several countries have recently modified their quota-levy system.[1] Recent modifications include an increase in the levy to be paid by companies not fulfilling their quota (*e.g.* France, Italy); an expansion of the quota regulation to cover the public sector (*e.g.* France, Poland); an expansion to smaller companies hitherto not covered by the regulation (*e.g.* Greece, Korea, Japan); and a broadening of the definition of disability used in the quota system to widen coverage (*e.g.* inclusion of persons with mental disorders in Japan, as from 2005).

Stronger employer incentives

Antidiscrimination legislation and employment quotas, despite recent changes, generate universal but not necessarily very strong or binding obligations for individual employers. Such obligations have been introduced in different ways in different countries. *Workplace accommodation* obligations, also for new job applicants, have often been strengthened in other legislation such as for example the Swedish Working Environment Act. Other countries have chosen to raise obligations by making employers responsible for *sickness benefit payment* for a period of varying length, *e.g.* most recently also in the Czech Republic (in exchange for reduced premia to sickness insurance). This period has been increased in steps in the Netherlands, where employers now have to pay sickness benefit for up to two years and even a third year in the case they cannot prove to have done everything to help the sick worker back into work. In some insurance systems, employers' contributions are increasingly related to the actual number of insurance cases they produce ("experience-rating of premiums"); this is true for disability benefit insurance in Finland and the Netherlands, and for various privately-provided schemes, *e.g.* in Canada and Switzerland.

Spreading of supported employment

A substantial number of countries have increased the range of employment programmes available to people with disability. Most noteworthy, *supported employment* programmes (also referred to as individual placement and support, or IPS, models) were introduced in many countries. These programmes are designed to help integrate people with disability into the regular labour market by first providing a trial workplace and then offering training and help on the job. This approach was also first introduced in the United States, where a revised programme in 1992 already included ongoing (at least twice monthly) support with site-based training and job coaching. Following the US model, several European countries have introduced supported employment-type models during the 1990s (*e.g.* the Nordic countries, Austria, Netherlands; Japan and Switzerland followed in 2002), often as a trial programme initially before being rolled-out country-wide.

Modernising sheltered employment

In the past 15 years, there has been an expansion of initiatives to help people integrate into the regular labour market. The strong focus on *sheltered employment* that many countries had taken was perceived as perpetuating the segregation of people with disability and hindering their integration into the regular labour market. In the United States, for example, sheltered employment is no longer considered as a measure of successful employment. Several countries have improved their sheltered employment regulations. Poland and Hungary, for instance, have introduced accreditation systems (as a prerequisite to receiving subsidies) to guarantee that the working environment is suitable for people with disability. Other countries have developed new forms of sheltered employment closer to the regular labour market, like the social enterprises in Finland and France; or strengthened the focus on progression into the open labour market (*e.g.* Norway which limits the share of people who can stay in sheltered employment permanently). In both cases, more emphasis is given to workers' professional development and the skills learned while in sheltered work. In the Netherlands, reforms emphasise the right to tailor-made sheltered employment which can also be offered by regular companies.

Improved wage subsidies

The main purpose of a wage subsidy – in most cases a subsidy to the employer, sometimes a subsidy given to the worker – is to change labour costs in favour of the targeted group (at the expense of others) so as to alter the composition of labour demand and create employment that would not have been possible without the subsidy. Several countries, *e.g.* Belgium and Denmark, expanded greatly *subsidised employment* for people with disability since the mid-1990s. In the latter country, generous wage subsidies (for so-called "flex-jobs") are provided for people who cannot perform their work under normal conditions, but subsidies are available only after exhaustion of rehabilitation possibilities. The effectiveness of wage subsidies depends on the degree of targeting and is typically much higher with a more restrictive system (such as in Finland) than a generous system like the Danish one, which invited large deadweight and required constant readjustment (*e.g.* a cap on the maximum subsidy) in response to sharp increases in the number of people holding such jobs, which are *de facto* subsidised part-time jobs.

Earlier vocational rehabilitation

Vocational rehabilitation operates on the supply side of the labour market. It aims to increase the productivity of people with disability by restoring and developing their skills and capabilities so they can participate in the general workforce. In recent years, a number of OECD countries have focused on increasing rehabilitation options at an early stage, as well as strengthening rehabilitation requirements. In Austria, for instance, vocational rehabilitation became compulsory in 1996 and each claim for a disability benefit is automatically treated as a request for rehabilitation. Early intervention kicks in when the present job cannot be resumed. Hungary follows, since 2008, a similar rehabilitation-before-benefit principle with a comprehensive rehabilitation process. With the fifth reform of its disability insurance, Switzerland aimed to go a step further by shifting from rehabilitation-*before*-benefit to rehabilitation-*instead-of*-a-benefit. This shift in Switzerland went hand-in-hand with the promotion of early intervention and the introduction of new measures (including job adaptation, placement and socio-professional rehabilitation). The Netherlands is an example of a country that expanded (previously largely non-existent) vocational rehabilitation considerably in the past decade; employers must do their utmost to reintegrate sick employees and – in line with the sick-pay obligation – are responsible for retraining during the two years.

Improving the institutional setup

The expansion of employment measures was, in many cases, complemented by changes in the structure of systems and service provision to make the use of new or expanded services more effective and more likely. Financing mechanisms were also changed in a few countries to strengthen the incentives of public authorities and service providers.

One-stop-shop service provision

Several countries have taken major steps towards a *one-stop-shop* benefit and service provision for people with disability. New Zealand engaged in a more co-ordinated delivery of income support and employment assistance to clients, with the merger of the Employment Service and the Work and Income Authority into the Department of Work and Income in 1998. Similarly, in the United Kingdom the creation of a new agency – Job Centre Plus – that operates on a far more customer-oriented basis provided a single point of delivery for jobs, benefits advice and support for people of working age. Norway has tried to fully merge the Public Employment Service and the National Insurance Authority into one new public administration to ensure streamlined and better co-ordinated services in order to minimise the possibility that clients are continually shuffled between agencies. Initial results are disappointing though this is mostly because such major institutional change will take a long time to deliver.

Better incentives for benefit authorities

Incentives for public institutions granting benefits or assisting persons with partial work capacity to resume employment have also been revised in several countries. Municipalities in Denmark became responsible in 1998 for both employment supports and benefit grants. Reimbursement rates from the central government are higher for active intervention so that municipalities have a vested interest in avoiding benefit payments. These reimbursement rates have been re-adjusted over the years as new policy challenges emerged; for instance, with the increased number of people on subsidised flex-jobs, the rate of reimbursement for this particular type of intervention was reduced in case of insufficient documentation in the application for a flex-job. In a similar but less developed way, and not related to disability policy as such, Dutch municipalities are given incentives to make better use of the work-related programmes available to their clients.

Outcome-based funding of services

A more recent development in some countries is a move away from *bulk funding* of employment services, provided by either public or non-profit institutions, to *outcome-based funding* of services, sometimes but not necessarily provided by private providers. To a varying degree, countries including Australia, the Netherlands and the United Kingdom have started to reimburse service providers for the actual employment outcomes (or sometimes participation outcomes) delivered, with payments often split into several components including an upfront payment and one or several payments along the road tied to performance, when a client has achieved an outcome or stayed in employment for a predefined period.

Freedom of choice for clients

Another development in a few countries is towards giving clients seeking and in need of services the possibility to select the provider of *choice* and, more importantly, the service they need. In the United States, for a number of years disability benefit recipients are now entitled to a voucher (the so-called "ticket-to-work") which they can use for services offered by certified providers. In a similar vein, individual reintegration plans in the Netherlands allow clients to choose their own service pathway, though requiring the consent of the insurance authority; seven out of ten clients are choosing this option. A few other countries, like Germany and the Czech Republic, are experimenting with similar policies on a smaller scale.

Tightening compensation policy

Fewer countries have also implemented changes to their benefit systems, which typically take the form of a tighter access to the system in one way or another. Benefit levels remained untouched in almost all cases but assessment criteria are applied more stringently, including a stricter way of managing the sickness absence phase, the main pathway into long-term disability benefits.

More objective medical criteria

Several countries have chosen to tighten the *medical criteria* used to determine disability benefit entitlement. More particularly, countries which have hitherto relied on assessments by general practitioners have moved to a more uniform evaluation. In Spain, for instance, with the creation of the National Institute of Social Security in 1997, disability is assessed by benefit administrators based on a medical assessment performed by the institute's own doctors. Switzerland did not go as far but in a similar vein an increasing number of the medical assessments are performed by the special regional medical services operated by the cantonal authorities, introduced in 2004. Similarly, New Zealand has seen a gradual shift since the mid-1990s in the decision-making process, from eligibility determined by medical practitioners completing certificates for clients, to case-managers determining eligibility on the basis of advice from medical practitioners, interviews with the client, and other relevant assessments.

More stringent vocational criteria

In terms of *vocational assessment*, several countries are taking an ever broader perspective by considering more and more jobs in the labour market as a reference in determining disability benefit eligibility. In the Netherlands, as of 1993 eligibility for benefits requires that a person could not do any theoretically available job. Similarly, a 1994 reform in Norway, through which the labour market authorities were given the overall responsibility for employment measures, changed the system from strict own-occupation assessment to a labour market-related criterion. Implementation of such change, which is quite radical in principle, is lagging behind. Germany introduced a similar reform in 2001 but the own-occupation approach was kept for all insured older than 40 years at the time of the reform and persons entitled to a partial benefit, who do not find proper part-time work, continue to receive a full disability benefit.

Changes to benefit payments

Reforms have also affected the duration of benefit payment and the level of disability required for benefit entitlement. In Austria, Germany and Poland, disability benefits were *de facto* permanent but became strictly *temporary* – except in the case of full disability in Austria and Germany – in 1996, 2001 and 2005, respectively. In Poland, a temporary benefit is usually granted for three years and upon expiration, payments are terminated, individuals have to reapply and their case will be fully re-examined. A few countries have also modified *minimum levels of disability* required for a disability benefit entitlement. Since the early reform of 1984 in Italy, Australia and Luxembourg restricted the access to benefits for those with partially-reduced work capacity. Since 2006, eligibility to disability benefits in Australia is based on not being able to work at least 15 hours a week, instead of 30 hours prior to reform. Similarly, in the Netherlands following a reform in 2006, the then very low minimum earnings capacity loss required for a disability benefit entitlement was raised, from 15% to 35%. Finally, the generosity of the benefit itself was only modified in a handful of countries. Recent broad benefit reforms in Denmark and the Netherlands included a reduction in the level of benefit payments. Some of the countries with flat-rate payments have made efforts to equalise sickness and/or disability benefit levels with unemployment benefit levels (*e.g.* New Zealand).

Stronger work incentives

Promoting *work incentives* for people on disability benefits has also been pursued by a group of countries. This was a high priority in the United Kingdom, which introduced a special tax credit in 1999 which later on was merged into the general Working Tax Credit. In addition, a new temporary earnings supplement – the Return-to-Work-Credit – was introduced in 2003. Both credits constitute a wage top-up for people with disability in low-paid employment to ensure work pays. The biggest problem with such tax schemes, however, is the low take-up rate. The latest disability benefit reform in the Netherlands, in 2006, improves work incentives by providing what is *de facto* a permanent in-work benefit for individuals with partial or temporary disability through a wage-related benefit payment. Other countries made it easier to combine disability benefit receipt with income from work, sometimes by introducing or increasing earnings disregards (*e.g.* Ireland, New Zealand, Portugal and the Slovak Republic). In addition to the combination of work and benefits, countries have sought to promote employment of people with disability by extending the possibility to put the benefit on hold while trying work for a certain period of time and being able to return to the benefit without reassessment. Such possibility was extended to two years or more at the end of the 1990s in Finland and Norway and more recently in Canada and is now possible without any time limit in Denmark and Sweden. Finally, a few countries have introduced special rehabilitation benefits paid at a higher level than disability benefit to encourage people to take employability-improving rehabilitation measures (*e.g.* Norway and recently Hungary).

Stricter sickness absence monitoring

Several countries concluded that to tackle the number of people claiming a disability benefit it is necessary to address the issue of long-term sickness absence. These countries have increased their efforts to reduce sickness absence by making drastic modifications in their *sickness monitoring policy*. In Denmark, municipalities have been given more and more incentives to monitor absence rigorously and introduce steps for early intervention.

Since 2005, the sickness monitoring process includes the categorisation of sickness into three categories with more work-relevant focus and closer follow-up rules (every four rather than eight weeks as is used otherwise) being applied for the category most at risk. A similar mechanism was established in Spain in 2004 when a new department at the National Institute of Social Security was created with the sole purpose of better monitoring and reducing absence rates. A new monitoring tool with daily updated complete individual sickness absence histories allows online selection of cases for reviews on the basis of longer-than-expected recovery phases. In addition, in 2005 a general absence control was put in place when the duration of absence was greater than six months. Other countries, including especially the Netherlands and Sweden, have recently put in place very detailed medical guidelines for sick-leave certificates by general practitioners for a range of diagnoses so to ensure that sick workers do not stay out of work for longer than is necessary, as judged by expert opinion.

3.2. Policies converge despite continuing differences

The sickness and disability reform intensity has increased all across the OECD, and changes in policy tools and institutional reforms suggest a gradual shift in policy orientation in many cases. While policies used to be very passive, the need for better supports for people with disability to help them stay in or enter the labour market is now widely accepted.

This section explores the extent to which the many reforms and changes in policy tools described above have indeed changed the overall policy setup, by looking at the following questions:

● How much have the changes observed in the past 15 years or so influenced the generosity and accessibility of sickness and disability benefits and the nature, availability and accessibility of employment and vocational rehabilitation programmes?

● Have the observed changes resulted in a convergence in policies across the OECD, within and between groups of countries with different practices, priorities and institutional setups?

To measure the extent of change and convergence in disability policy in the period 1990 to 2007, this section draws on the policy typology developed in OECD (2003). This typology is based on two qualitative policy indicators, which capture a comprehensive selection of disability-related policies and allow for comparisons across countries and over time. The first indicator provides an overall assessment of policy features related to the benefit system whereas the second captures the intensity of integration measures for benefit recipients and those applying for benefits (see Box 3.1 for further details).

Measuring policy change in the past 15 years

There is significant variation across countries in both policy indicators (Figures 3.1 and 3.2). Scores on the first dimension, encapsulating the benefit or compensation policy tools, range from around or below 20 in most of the English-speaking countries, Korea and Japan (countries with the least generous and least accessible benefit systems) to over 30 in most of the Nordic countries, Portugal, Germany and Switzerland. Scores on the second dimension, summarising employment-oriented or integration policy tools, span a slightly broader range; from around 15 in many south-European countries, Ireland and Korea (and

Box 3.1. **OECD disability policy indicators**

Two disability policy indicators are constructed: the first covers compensation measures or benefit programmes, and the second employment or integration measures. These indicators were originally constructed for *Transforming Disability into Ability* (OECD, 2003) for two years, 1985 and 2000. They have been extended to cover the whole period between 1990 and 2007 and have been slightly modified for the purpose of the regression analysis presented later in this chapter. Each of the two indicators is composed of ten sub-components. Each sub-component is measured according to a predefined quantitative and/or qualitative scale, resulting in a certain number of points, ranging from zero to five points for each sub-component. The criteria for each sub-component are spelled out in detail in Annex 3.A1, and the country-specific scores in Annex 3.A2. The points for each sub-component are added to obtain the overall score for each indicator; hence, each sub-component receives the same weight. Tests for correlation and internal consistency have been performed and have revealed no particular problems with the chosen sub-components.

The compensation dimension is split into the following ten sub-components: i) *coverage;* ii) minimum *degree of incapacity* needed for benefit entitlement; iii) degree of incapacity needed *for a full benefit;* iv) *disability benefit level* (in terms of replacement rate for average earnings with a continuous work record); v) *permanence of benefits* (from strictly permanent to strictly temporary); vi) *medical assessment* (from exclusive responsibility of treating doctors to that of teams of insurance doctors); vii) *vocational assessment* (from strict own-occupation assessment to all jobs available); viii) *sickness benefit level* (distinguishing short- and long-term sickness absence); ix) *sickness benefit duration* (including the period of continued wage payment); and x) *sickness monitoring* (from no checks on sickness absence to strict steps for monitoring and early intervention). A higher score means greater system generosity, with 50 being the score for maximum generosity.

The integration dimension distinguishes the following ten sub-dimensions: i) *coverage consistency* (access to different programmes and possibility to combine them); ii) *assessment structure* (responsibility and consistency); iii) *anti-discrimination legislation* covering employer responsibility for work retention and accommodation; iv) *supported employment* programme (extent, permanence and flexibility); v) *subsidised employment* programme (extent, permanence and flexibility); vi) *sheltered employment* sector (extent and transitory nature); vii) *vocational rehabilitation* programme (obligation and extent of spending); viii) *timing of rehabilitation* (from early intervention to late intervention only for disability benefit recipients); ix) *benefit suspension* regulations (from considerable duration to non-existent); and x) additional *work incentives* (including possibilities to combine work and benefit receipt). Again, a higher score indicates a more active approach, with 50 being the possible maximum score.

half this value in Mexico) to 35 points or more in Denmark, Germany, the Netherlands and Norway.

The ranking of countries on the two indicators shows some resemblance, with several of the 28 countries covered in this study having either a high or a low score on both policy dimensions. Countries with high scores on both scales have a comparatively strong integration policy in place, but the generosity and accessibility of benefits is likely to devalue the potential of these policies. Similarly, some countries have very stringent

Figure 3.1. **Large variation in disability policy orientation across the OECD**

Compensation (X axis) and integration (Y axis) policy codes in 2007 for 28 OECD countries, country values on the two ordinal 50-point scales of the OECD disability policy typology indicator

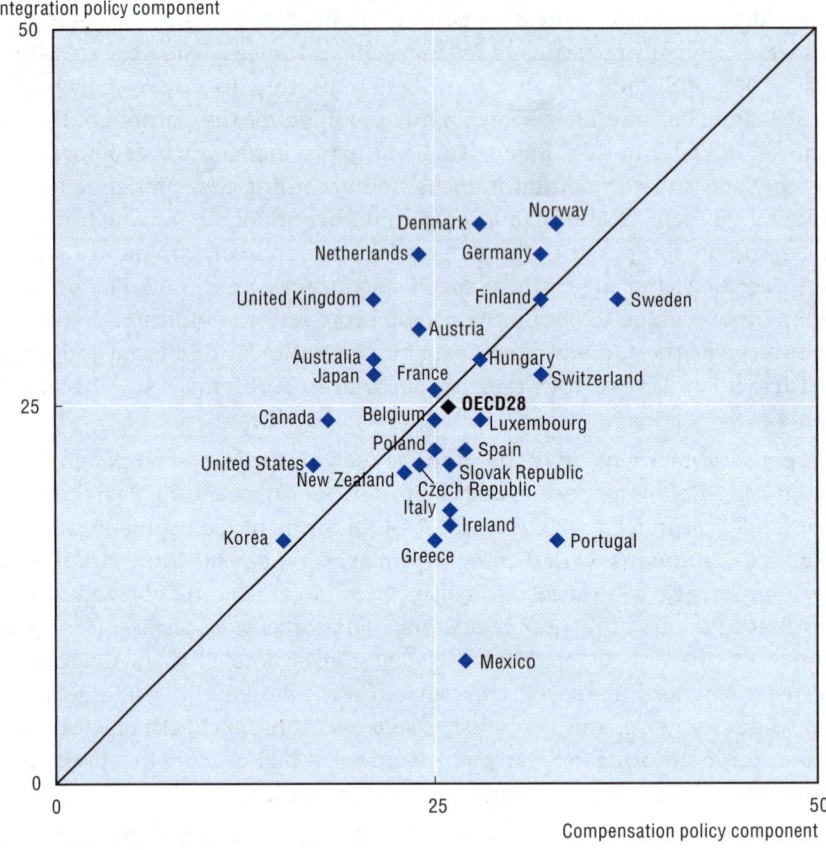

Note: The higher the score, the more generous and accessible the benefit system (X axis) and the more developed the rehabilitation and employment stance of the policy (Y axis). The maximum score is 50 on both scales. The difference between the two indices is an indication of policy orientation, *e.g.* a compensation index that is significantly higher than a country's integration index indicates a strong compensation focus, and *vice versa*.

Source: OECD estimates based on information from national authorities as well as OECD (2006, 2007 and 2008), *Sickness, Disability and Work: Breaking the Barriers* (Vol. 1-3), OECD Publishing, Paris.

benefit schemes and mediocre payments levels, but the lack of stronger employment policies still implies a relatively passive policy setup.

The *difference* between the two scores could be interpreted as a measure of policy orientation: The higher the integration score relative to the compensation score, the more pronounced is the integration orientation of a policy setup, and *vice versa*. On this account, only a few countries seem to have a more dominant – either compensation or integration – focus in their policies. Portugal and Mexico, followed by Greece, Ireland and Italy, have the strongest compensation orientations. On the other side of the spectrum are the Netherlands and the United Kingdom, followed by Denmark, Canada, Australia, Japan and Austria, with the strongest integration orientations in their policy setup.

Figure 3.2 shows how the various reforms and changes in policy tools since 1990 have changed the scores on the two dimensions of the policy typology. The picture arising from this chart is very clear. Sickness and disability policy reforms across the OECD during the past 15 years have led to a strong shift in policy in many countries. Changes in the integration policy score are all positive and sometimes very large, while changes in the

Figure 3.2. **Disability policy is changing fast in many OECD countries**

Integration and compensation policy scores in 2007 and 1990

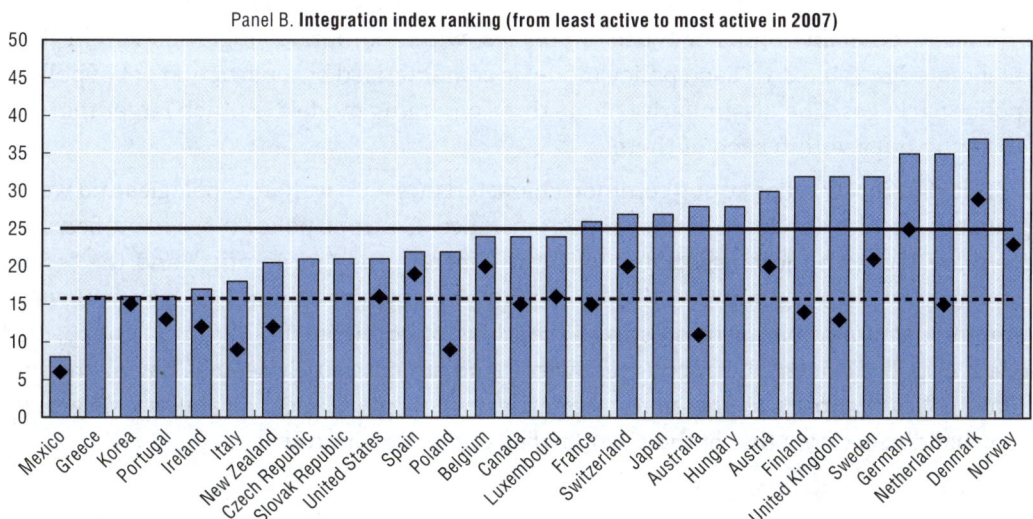

Source: OECD estimates based on information from national authorities as well as OECD (2006, 2007 and 2008), *Sickness, Disability and Work: Breaking the Barriers* (Vol. 1-3), OECD Publishing, Paris.

compensation policy score are predominantly negative, though on average less pronounced. As a result, most countries have seen a – sometimes very considerable – shift in policy orientation from compensation to integration, *i.e.* from a largely passive to a more active disability policy.

In two-thirds of the countries, integration scores have increased by over five points, and the Netherlands, the United Kingdom, Finland and Australia recorded increases of over 15 points.[2] The latter are large changes on a 50-point scale in a period of only 15-20 years. Similarly, two-thirds of the countries have experienced at least some decline of their compensation scores, with the largest drops of 10 points or more observed in the

Netherlands, Luxembourg and Italy. On the contrary, little change occurred in Korea and the Southern European countries.

This big shift in policy orientation towards a more employment-oriented approach does not or not yet seem to be reflected in the labour market outcomes of people with disability. This has several co-existing explanations, which are elaborated in more detail in subsequent chapters. First, it appears that policy implementation is lagging behind policy intentions. The big shift in rhetoric and policy has yet to translate in many cases to an actual shift in everyday practice of doctors, caseworkers, benefit-granting authorities and service providers. This will require very significant additional change addressing the financial incentives of the main stakeholders. Moreover, the policy shift has not been accompanied to the necessary degree by a corresponding shift in resources – contributing to the very low take-up in most cases of new and modified services. This suggests that the shift to a more active stance as identified by the policy typology is probably somewhat exaggerated.

Policy clusters and policy convergence

Do these changes imply that policies have converged across the OECD, or do we continue to find very distinct groups of countries with different sets of disability policies? These questions are explored in the following, concluding that convergence is found both within and between groups of countries.

A cluster analysis over the 20 sub-dimensions of the OECD disability policy typology identifies three main groups or types of policies, with additional subgroups within these, as elaborated in Table 3.1.[3] Each policy model is characterised by a particular set of policies, or policy packages. The dissimilarity of the three emerging models is much larger than that of the subgroups within each of them.

This classification has strong common characteristics with welfare typologies and welfare regime taxonomies developed elsewhere. For instance, the three policy types identified above largely overlap with those associated with the "liberal", the "corporatist" and the "social-democratic" welfare regimes described in Esping-Andersen's seminal 1990 paper. However, there are also a number of interesting exceptions of countries falling into "unexpected" models, or policy clusters. Germany and Switzerland are not usually seen as having the same welfare policy approach as the Nordic countries; whereas Ireland's disability policy seems somewhat distinct from that of the other English-speaking countries.[4]

Table 3.1. **Three distinct disability policy models across the OECD**

Results from a cluster analysis based on the OECD disability policy typology

"Social-democratic" model (mostly north European countries)		"Liberal" model (OECD Pacific and English-speaking countries)		"Corporatist" model (mostly continental European countries)		
Sub-group A	Sub-group B	Sub-group A	Sub-group B	Sub-group A	Sub-group B	Sub-group C
Denmark	Finland	Australia	Canada	Austria	France	Czech Republic
Netherlands	Germany	New Zealand	Japan	Belgium	Greece	Ireland
Switzerland	Norway	United Kingdom	Korea	Hungary	Luxembourg	Italy
	Sweden		United States		Poland	Portugal
						Slovak Republic
						Spain

Source: OECD calculations.

The *Social-democratic* disability policy model is broadly characterised by i) a relatively generous and accessible compensation policy package, with largely universal benefit coverage, a low entry threshold for a partial disability benefit and generous sickness and disability benefits; and ii) a broad and equally accessible integration policy package, with particularly strong focus on vocational rehabilitation. It provides good supports for those who can and want to work, but also considerable incentives to apply for, or remain on, long-term benefits. Such policy is potentially expensive and will not necessarily result in the highest possible labour market participation. Two variants of this model are distinguished in Box 3.2.

The *Liberal* disability policy model is characterised by a much less generous compensation policy setup compared with the other policy models, with lower benefit levels and a much higher threshold to get onto benefits, including an assessment of work capacity with regard to any job on the labour market. Absence monitoring is not well developed. Employment policies are on an intermediary level and vocational rehabilitation is, by and large, relatively underdeveloped; but work incentives are strong and benefit

---

Box 3.2. **Several variants of the three main disability policy models**

The *Social-democratic* policy model comes in two variants. One group, including Denmark, Switzerland and the Netherlands, is less generous than the other one on both policy dimensions (benefits and employment supports are less accessible) but provides better work incentives. It also has the strongest sickness absence monitoring and/or sick-pay eligibility control focus of all models and sub-models. Germany, according to this typology, belongs to the second Nordic sub-model, together with Finland, Sweden and Norway. This sub-model is the most generous in the OECD (with full population coverage, low entry thresholds, high benefits, generous benefit suspension, comprehensive employment and vocational rehabilitation programmes), but also has the strongest employer obligations of all models and sub-models.

The *Liberal* policy model also has two variants. One, covering Australia, New Zealand and the United Kingdom, has far better organised and co-ordinated and thus better accessible services. Benefit levels are even lower for this than for the other subgroup but benefit coverage is almost universal. The other sub-model, comprising Canada and the United States on the one hand and Japan and Korea on the other, has the most stringent eligibility criteria for a full disability benefit, including the most rigid reference to all jobs available in the labour market, and the shortest sickness benefit payment duration, compared with all other models and sub-models.

Within the *Corporatist* policy model, three subgroups can be distinguished. Policies in the first group, including Austria, Belgium and Hungary, stand out in having well developed rehabilitation as well as employment programmes coupled with lower benefit levels, thus having a stronger employment orientation than the other countries in this policy cluster. The countries in the second subgroup, France, Greece, Luxembourg and Poland, pay the most generous sickness and disability benefits of all the countries in the Corporatist cluster; other distinguishing policy features include a focus on temporary disability benefits, more attention to sickness absence monitoring and a lack of benefit suspension possibilities. The third and biggest subgroup, covering the Czech Republic, Ireland, Italy, Portugal, the Slovak Republic and Spain, has comparatively underdeveloped employment and rehabilitation policies. This makes for a stronger compensation orientation even though the sickness benefit level is lower than in the other subgroups of this cluster (but with longer sickness benefit payment duration).

---

suspension rules very flexible. This policy setup is less expensive overall but the stronger inbuilt employment incentives resulting from less generous benefits are only partly harvested with an intermediary integration policy focus. Again, two sub-groups of this model are distinguished in Box 3.2.

The *Corporatist* disability policy model can be interpreted as intermediate, relative to the other two models. Benefits are relatively accessible and relatively generous but not at the level of the Nordic model. Similarly, employment programmes are quite developed but the focus on vocational rehabilitation and supported employment is not nearly as strong as in the Nordic model. Employment and beneficiary outcomes of such a setup can be rather mixed. Outstanding system features are a relatively strong focus on own-occupation assessment in many of the countries in this group and a lower population coverage, but also limited benefit flexibility and work incentives features. The Corporatist model covers a large number of countries mostly in the south, east and west of Europe with considerable differences in their policy setup, as described in Box 3.2.

Figures 3.3 shows how policy has changed for the groups of countries identified through cluster analysis. On the integration policy dimension, policy is moving in largely

Figure 3.3. **Disability policy is converging in the same direction**

Changes in integration and compensation policy scores 1990-1999 and 1999-2007 for the three policy models: Social-democratic (Soc), Liberal (Lib) and Corporatist (Cor)

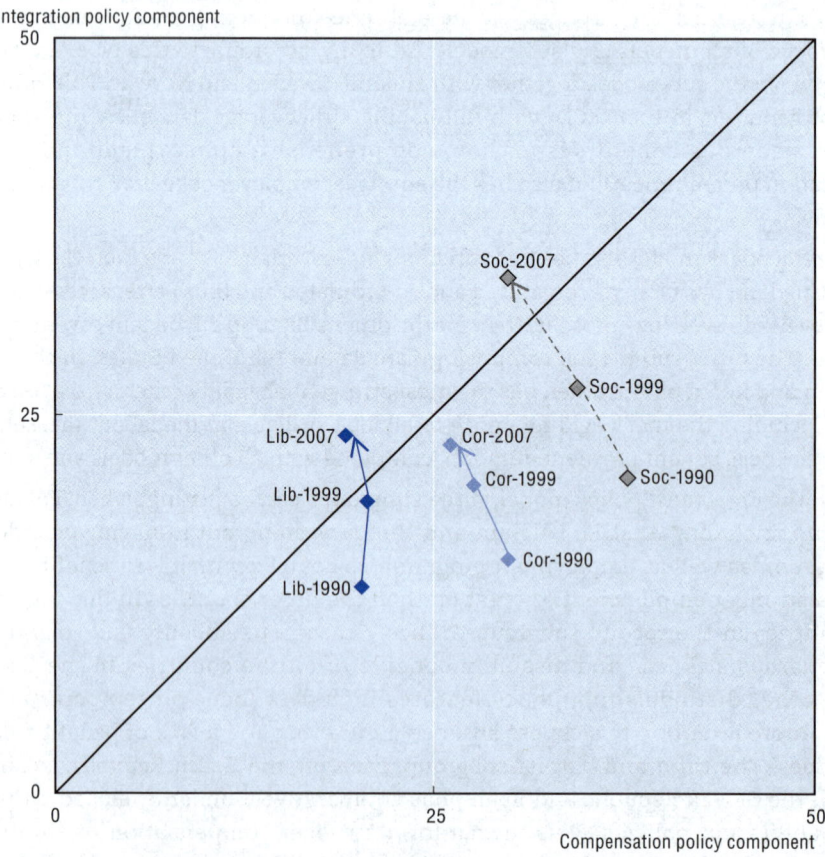

Source: OECD estimates based on information from national authorities as well as OECD (2006, 2007 and 2008), *Sickness, Disability and Work: Breaking the Barriers* (Vol. 1-3), OECD Publishing, Paris.

the same direction in all models and sub-models. Since the upwards move is also comparable in size, differences across policy models have essentially remained unchanged. Thus, there is convergence in trends but not in indicator levels. On the compensation policy dimension, however, considerable convergence is found, due to differences in both the extent and direction of change. Countries belonging to a model with more generous benefit systems have seen more downward change, and the least generous group back in 1990 has even seen an upward shift. In conclusion, therefore, policy models remained distinct but they are more similar now than some 15-20 years ago.

3.3. The effect of policy changes on disability benefit rolls

The key question for policy makers is whether the reforms they are legislating and implementing are having the intended effect of lowering benefit dependency and raising employment of people with disability. This section investigates the potential impact of the different reforms introduced in the disability system in the past 10-20 years on one key outcome, the number of working-age people claiming disability benefit.[5] Features of the sickness and disability benefit system potentially play a major role in depressing labour force participation. They can reduce the willingness to work or engage in job search not only for current beneficiaries but also for current jobholders with or without disability, by modifying the relative advantage of working *versus* not working. Similarly, the new integration approach with expanded, more accessible employment services and at times more mandatory elements of rehabilitation can have the opposite effect of making the non-work option less attractive and less likely.

The results of a multivariate regression show that the overall compensation features of disability policy matter as they are positively related to the resulting number of disability beneficiaries (Table 3.1, model I).[6] The effect of compensation policy holds after controlling for a range of economic conditions, although it is significantly reduced (compare model I, with/without controls).[7] At the same time, integration policy taken as a whole has only a very modest and non-significant effect on resulting disability benefit recipiency rates. This confirms that policy implementation is lagging behind policy change in regard to its employment-oriented components.

Model II while controlling for the same economic conditions looks into the impact on beneficiary outcomes of the specific elements of compensation and integration policy. In line with previous findings (OECD, 2003), it appears that changes in accessibility to disability benefit programmes and benefit generosity are both positively associated with disability beneficiary rates. This is also confirmed by single-country experiences, with a sharp drop in beneficiary rolls in the aftermath of a reform introducing a much more restrictive approach to granting permanent disability benefits (Poland after 1999) or much stricter access to disability benefit for people with partially-reduced work capacity (Luxembourg after 1997).

A more generous and lenient sickness policy (combined "sickness policy indicator" in Table 3.2) also contributes to higher disability beneficiary levels. The link in this case is often a longer-term sickness absence, which then leads to a disability benefit claim. This finding is in line with other studies, for instance, for Sweden on a strong positive relationship between the sick-leave compensation rate and the resulting absence level (Hesselius and Persson, 2007), or the Netherlands where the increasing sickness absence

Table 3.2. **What explains changes in disability benefit recipiency rates?**

Fixed-effect regression coefficients[a, b, c]

	Model I		Model II	Model III
	No controls	With controls		
Indicators				
Compensation indicator	0.117**	0.081**		
Integration indicator	−0.007	−0.011		
Detailed policy indicators				
Benefit accessibility/generosity			0.184***	0.185***
Medical and vocational assessment			−0.160***	−0.149***
Sickness indicator			0.245***	0.211***
Anti-discrimination legislation			0.172**	0.131*
Vocational rehabilitation programme			−0.239*	−0.216*
Sheltered/Subsidised/Supported			−0.115***	−0.117***
Incentives indicator			−0.125***	−0.152***
Gross replacement rates (UB)				−3.604*
Constant	−0.102	−4.945	−10.002***	−3.806
Observations	330	300	300	277
R-squared	0.928	0.938	0.958	0.956

*, **, ***: statistically significant at the 10%, 5%, 1% level, respectively.

a) The dependent variable is annual disability beneficiary rates in 19 OECD countries (Australia, Austria, Belgium, Canada, Denmark, Finland, Germany, Ireland, Korea, Luxembourg, the Netherlands, Norway, Poland, Portugal, Spain, Sweden, Switzerland, the United Kingdom and the United States) in the period 1990-2007. The following years are included for each country: 1994-2007 for Austria; 1990-2007 for Australia, Belgium, Denmark, Finland, the United Kingdom, Ireland, Netherlands, Norway, Portugal and Sweden; 1996-2006 for Canada; 1996-2007 for Switzerland; 1995-2007 for Germany and Spain; 1995-2006 for Korea; 1990-2005 for Luxembourg; and 1990-2006 for the United States.

b) All regressions also include year and country dummies and are weighted by population size. Female labour force participation rates, the share of people aged 55 and above in the population and the share of employment in manufacturing are used as controls for economic conditions and demographic trends. In particular, the share of jobs in manufacturing is also used as a proxy for structural changes in the economy. GDP per capita is capturing a wealth effect. Gross replacement rates for unemployment are used as a crude measure of alternative benefit options only in model III. Differences in the sample size are explained by the non-availability of certain economic indicators and gross replacement rates for some of the countries.

c) The detailed policy indicators used in this table group the sub-components described in Annex 3.A1 into meaningful sub-indicators. Benefit accessibility/generosity includes coverage; minimum disability level; disability level for a full benefit; maximum benefit level; and permanence of benefits. Medical and vocational assessment includes those two components, whereas the sickness indicator includes sickness benefit level; sickness benefit duration; and sickness monitoring. The choice of these sub-components is based on the low correlation that exists between them and the fact that they cover a broad range of elements. Because of the lack of available yearly time series, integration coverage and institutional assessment are not included.

Source: OECD estimates based on OECD Economic Outlook Database, OECD Labour Force Statistics, Labour Force Survey for Australia and OECD STAN Database for all other countries. Disability beneficiary rates are OECD Secretariat estimates based on information provided by national authorities as well as OECD (2006, 2007 and 2008), Sickness, Disability and Work: Breaking the Barriers (Vol. 1-3), OECD Publishing, Paris.

monitoring responsibilities of the employer were found to be one of the main factors in the recent drop in the number of new disability benefit claims (Jehoel-Gijsbers, 2007).

The recently tightened way in which disability is assessed – in some case more stringent medical, in others tighter vocational assessment – appears to be correlated with an increasing beneficiary caseload. This is in contradiction with observations from specific countries like Switzerland, for example, where the introduction of new regional medical services providing more uniform and qualitatively better disability assessments throughout the country was shown to have contributed to the fall in new disability benefit claims as of 2004. However, capturing the effect of changes in the assessment process is notoriously difficult, not only because such changes take a while to be implemented properly, but also because of the difference in many cases between legislation (on which the indicator is based) and actual implementation.[8]

With respect to integration, the expansion of employment programmes and vocational rehabilitation is correlated with a decreasing number of persons receiving a disability benefit. The same is true for changes in work incentives which are also associated with reduced levels of disability benefit recipiency rates. This confirms findings for the United Kingdom according to which the recent reversal in the upward trend in disability beneficiaries is related to a range of policies focusing on labour market integration – including the New Deal for Disabled People rolled out nationally as of 2001 (which *e.g.* includes the use of unpaid work trials and temporary job-match payments for part-time work); the mandatory work-focused interviews eight weeks after the initial benefit claim introduced in the mid-2000s; and a new although temporary earnings supplement for incapacity benefit recipients moving into paid work.

Anti-discrimination legislation, on the other hand, is associated with higher shares of disability benefit recipients. Again, this is not dissimilar from evidence elsewhere (mainly for the United States) showing mixed results in terms of employment outcomes for people with disability (*e.g.* Begle and Stock, 2003; Jolls and Prescott, 2004). One plausible explanation is that such legislation, while protecting workers in existing employment, may hinder the hiring of workers with health problems, even though the Americans with Disabilities Act also protects job applicants with disability.

The regression analysis shows that some elements of disability policy reform are associated with a change in disability beneficiary rates. However, these beneficiary rates are also related to policies in other areas, in particular the availability of other working-age benefits such as for example unemployment benefit (Bound and Burkhauser, 1999). Adding into the model's equation gross replacement rates for unemployment benefits, as a crude measure of alternative benefit options, does not alter significantly the results (Table 3.2, model III). A more generous unemployment benefit is associated with lower disability beneficiary rates (significant at the 10% level), confirming findings discussed earlier in the report according to which increases in disability benefit rolls coincided with a fall in the number of people receiving unemployment benefit.[9]

3.4. The political economy of reform

Sickness and disability system reform is a huge task, for several reasons. First, the underlying policy goals are potentially contradictory: to provide income security during periods of short or long-term work incapacity, while at the same time helping people to stay in the labour market or to enable them to return to it as quickly as possible. Second and partly related to this, the group of people to be helped is extremely heterogeneous, requiring a wide range of different forms of incentives, supports and services to be provided by one and the same system. Third, the group of stakeholders involved is broader than in other policy fields; not only are social and employment issues at stake but the medical sector is also involved, both in assessing eligibility and in rehabilitating workers. Fourth, changing one parameter of the system (*e.g.* eligibility assessment) can have complex effects on other parameters (*e.g.* early intervention). Finally, reforms of *other* social assistance and social insurance systems often have a major impact on sickness and disability benefits, which have become in several cases the "benefit of last resort".

For these reasons, it is difficult to make structural system reform happen. Successful change not only needs the right elements of reform but also has to pay sufficient attention to the way in which reform is being argued, designed and put in place.[10] Only rigorous implementation of reform can guarantee its intention will be followed and outcomes improved. It is too easy for stakeholders to continue business as usual, and there are incentives in the system for stakeholders to err on the side of leniency when granting a benefit.[11] Therefore, structural reform needs a change in attitudes and mind-sets of all the actors involved at different stages. In turn, this makes the study of sickness and disability reform paths and processes and of the political economy of system reform particularly interesting.

An issue that arises when governments are considering comprehensive reform is the ability to communicate clearly and convincingly to stakeholders both the need for reform and the desirability of the proposed solutions. The rigor and quality of the analysis underlying a reform can affect both the prospects for its adoption and the implementation and the quality of the policy itself. At any given moment, the political context will also influence the reception by the general public, by stakeholders and by policy elites of any particular piece of analysis and policy recommendation. Drawing on Prinz and Tompson (2009), Box 3.3 exemplifies some of these problems by looking at the reform pathways in selected OECD countries – demonstrating the iterations of reform in most cases.

Box 3.3. **Policy process lessons from selected OECD countries**

Switzerland, after 40 years of little change in its disability policy regime, undertook a series of increasingly successful reforms in recent years. To a considerable degree, these reforms were motivated by accusations of widespread benefit fraud that, although never proven, triggered a more thorough public debate. Public discussion of the issue became increasingly intense in response to the steady increase in numbers of beneficiaries and the fast rise in the deficit of public disability insurance. These helped to convince most stakeholders of the need for reform. At the same time, new data were being collected and a large body of new scientific evidence was being produced. Much attention was paid to benchmarking outcomes and policies against other OECD countries. Placed in a comparative context, policies, institutions and practices that seemed normal until then came to be looked at through a more critical lens. Such discussion made it possible to generate consensus on the direction of reform, its main characteristic being a new focus on early identification and intervention in order to prevent people flowing onto long-term disability benefit.

Norway has yet to undertake major reform, despite the highest sickness absence and disability beneficiary rates in the OECD. A Royal Commission report in 2000 presented far-reaching reform proposals, especially regarding the benefit system and the incentives for workers and employers, but successive governments have left it to the social partners to solve the problems the Commission identified. This approach has brought very limited success so far: Sickness absence has not really fallen and disability beneficiary rates continued to increase. Government shied away from more comprehensive structural reform, even though an increasing body of national evidence suggests that such change is needed to alter the incentives facing the key players in the system. Hence, the need for change and also the direction of necessary reform is well recognised by most experts but the political culture of consensus-driven reform (via social dialogue) hinders enactment of some unavoidable but unpopular system restructuring. A renewed tripartite agreement aims to strengthen further the focus on partial sickness absence and closer follow-up during sick leaves.

Box 3.3. **Policy process lessons from selected OECD countries** (cont.)

Australia has experienced steady economic growth since the early 1990s. However, as unemployment was falling, the disability beneficiary rate was rising, and at a roughly similar rate. What is more, this happened despite an important reform in 1991 that provided significant resources and introduced a series of new programmes to promote the employment of people with disability. Much of the reform effort since then has involved attempts to expand the more successful elements of labour market programmes to assist people with reduced work capacity to find work. This idea encountered lots of resistance, but the accumulation of a growing body of national evidence supporting such change enabled the government to introduce a comprehensive welfare-to-work reform in 2006. Under the new arrangements, many of those with partially-reduced work capacity are now treated like the regular unemployed, with corresponding part-time work, job-search and participation requirements. However, adoption of this very contentious reform was made possible only by leaving untouched the entitlements of those already on a disability benefit.

The *United Kingdom*, too, has seen a significant part of the rapid fall in unemployment since 1993 offset by increased use of disability benefits – with the result that the share of the working-age population on such benefits far exceeded the OECD average. This has generated a vast literature on various elements of the system, including a series of evaluations of the impact of interventions of all kinds showing, *inter alia*, that employment programmes could be effective also for people with reduced work capacity and work was generally good for people's health. The accumulation of an evidence base enabled the government to push forward with reform, often using trials and pilots in an initial stage, and including a proposal to move in the direction of a single working-age benefit. Reliance on pilot programmes means that the universal or comprehensive roll-out of an initiative is evidence-based, even though the effectiveness might be less pronounced on a nationwide scale.

In *Sweden*, since the beginning of the 1990s successive governments have tried to tackle the problem of rapidly rising expenditure on sickness benefits, as well as the concomitant growth in the number of work days lost as a result of sickness. During the 1990s, these efforts – triggered by an acute fiscal crisis – were ineffective; a series of reforms or reform attempts were either reversed or blocked. Back then, there was no consensus on the need for reform. Since 2002, however, there have been renewed attempts at sickness insurance reform, recently with very impressive results. There are many reasons for the frustration of reform efforts in the 1990s and the – so far – promising outcomes observed since 2002. These include a gradual shift in the political consensus from a commitment to passive income assistance with respect to people with disability to the application of the kind of mutual-obligations approach already used with respect to unemployed people. There is also a strong case for arguing that the more recent reforms were possible because the failed reforms of the 1990s gave rise to a large and sophisticated body of empirical work on the weaknesses in the sickness insurance system.

The *Netherlands*, finally, has long had one of the most generous disability insurance systems in the OECD. By 2000, around 11% of the working-age population was drawing disability benefits. A major reform to the system was agreed by the government and the social partners in 2003-04, and took effect in 2006. The reform, which applied only to persons who suffered disability in 2004 or later, reduced the inflow into the disability benefit scheme from the 70 000-100 000 per year that had prevailed over the preceding decade, to some 40 000 in 2007 and 2008 – a major accomplishment. Those already receiving benefits at the time of the reform continued to receive benefits defined under the old rules, but most of those younger than age 45 have had their entitlement re-assessed under the criteria used in the new system. Again, there is a strong case for arguing that the success of the latest reforms which have changed the incentives facing employers and employees drastically was made possible by the (failed) earlier reform which, building on fast growing new scientific evidence, have created a consensus for the need for change.

3.5. Conclusion

This chapter finds that sickness and disability policy is changing in most OECD countries, and in largely the same direction. To a varying degree and at varying speed, countries are transforming their systems gradually in a search for a better balance in the provision of income support and work incentives. Most countries have expanded considerably the array of employment supports available for people with chronic health problems or disability, and some countries have also – to a lesser extent – started to control more stringently access to hitherto easy – to-get sickness and disability benefits. The chapter also finds evidence of some convergence in policies even though distinct policy models continue to exist.

However, despite a number of efforts, in most countries reforms have not gone far enough to change sufficiently the continuously disappointing outcomes in terms of low employment and high rates of benefit dependency. The message given by many systems to workers, employers and public authorities administering the system continues to be slightly contradictory in terms of whether or not employment is seen as the best way to tackle disability. The lack of more far-reaching reform in several countries is to a considerable degree the consequence of the difficult policy process involved in changing a passive system that was designed for a narrow group and is now serving a highly heterogeneous target group.

The good news on which further structural reform should build is that policy matters: Countries which embarked on comprehensive reform involving both the benefit and the employment support system have seen the biggest changes in outcomes.

Notes

1. Quota-levy systems aim to influence labour demand by mandating employers to employ a certain share of workers with disability, typically in the range of 2%-7% of the company workforce. However, systems allow employers to opt out by contributing money (a levy) to a special fund. These funds usually disperse resources to workers with disability, service providers, and employers.

2. It should be kept in mind that not each and every single policy change has an impact on the indicator values and also that the indicator is more sensitive to some types of changes than others. Hence, these results should be taken as indicative of the overall size of change in each country.

3. Cluster analysis is a method to group data (in this case, a series of policy typology scores) into subsets or "clusters", such that those within each cluster are more closely related (or more similar) to one another than objects assigned to different clusters. Cluster analysis discovers structures in data without explaining why they exist. The estimates are based on hierarchical clustering using the classic complete linkage method whereby distance between groups is defined as the distance between the most distant pair of objects. Hierarchical clustering means that more and more objects are being aggregated together into larger and larger clusters of increasingly dissimilar elements.

4. A classification like this obtained through cluster analysis should be interpreted carefully. It can help identify broad commonalities and differences but can also react very sensitively to small changes in indicator values in one or several countries.

5. Due to data limitations, the dependent variable used is the total disability benefit caseload not the flow of new claimants of disability benefits which reacts more sensitively to policy change. However, flow data are not available for a long enough period for a large enough number of countries.

6. The analysis describes multivariate correlations between changes in system and policy features and changes in the beneficiary caseload. Results cannot be interpreted as causal, again because of data limitations.

7. Several sensitivity tests have been performed, based on disaggregated data by gender and age and excluding one country at a time. Labour market factors may play an important role in explaining changes in disability recipiency rates since decreases in work options, or work options that are low paid, are found to be a major explanation for lower participation rates for the low-skilled and higher applications to disability benefits (Autor and Duggan, 2003; Faggio and Nickell, 2005). Labour demand and alternative benefit options (such as early retirement) are *not* controlled for in this analysis because of the lack of appropriate indicators. Unemployment rates could be used as a proxy for labour demand conditions, but they may capture more general economic change more than the relative attractiveness of unemployment *versus* disability benefits. Concerns about using time-series data for such analysis exist (Disney and Webb, 1991) and would be particularly problematic given the short time-span and the cross-country nature of the data.

8. Taking the example of the Netherlands, changes in the definition of disability reduced the number of new benefit awards by 7% in 1993. However, the slowdown was reversed at the end of the 1990s and the number on disability rolls reached almost 1 million in 2002. The reversal is believed to be partly attributed to a more lenient interpretation of the assessment rules.

9. The causality between disability and other beneficiary trends can also be influenced by policy decisions, for instance, easier access to unemployment benefit during a downturn reducing the need for disability benefit in the short run, or stricter application of entitlement rules for social assistance payments contributing to a shift of some people onto disability benefit, as has been shown for Finland (Gould, 2003).

10. The right timing of reform can be another critical parameter. The coincidence of a jobs crisis does not appear to be the best moment to embark on structural reform but this report tries to argue why ongoing disability reform cannot be halted at this stage in view of the long-term structural risks (of a higher structural disability beneficiary rate) and challenges (of a falling labour force).

11. This problem is closely related to the challenge of assessing work capacity. Ideally, a system should neither deny benefits to people who deserve them (exclusion error) nor award benefits to those who do not (inclusion error). Both errors involve welfare losses, but the consequences of exclusion errors are likely to be more serious for those administering the system: deserving applicants who are denied benefit may contest the decision, whereas undeserving applicants who are awarded benefits will not draw attention to themselves. Moreover, doctors and others involved in screening are likely to face more serious consequences if they are found to have denied assistance to a genuinely needy individual, who then suffers further health problems or loss of capacity as a result. The agents administering the system thus have incentives to err on the side of leniency and grant the benefit of doubt.

Bibliography

Autor, D. and M.G. Duggan (2003), "The Rise in the Disability Rolls and the Decline in Unemployment", *Quarterly Journal of Economics*, Vol. 118, No. 1, pp. 157-206.

Begle, K. and A. Stock (2003), "The Labour Market Effects of Disability Discrimination Laws", *Journal of Human Resources*, Vol. 38, pp. 806-859.

Bound, J. and R. Burkhauser (1999), "Economic Analysis of Transfers Programs Targeted on People with Disabilities", in O. Ashenfelter and D. Card (eds.), *Handbook of Labor Economics*, Vol. 3, No. 1, Chapter 51, Elsevier, pp. 3417-3528.

Disney, R. and S. Webb (1991), "Why Are there So Many Long-term Sick in Britain?", *The Economic Journal*, Vol. 101, pp. 252-262.

Esping-Andersen, G. (1990), *The Three Worlds of Welfare Capitalism*, Polity Press, Cambridge.

Faggio, G. and S. Nickell (2005), "Inactivity among Prime Age Men in the UK", *CEP Discussion Paper*, No. 673, London School of Economics, London.

Gould, R. (2003), "Disability Pensions in Finland", in C. Prinz (ed.), *European Disability Pension Policies. 11 Country Trends 1970-2002*, European Centre Vienna, Ashgate, Aldershot.

Hesselius, P. and M. Persson (2007), "Incentive and Spill-over Effects of Supplementary Sickness Compensation", *IFAU Working Paper*, No. 16, Institute of Labour Market Policy Evaluation, Uppsala.

Jehoel-Gijsbers, G. (2007), "Beter aan het werk. Trendrapportage ziekteverzuim, arbeidsongeschiktheid en werkhervatting", Social and Cultural Planning Bureau, The Hague.

Jolls, C. and J.J. Prescott (2004), "Disaggregating Employment Protection; The Case of Disability Discrimination", *NBER Working Paper Serie*, No. 10740, Cambridge, MA.

OECD (2003), *Transforming Disability into Ability*, OECD Publishing, Paris.

OECD (2006), *Sickness, Disability and Work: Breaking the Barriers. Vol. 1: Norway, Poland and Switzerland*, OECD Publishing, Paris.

OECD (2007), *Sickness, Disability and Work: Breaking the Barriers. Vol. 2: Australia, Luxembourg, Spain and the United Kingdom*, OECD Publishing, Paris.

OECD (2008), *Sickness, Disability and Work: Breaking the Barriers. Vol. 3: Denmark, Finland, Ireland and the Netherlands*, OECD Publishing, Paris.

Prinz, C. and D. Tompson (2009), "Sickness and Disability Programmes: What is Driving Policy Convergence?", *International Social Security Review*, Vol. 62, No. 4, pp. 41-6.

ANNEX 3.A1

Table 3.A1.1. **OECD disability policy typology: classification of the indicator scores**

DIMENSION	5 points	4 points	3 points	2 points	1 point	0 points
X. Compensation						
X1. Population coverage	Total population (residents)	Some of those out of the labour force (e.g. congenital)	Labour force plus means-tested non-contrib. scheme	Labour force with voluntary self-insurance	Labour force	Employees
X2. Minimum required disability or work incapacity level	0-25%	26-40%	41-55%	56-70%	71-85%	86-100%
X3. Disability or work incapacity level for full benefit	< 50%	50-61%	62-73%	74-85%	86-99%	100%
X4. Maximum disability benefit payment level	RR > = 75%, reasonable minimum	RR > = 75%, minimum not specified	75 > RR > = 50%, reasonable minimum	75 > RR > = 50%, minimum not specified	RR < 50%, reasonable minimum	RR < 50%, minimum not specified
X5. Permanence of benefit payments	Strictly permanent	De facto permanent	Self-reported review only	Regulated review procedure	Strictly temporary, unless fully (= 100%) disabled	Strictly temporary in all cases
X6. Medical assessment criteria	Treating doctor exclusively	Treating doctor predominantly	Insurance doctor predominantly	Insurance doctor exclusively	Team of experts in the insurance	Insurance team and two-step procedure
X7. Vocational assessment criteria	Strict own or usual occupation assessment	Reference is made to one's previous earnings	Own-occupation assessment for partial benefits	Current labour market conditions are taken into account	All jobs available taken into account, leniently applied	All jobs available taken into account, strictly applied
X8. Sickness benefit payment level	RR = 100% also for long-term sickness absence	RR = 100% (short-term) > = 75% (long-term) sickness absence	RR > = 75% (short-term) > = 50% (long-term) sickness absence	75 > RR > = 50% for any type of sickness absence	RR > = 50% (short-term) < 50% (long-term) sickness absence	RR < 50% also for short-term sickness absence
X9. Sickness benefit payment duration	One year or more, short or no wage payment period	One year or more, significant wage payment period	Six-twelve months, short or no wage payment period	Six-twelve months, significant wage payment period	Less than six months, short or no wage payment period	Less than six months, significant wage payment period
X10. Sickness absence monitoring	Lenient sickness certificate requirements	Sickness certificate and occupational health service with risk prevention	Frequent sickness certificates	Strict follow-up steps with early intervention and risk profiling, but no sanctions	Strict controls of sickness certificate with own assessment of illness if necessary	Strict follow-up steps with early intervention and risk profiling, including sanctions

Note: RR = replacement rate.

Table 3.A1.1. **OECD disability policy typology: classification of the indicator scores** (cont.)

DIMENSION	5 points	4 points	3 points	2 points	1 point	0 points
Y. Integration						
Y1. Consistency across supports in coverage rules	All programmes accessible	Minor discrepancy, flexible mixture	Minor discrepancy, restricted mixture	Major discrepancy, flexible mixture	Major discrepancy, restricted mixture	Strong differences in eligibility
Y2. Complexity of the benefits and supports systems	Same agency for assessment for all programmes	One agency for integration, benefits co-ordinated	Same agency for benefits and vocational rehabilitation	One agency for integration, benefits not co-ordinated	Different agencies for most programmes	Different agencies for all kinds of assessments
Y3. Employer obligations for their employees and new hires	Major obligations towards employees and new applicants	Major obligations towards employees, less for applicants	Some obligations towards employees and new applicants	Some obligations towards employees, none for applicants	No obligations at all, but dismissal protection	No obligations of any kind
Y4. Supported employment programmes	Strong programme, permanent option	Strong programme, only time-limited	Intermediary, also permanent	Intermediary, only time-limited	Very limited programme	Not existent
Y5. Subsidised employment programmes	Strong and flexible programme, with a permanent option	Strong and flexible programme, but time-limited	Intermediary, either permanent or flexible	Intermediary, neither permanent nor flexible	Very limited programme	Not existent
Y6. Sheltered employment programmes	Strong focus, with significant transition rates	Strong focus, but largely permanent employment	Intermediary focus, with some "new" attempts	Intermediary focus, "traditional" programme	Very limited programme	Not existent
Y7. Comprehensiveness of vocational rehabilitation	Compulsory rehabilitation with large spending	Compulsory rehabilitation with low spending	Intermediary view, relatively large spending	Intermediary view, relatively low spending	Voluntary rehabilitation with large spending	Voluntary rehabilitation with low spending
Y8. Timing of vocational rehabilitation	In theory and practice any time (e.g. still at work)	In theory any time, in practice not really early	Early intervention increasingly encouraged	Generally *de facto* relatively late intervention	After long-term sickness or for disability recipients	Only for disability benefit recipients
Y9. Disability benefit suspension option	Two years or more	At least one but less than two years	More than three but less than 12 months	Up to three months	Some, but not for disability benefits	None
Y10. Work incentives for beneficiaries	Permanent in-work benefit provided	Benefit continued for a considerable (trial) period	Income beyond pre-disability level allowed	Income up to pre-disability level, also partial benefit	Income up to pre-disability level, no partial benefit	Some additional income allowed

Note: RR = replacement rate.

ANNEX 3.A2

Table 3.A2.1. **OECD disability policy typology: country scores around 2007**

Panel A. Compensation policy dimension (values from 0-5 for each sub-component and 0-50 for the total)

	1	2	3	4	5	6	7	8	9	10	Sum
	Benefit system coverage	Minimum disability benefit	Level for full disability	Disability benefit generosity	Disability benefit permanence	Medical assessment rules	Vocational assessment rules	Sickness benefit generosity	Sickness benefit duration	Sickness benefit monitoring	
Australia	4	1	2	1	2	3	1	1	1	5	21
Austria	2	3	4	2	1	1	4	3	2	2	24
Belgium	3	2	3	1	4	2	4	2	2	2	25
Canada	3	1	1	1	4	1	0	1	1	5	18
Czech Republic	1	4	3	3	0	2	1	0	5	5	24
Denmark	5	2	1	3	4	4	2	4	3	0	28
Finland	5	4	4	3	2	3	2	3	3	3	32
France	3	2	1	3	1	2	4	2	5	2	25
Germany	3	5	3	2	1	3	2	4	4	5	32
Greece	3	3	2	5	2	1	3	2	2	2	25
Hungary	1	3	2	3	2	1	4	3	5	4	28
Ireland	3	1	2	1	4	3	2	1	5	4	26
Italy	3	2	0	3	1	1	3	3	5	5	26
Japan	4	1	0	1	2	2	0	2	5	4	21
Korea	3	3	0	1	2	1	0	0	1	4	15
Luxembourg	2	1	2	5	3	2	2	5	4	2	28
Mexico	0	3	4	0	3	2	5	2	3	5	27
Netherlands	4	4	2	3	2	1	0	4	4	0	24
New Zealand	5	1	2	1	2	3	1	1	5	2	23
Norway	5	3	2	4	2	4	2	5	4	2	33
Poland	3	3	4	4	0	1	3	3	2	2	25
Portugal	3	2	3	5	4	1	4	1	5	5	33
Slovak Republic	1	4	3	2	4	2	1	2	5	2	26
Spain	3	4	1	4	5	0	3	2	4	1	27
Sweden	5	5	1	5	4	3	1	4	4	5	37
Switzerland	5	4	3	3	4	3	2	3	4	1	32
United Kingdom	3	1	2	1	2	3	1	1	2	5	21
United States	3	0	1	3	2	4	0	3	0	1	17
OECD average (28)	3.1	2.6	2.1	2.6	2.5	2.1	2.0	2.4	3.4	3.0	25.8

Table 3.A2.1. **OECD disability policy typology: country scores around 2007** (cont.)

Panel B. Integration policy dimension (values from 0-5 for each sub-component and 0-50 for the total)

	1	2	3	4	5	6	7	8	9	10	Sum
	Access to employment programmes	Agency responsibility structure	Degree of employer responsibility	Supported employment programme	Subsidised employment programme	Sheltered employment programme	Vocational rehabilitation programme	Vocational rehabilitation timing	Benefit suspension rules	Work incentives rules	
Australia	4	5	3	1	2	3	1	3	5	1	28
Austria	2	3	3	4	4	2	5	4	0	3	30
Belgium	3	3	3	1	5	2	2	3	2	0	24
Canada	1	1	3	3	2	2	1	2	5	4	24
Czech Republic	3	1	4	1	1	3	1	4	0	3	21
Denmark	4	4	2	3	5	2	5	4	5	3	37
Finland	2	2	4	3	3	3	4	4	5	2	32
France	3	2	3	3	5	4	1	2	0	3	26
Germany	4	0	4	5	4	3	5	5	3	2	35
Greece	3	2	3	0	2	3	0	1	0	2	16
Hungary	2	3	4	3	3	2	3	2	4	2	28
Ireland	3	2	2	1	3	2	0	1	1	2	17
Italy	4	2	4	1	1	2	0	2	0	2	18
Japan	3	1	1	3	3	2	2	4	5	3	27
Korea	0	1	1	2	3	2	1	2	1	3	16
Luxembourg	2	4	3	2	4	3	2	3	0	1	24
Mexico	2	2	0	0	0	0	0	1	0	3	8
Netherlands	4	4	4	2	2	4	4	4	2	5	35
New Zealand	3	5	2	2	2	1	0	0	3	3	21
Norway	4	5	4	2	4	4	5	4	5	0	37
Poland	4	2	2	0	3	4	2	2	0	3	22
Portugal	3	2	2	1	2	2	1	1	1	1	16
Slovak Republic	3	2	4	2	2	3	0	2	0	3	21
Spain	4	3	3	1	2	3	2	2	0	2	22
Sweden	3	4	5	2	4	3	3	3	5	0	32
Switzerland	4	4	2	1	1	3	5	4	0	3	27
United Kingdom	4	4	4	3	1	2	1	3	5	5	32
United States	0	0	3	4	1	2	1	1	5	4	21
OECD average (28)	2.9	2.6	2.9	2.0	2.6	2.5	2.0	2.6	2.2	2.4	24.9

Chapter 4

Transforming Disability Benefits into an Employment Instrument

This chapter addresses the key challenges and recent developments in changing the current disability benefit schemes, which are still too passive in nature, into employment-promoting policy tools. Key elements in the transformation process are a new way of assessing work capacity implemented, thus, benefit eligibility; a new activation and mutual-obligations stance applied at the application phase; a stronger focus on reassessments of benefit eligibility and work capacity of current or long-term benefit recipients; and improved work incentives to make sure work always pays. The chapter concludes that what is needed is to bring the disability benefit scheme closer in all its aspects to existing unemployment benefit schemes and questions the need for distinguishing unemployment and disability as two distinct contingencies.

As noted earlier, the vast majority of persons who take up disability benefits never return to work. This would not seem surprising were disability benefits only granted to those without any remaining work capacity. However, this is not the case for the majority of the large and increasing numbers of recipients today who do have partial work capacity. Contrary to its intended purpose, disability benefit systems seem to be having a *disabling* effect on people, steering them into welfare dependency and labour market exclusion.

How can countries halt the rising practice of disability benefit dependency? One way forward is to improve the process of identifying applicants potentially able to work and thereby avoiding their initial entry into long-term incapacity benefit status. Assessment procedures in several countries have started to shift to looking at the remaining capacity of people applying for a disability benefit. Given that people rarely move off disability benefit once they have been granted it, limiting new entries into the disability benefit system will be the most effective way forward, even though it will take a while for this to reduce the beneficiary caseload.

Secondly, although disability policy across the OECD has moved towards a stronger employment orientation in the past decade, disability schemes continue to be very passive when it comes to expectations for persons with partial work capacity. To prevent the disability benefit trap, this group should be made subject to participation requirements matching their capacity, similar to the requirements facing recipients of unemployment benefits.

Limiting access to disability benefits and increasing participation requirements alone will not be sufficient to promote employment opportunities for persons with disability. If work does not pay, people will be reluctant to work, or to seek work. Providing the right financial incentives can be particularly important for workers with disability since many of them are likely to enter low-paid jobs.

This chapter sequentially address these key challenges. Policy issues in relation to sickness benefit, the main precursor to a disability benefit claim, are discussed in Chapter 5, in the context of the role of employers in retaining sick workers.

4.1. From disability assessment to work-capacity assessment

The significant rise in the number of disability beneficiaries in recent decades has required countries to rethink their approach to addressing working-age disability. A key reason why people with health problems but meaningful work capacity became, in effect, pensioned off by disability benefit schemes is that entitlement was *not* determined according to a reliable and valid assessment of a person's labour market competitiveness. Instead, there was and still is too much focus on a medical diagnosis of loss of physical and/or mental functioning, as assessed by a medical practitioner with no or limited expertise in rehabilitation. This medically-driven judgement can either lead directly to the granting of a disability benefit, or in any case will be a major factor in the award procedure.

A second problem, related to this, is that disability benefits are awarded with a number of implicit preconditions that presuppose a claimant's health is unlikely to improve and will permanently preclude them from undertaking any work. This is a wrong assumption for many of the most prevalent health conditions today. To avoid having their benefits cut, claimants must, firstly, maintain that they are unable to work; secondly, they must not participate in any activity that would significantly boost their income, even if they are living close to poverty; and lastly, they must not report any improvement in their health status. In exchange, the claimant receives what in many countries amounts to a *de facto* lifetime disability payment.

Assessing for capacity

Among the flaws with this approach is that medical diagnoses are typically unrelated to a person's likelihood of returning to work. Moreover, in practice such decision-making varies considerably and unreliably across medical assessors (*e.g.* Hunt *et al.*, 2002) and patient demand may be playing a significant role in shaping the medical decisions that determine entitlements (*e.g.* Campbell and Ogden, 2006). As a result, there is a high likelihood that many people who could work are being granted a disability benefit that effectively excludes them from the labour market. Persons with chronic health problems or disability may need medical care and rehabilitation, but using a predominantly medical assessment that is inconsistently variable as the primary determinant of benefit entitlement is not an effective approach.

Recognising this, several countries have recently made efforts to move away from assessing a person's disability to exploiting better the person's remaining work capacity. Such a change in orientation also shifts the focus of supports and resources to rehabilitating people back to part or full-time work rather than supporting them to stay out of work. Denmark has perhaps gone furthest in this shift to a broader approach to capturing the applicant's remaining work capacity:

- Following comprehensive reform in 2003, disability assessment in Denmark now focuses on the person's *remaining functions* and the *possible jobs* the person can still perform. A comprehensive individual resource profile is put together covering a range of health, social (network) and labour-market experience and proximity criteria. Health is only one of many elements involved though it is a key factor in 95% of all new disability benefit grants.

- Similarly, in the Netherlands disability assessment is based on the person's functional abilities which are matched to job requirements in order to determine the residual earnings capacity (with 35% capacity loss required for a partial disability benefit). The job-matching process is based on hypothetical jobs in the economy, not actual jobs available.

Several other countries have changed their assessment procedures in different ways, moving away from a medical focus to a more interdisciplinary one taking social aspects and labour market contexts into account (*e.g.* Hungary, Slovak Republic). In many cases this shift is complemented with a shift in responsibilities, with decisions increasingly taken by case-managers of benefit authorities taking into account not only the medical file but also clients' abilities and work aspirations (*e.g.* New Zealand). This is important in countries which used to rely heavily on the assessment of general practitioners, such as Norway and Switzerland, for example.

Assessment criteria

The Dutch example cited above raises an important issue – whether or not to take into account the actual *availability* of a job matching the person's capabilities. To avoid premature labour market exclusion, most countries today refer to a "theoretical" labour market when assessing disability benefit eligibility, *i.e.* to jobs that exist in principle in the economy, rather than actually available jobs. However, in some countries this principle is violated by regulations according to which a full benefit is paid temporarily until a matching job is found (see "Requirements to participate in work-related activities" in Section 4.2 below).

Another general development is the move away from usual-occupation assessment where entitlement is determined *vis-à-vis* the applicant's ability to perform the *usual* job or a job in the usual occupation, to a broader assessment taking *all* jobs in the economy as a reference. Most countries today use an "any-occupation" criterion for determining eligibility for a (typically long-term) disability benefit but an "own-job" criterion to determine sickness benefit entitlement, which is now a temporary payment in virtually all OECD countries. Depending on the duration of sick pay, this can imply a significant loss in time before a broader assessment against all jobs can be undertaken, time during which the person in question is usually inactive and could have been activated. To shorten this period, Sweden is currently trying to implement an innovative approach:

● Under what is called the new "rehabilitation chain", sickness benefit is initially paid for a period of 90 days in which a person is given time to resume their existing job, possibly with some modification in duties. In the next 90 days, if workers cannot perform their previous jobs, they are expected to accept another job in the same business or to try out another job with another employer. After 180 days, clients are assessed against all jobs in the labour market.

The Swedish reform is facing massive opposition during its implementation, partly because this change marked a very big shift given that sickness benefit was previously paid without any time limit. However, sickness absence rates have recently fallen at a very rapid pace down from twice to just around the OECD average, and the trend is expected to continue (OECD, 2009). This suggests that there is great potential in trying to transfer people on long-term sick leave to other jobs earlier.

In trying to strengthen the identification of remaining work capacity, with the aim to better activate those with some capacity, several countries try to screen out people with full and permanent work incapacity for whom a passive disability benefit is the most appropriate choice. This is understandable, but it is not straightforward to set the level of capacity below which it is impractical to expect a person to participate in the labour market. Part of the difficulty arises from the confounding effect of individual motivation. Even severe physical or mental health problems do not consistently prevent some sufficiently-determined persons from performing in the open labour market, albeit often in low-skilled jobs. Yet, countries like the Netherlands and the United Kingdom have chosen to separate, in the course of the assessment, people who are fully incapacitated and who will receive a disability benefit, which is paid permanently and at a higher level and without any activation elements. This should facilitate the implementation of a more active approach for those with meaningful work capacity. Other countries like Austria and Italy have long had an implicit distinction of this kind, paying benefits permanently to those with full and permanent disability but temporarily otherwise (see "Temporary benefits and regular assessment of medical conditions" in Section 4.2 below).

To summarise the trends in regard to disability assessment, most countries are implementing changes which one way or the other aim to assess remaining work capacity – bringing the assessment forward in time and/or strengthening the non-medical elements and/or broadening the labour market reference. These changes which are ongoing will all help in establishing a system with a stronger focus on employment and activation. However, changes have to be continued, in particular in view of the rapid increase in the share of mental health problems causing disability benefit applications.

4.2. Moving to an activation stance

Disability and unemployment benefits both offer income replacement to working-age people without a job who are in many cases able to work. Disability schemes, however, differ drastically in how they operate and the outcomes they produce. Unemployment benefits are paid so long as a beneficiary engages in job-search activities, training or other obligatory activation measures. In most countries, this is not the case for a person on, or applying for, a disability benefit who tends to be viewed as incapacitated and inactive, irrespective of his or her actual work capacity. As a consequence, employment supports are offered on a voluntary basis, in turn explaining at least in part the low take-up of these services.

In terms of competitiveness in the labour market, the distinction between persons with partial work capacity and the long-term unemployed is not necessarily useful and becoming increasingly blurred. In order to limit the disincentives inherent in current disability benefit and employment support schemes and thereby improve labour market outcomes, some countries are beginning to explore approaches for tackling this, in two ways: i) by managing persons with partial work capacity in a different way, expecting more from benefit applicants or beneficiaries, in return for better supports being offered; and ii) by seeking ways to turn disability benefit payments into more temporary payments, like unemployment benefit.

Requirements to participate in work-related activities

Contrary to the unemployed, disability beneficiaries are exempt from job-search requirements, further increasing the likelihood of permanent labour market exclusion. Imposing job-search requirements for all disability beneficiaries or benefit applicants is impossible, given that some people cannot reasonably be expected to work. But requirements targeted to the person's remaining work capacity are a different matter and can be implemented as a part of a mutual-obligations strategy. Several OECD countries have gone down this route with the aim of raising people's expectations and requirements.

Strengthening participation requirements

Some countries in Europe, e.g. Austria, Germany, Hungary and Switzerland, have long had formal requirements for disability benefit applicants by applying a vocational rehabilitation-before-benefit principle. Also in Denmark regulations say that possibilities for rehabilitation must have been exhausted before a disability benefit can be granted.[1] These requirements have recently been strengthened in some cases:

• Switzerland, for example, is moving to a more binding rehabilitation-*instead-of*-benefit principle. It is in the process of introducing new responsibilities for persons with health conditions that could lead them to taking up disability benefits. Under a reform adopted in 2008, these persons are now obliged (as the legislation states) "to participate actively in reasonable measures aimed at maintaining the workplace or their reintegration into professional life (or activities comparable to working life)"; obligations are listed explicitly, together with sanctions for non-compliance.

• Similarly, in Luxembourg, people with partial work capacity are now obliged to enrol in training and reintegration measures.

Both countries have seen falling disability benefit inflow rates recently, though this change was only one of several changes and the impact of the strengthened obligations themselves is not known. Countries which hitherto have not had any such requirements in their systems may instead opt for a milder version initially, to test the acceptability and impact of such approach, like the United Kingdom did a few years ago:

• The United Kingdom's Pathways-to-work process trialled as from 2003 is one such example. The key feature of this policy is a series of six, ordinarily monthly, mandatory work-focused interviews, usually starting eight weeks after the benefit claim. These interviews are led by an incapacity benefit adviser whose aim is to develop a personal action plan. A range of programmes can be accessed afterwards to support return to work but so far any such action taken in response remains non-compulsory.

Pathways-to-work is targeting new benefit applicants, but people already receiving a disability benefit can volunteer to go through the same process.[2] Evidence on the impact of the new process, based on the initial trials, suggested that the chances of being in employment 18 months after starting the benefit claim were increased by 7 percentage points and benefit outflow accordingly (Blyth, 2006). However, newer results – still referring to a pre-recession year – after the full rollout are inconclusive (Bewley *et al.*, 2009).

Combining partial disability benefits with work-availability requirements

A number of OECD countries have long used partial disability benefits as a way to encourage people to remain in work, or to return to employment, to some degree (Table 4.1). Partial benefits function in different ways. Most countries with such systems, especially Nordic and eastern European countries but also the Netherlands and Switzerland, offer a full benefit for those more or less fully unable to work and various degrees of partial benefits in line with reduced work capacity. Most countries offer 1-3 steps of such partial benefit, while some use a finer grid (*e.g.* at 5% steps in Norway). Partial work capacity is defined in different ways, *e.g.* in terms of the number of hours a person is still able to work (Germany, Sweden) or in relation to the remaining percentage of work capacity, or earnings capacity.

Other countries, including France, Poland and Spain, have a quasi-partial benefit for people who are unable to work in their *usual* occupation and a full benefit only for those unable to work in *any* occupation. Hence, the capacity threshold is the same for both benefits but the reference is different. The partial benefit is *de facto* a full benefit paid at a reduced rate, and the benefit can be topped up to some extent by earnings from a job in another occupation (even without income limit in the case of Spain). Most other countries

Table 4.1. **Partial disability benefit regulations vary considerably across OECD countries**

Regulations on the disability definition and the availability of partial disability benefits

Australia	No partial benefit. Full benefit only if unable to work at least 15 hours per week within the next two years. (Before 2006, full benefit if unable to work at least 30 hours per week within the next two years.)
Austria	No partial benefit. Full benefit for at least 50% work-capacity reduction (earnings-capacity reduction for unskilled workers).
Belgium	No partial benefit. Full benefit with 66% earnings-capacity reduction in the usual occupation.
Canada	No partial benefit. Full benefit with severe and prolonged mental or physical disability that prevents individuals from regularly pursuing any substantially gainful occupation.
Czech Republic	Three levels of disability benefit: 1st level – work capacity decline 35-49%; 2nd level – work capacity decline 50-69%; 3rd level (full benefit) – work capacity decline at least 70%.
Denmark	No partial benefit (partial benefit abolished in 2003). Full benefit only if, after activation attempts have failed, permanently disabled and unable to perform a part-time job or a job with a permanent wage subsidy.
Finland	Full benefit if work capacity is reduced by at least 60%; half benefit if it is reduced by 40-59% (only for the earnings-related pension).
France	Reduced quasi-partial benefit (worth 60% of a full benefit) with 66.6% earnings-capacity reduction and unable to carry out the usual occupation; can be combined with income from another job to some extent. Full benefit only for those unable to carry out any occupation.
Germany	Full benefit: person only able to work less than three hours per day, partial benefit: person able to work 3 to 6 hours per day (partial benefit in full if no matching part-time work can be found).
Greece	Three levels of disability benefit. 1st level – 50-66% earnings-capacity reduction with respect to own occupation (strength, skills and education) with a strong medical focus; 2nd level – 67-79% earnings-capacity reduction; 3rd level (full benefit) – earnings-capacity reduction of 80% or more.
Hungary	Full benefit with more than 79% of damage on health. Partial benefit with 50-79% damage and person cannot be employed without rehabilitation.
Ireland	No partial benefit. Full benefit only for those unable to work (Invalidity Pension) or if, because of a disability, person is at a disadvantage in unertaking suitable work (non-contributory Disability Allowance).
Italy	No partial benefit. Full benefit with 100% total and permanent incapacity to perform any work (disability pension) or 66.6% work-capacity loss (means-tested disability allowance).
Japan	No partial benefit. Full benefit with a medically-determined degree of disability that severely restricts the person's ability to work (supplements if person's ability to live independently is also restricted).
Korea	Three degrees of benefit depending on the medically-determined degree of disability, paying 100%, 80% and 60% of the insured's basic pension amount for total, moderate and minor disability, respectively.
Luxembourg	Full benefit only for those unable to carry out their former occupation or another occupation commensurate with their abilities. Quasi-partial benefit in respect to the last workplace if redeployed either in the own or another company (with special allowance paid at the level of a full disability benefit for as long as the person otherwise would be entitled to an unemployment benefit).
Mexico	No partial benefit. Full benefit if 50% earnings-capacity reduction in previous job.
Netherlands	Full benefit for permanent earnings capacity reduction of at least 80%. Reduced benefit for those with a full but temporary capacity reduction or a partial capacity reduction of 35-79%. Higher benefit payment for those who utilise at least half of their partial capacity.
New Zealand	No partial benefit. Full benefit if permanently and severely restricted in work-capacity. Disability expected to last at least 2 years and the individual cannot regularly work 15 hours or more in open employment. However, people who are unable to work full-time but more than 15 hours, so do not qualify for Invalids Benefit, are able to access Sickness Benefit.
Norway	Partial benefit granted in 5% intervals for work-capacity reduction of 50-94%; full benefit for at least 95% reduced work capacity (but the benefit level is determined by the level of *earnings*-capacity reduction).
Poland	Reduced quasi-partial benefit (worth 75% of a full benefit) if unable to carry out the usual occupation; can be combined with income from another job to some extent. Full benefit if unable to carry out any work.
Portugal	Partial benefit if 66.6% earnings-capacity reduction in the usual occupation; full benefit for 100% permanent incapacity to carry out any working activity (with the same benefit calculation rules for both situations).
Slovak Republic	No partial benefit. Full benefit for more than 40% earnings-capacity reduction which is expected to last for more than one year, taking into account possibilities for vocational rehabilitation.
Spain	Reduced quasi-partial benefit (worth 55% of a full benefit) if unable to carry out the usual occupation; can be combined with income from another occupation. Full benefit if unable to carry out any work.
Sweden	Full benefit if unable to work at least 2 hours a day. Partial benefits (25/50/75% of a full benefit) determined in relation to the daily number of hours a person can work.
Switzerland	Full benefit if earnings-capacity reduced by at least 70%; three-quarter benefit for reduction of 60-69%; half benefit for 50-59%; and quarter benefit for 40-49%. (Three-quarter benefit introduced in 2004.)
Turkey	No partial benefit. Full benefit for 40 % work-capacity reduction.
United Kingdom	No partial benefit. Full benefit only for people with severe functional limitations at such a level that they cannot be expected to seek work in the open labour market.
United States	No partial benefit. Full benefit for inability to engage in any substantial gainful activity (in any occupation) due to a medical impairment which has lasted or is expected to last for at least 12 months or result in death.

Note: Information relates to the main disability benefit programme; information on second typically non-contributory scheme also given for countries with a high beneficiary number on this scheme.
Source: Information provided by national authorities.

have abolished such own-occupation assessment altogether in the past two decades, with the major exceptions being Belgium and (for white-collar workers) Austria where a full benefit is paid in relation to incapacity in the usual occupation.

There is limited evidence that the labour market reference (usual *versus* any occupation) has any correlation with the ease of access to disability benefit. On the other hand, it appears that countries with a partial benefit system tend to have higher overall benefit recipiency rates. The problem with partial benefit schemes is that they often just provide lower benefits for people with only partially-reduced work capacity, without having a strong focus on the remaining capacity of those people or on imposing participation requirements. In most countries, people can choose to take the partial payment without having to be available for part-time work. There is also inconclusive evidence on the impact of partial benefits on employment rates. Data from Finland and the Netherlands, for example, suggest that between one-third and one-half of those people receiving a partial disability benefit are not in work.

Partial benefits could be accompanied by work-availability requirements for the remaining work capacity. However, this rarely happens unless the person is looking for work and choosing to seek employment support from the employment service, in which case the normal participation and job-search requirements would apply. Hence, there can be a partial work-availability requirement especially where a partial disability benefit can be, and is, combined with a partial unemployment benefit. But actual practice is very different. In Germany, for example, a person entitled to a partial benefit will receive a full benefit if he or she cannot find a corresponding part-time job.

Switzerland has recently introduced an additional intermediary partial-benefit level and is now considering a move to a more graduated system to allow for a gradual increase or reduction in benefit level in line with the person's work capacity. By having a more flexible system with improved financial incentives to increase work effort, they hope to reduce labour market barriers. However, there is no evidence available on the likely impact of such a change.

Turning partial disability benefits into in-work payments

The issue is how to turn a partial-benefit system into a more active tool, and transform it from an out-of-work payment to an in-work benefit – thereby as much as possible promoting work of those with reduced capacity while avoiding to draw too many people into benefit. There are various ways in which countries are tackling this issue. Denmark and the Netherlands provide two variants of largely the same idea, *i.e.* to make it more attractive for people with partial capacity to work while receiving income support:

- Denmark is the only country which, in 2003, has abolished a previously existing partial disability benefit in recognition of its inactivity-enhancing features. The partial benefit was replaced by a generous wage subsidy scheme (for so-called "flex-jobs") that has a very similar function but is related to whether or not a person is working, *i.e.* it is an in-work subsidy. Subsidies are available at two different levels (one-half or two-thirds of the previous wage); cover the full difference between the previous and the new wage; and require that the person has a permanent work incapacity, is unable to work under normal conditions and has exhausted all rehabilitation possibilities.

- The revised disability benefit system that came into operation in the Netherlands in 2006 has similar features. Workers with assessed earnings incapacity of 35-79%

receive a wage supplement depending on the amount of remaining work capacity actually used (at least half of the actual remaining capacity needs to be used). If not working, or not enough, a flat-rate benefit is paid instead which is considerably lower than the disability benefit used to be.

What are the lessons from these changes? In Denmark, the use of subsidised flex-jobs has increased very rapidly – but without a corresponding fall in disability beneficiary numbers. This is partly because, due to the attractiveness of the system, the wrong group of people was drawn into such jobs, and partly because the implicit work-availability requirement was nullified by regulations effectively paying a full benefit when the person seeking such a subsidy is unable to find a corresponding job. Similar to the regulation in Germany referred to earlier, Danes receive a special benefit effectively paid at the level of a disability benefit, the so-called waiting benefit, in such situation; this can easily become another quasi-disability benefit.

The regulation in the Netherlands is much tougher in this regard – the higher benefit is only paid when the person works. The outcome is indeed much more promising, including a rapid fall in the number of new disability benefit claims, but it is difficult to quantify the individual impacts of the various changes introduced in 2006. The work-incentives feature of disability benefit reform, however, is not that effective; especially for people with lower incomes, the threat of a benefit cut is often effectively compensated by higher housing benefit entitlements (OECD, 2008).

Unemployment benefit for people with partial work capacity

Other countries are trying to achieve better labour market integration via work-availability requirements for people with partially-reduced work capacity by treating more of this group in the unemployment benefit system. Some countries – like Germany or France – have always had more people with health restrictions on their unemployment records, thereby partly explaining the lower disability beneficiary rates and, equally, the higher rates of long-term unemployment. This is a good setup in principle in terms of making the most of peoples' work capacity, especially in times of an economic upsurge, provided the PES actually seeks to activate the long-term unemployed with health problems. Other countries in which this has not been the case hitherto are trying to get closer to such a situation:

- Welfare reform in Australia, in 2006, has been along these lines. People with significant work capacity who are able to work 15-29 hours per week are now no longer entitled to a disability benefit but, instead, classed as regular unemployed and supported and obliged to seek matching part-time work.[3]

- Similarly, in the Netherlands also since the 2006 reform workers with an earnings capacity reduction of 15-34% can no longer receive a disability benefit; in case of job loss they are, after exhaustion of sickness benefits, managed like other unemployed with normal job-search requirements.

- In Luxembourg, since 2002, people with remaining work capacity who were receiving sickness benefits were shifted onto job-search support in the form of a clearly-defined "redeployment" procedure which can have two outcomes: i) employment with a permanent payment to compensate for any difference between previous and new earnings (similar to the Danish flex-job subsidy); or ii) unemployment in which case they receive a waiting allowance set at the level of disability benefit but with availability requirements just like every other unemployed (OECD, 2007).

Effectively, in legal terms such shifts of a larger group of people with partial work capacity onto the more active unemployment benefit largely occurred in countries which used to have a very low entry threshold for a disability benefit (15% earnings-capacity reduction in the Netherlands, inability to work 15 hours a week in Australia, prior to reform). However, tighter administration of disability benefit applications can have a similar effect without any legal change. Luxembourg is an example of the latter where change was driven by changes in the way rules are being interpreted and implemented (*i.e.* the rules are now more strictly followed), rather than by changes in legislation.

Moving towards a single working-age benefit

One way or the other, all these attempts suggest that treating people along different contingencies – unemployed, sick and disabled, or otherwise – is not the most effective way to go about supporting people facing problems in the labour market. An alternative approach altogether would be to, first, offer a single working-age benefit to the entire working-age population in need of income and employment support, with contingency payments to cover the costs of managing various individual health conditions or other problems that limit a person's capacity to work; and secondly, offer employment supports in line with the person's needs and irrespective of the benefit category.

New Zealand gave active consideration a few years ago to the idea of integrating all of its working-age benefits, but eventually decided against going down this route. Several countries, however, are making attempts to simplify their benefit system, thereby moving closer to a single-benefit setup:

- The United Kingdom is perhaps the best example. With reform in 2008, the existing disability benefits (both contributory Incapacity Benefit and non-contributory Income Support) were replaced with the new Employment and Support Allowance. For clients assessed as having a limited work capacity, the new benefit works in a similar way to unemployment benefit, albeit paid at a slightly higher rate, recognising the additional obligation to engage in a mandatory work-related interview regime where sanctions ensue for non-attendance.

- Germany is another example. In 2005, unemployment and social assistance were combined into the basic security benefit for jobseekers, thereby generating a single benefit for all "employable" people of working age in need of assistance. Persons are considered employable if illness or disability does *not* prevent them from working for at least three hours per day for more than six months (in which case they would not be entitled to a disability benefit). In other words, this is a step towards a single working-age benefit but explicitly excluding disability benefit.

- Norway, with its latest reform in 2010, merged different types of medical and vocational rehabilitation benefits and the time-limited disability benefit into a single "Work Assessment Allowance". Increased weight is given to the person's workability profile in the assessment process as well as during the strengthened following-up requirements.

With the new benefit setup it has become easier in these countries to enforce work-availability requirements through sanctions, even small, which have tended to prove an effective tool for promoting re-employment chances of recipients of either unemployment benefits (Lalive *et al.*, 2002) or welfare payments (Reijenga *et al.*, 2004).

Follow-up of rejected claimants

One of the virtues of a single working-age benefit would be its ability to curb the big problem of *welfare-system movers*, i.e. people being shifted across different income support payments or between the authorities responsible for different contingencies. Such moves could include shifts from unemployment to disability benefit, because caseworkers of the employment service find the health restrictions too strong for an effective reintegration; from disability benefit to social assistance, because the health problem is not severe enough to qualify for a disability benefit; and from social assistance back to unemployment benefit, after an intermediary, albeit short, period of work.

The problem of welfare-system movers is well reflected in the extremely high rejection rates for disability benefits virtually all over the OECD. In most countries, between one-third and two-thirds of all disability benefit applications are declined; only in the Nordic countries are these shares significantly lower, around or even below 20% (Figure 4.1). Many of these people have been inactive for a long while and are unlikely to find their way back to the labour force easily.[4] On the contrary, there is a high likelihood that these people will stay on or move into another benefit, such as unemployment benefit or social assistance, and a good chance they will reapply for disability benefit at a later stage. As a result, after a few years of cycling between various working-age benefits, they will often end up on disability benefit eventually.

Figure 4.1. **In many OECD countries, more than one in two applicants for a disability benefit are rejected**

Benefits rejected as a share of all benefit applications, 2008 or latest year available[a, b]

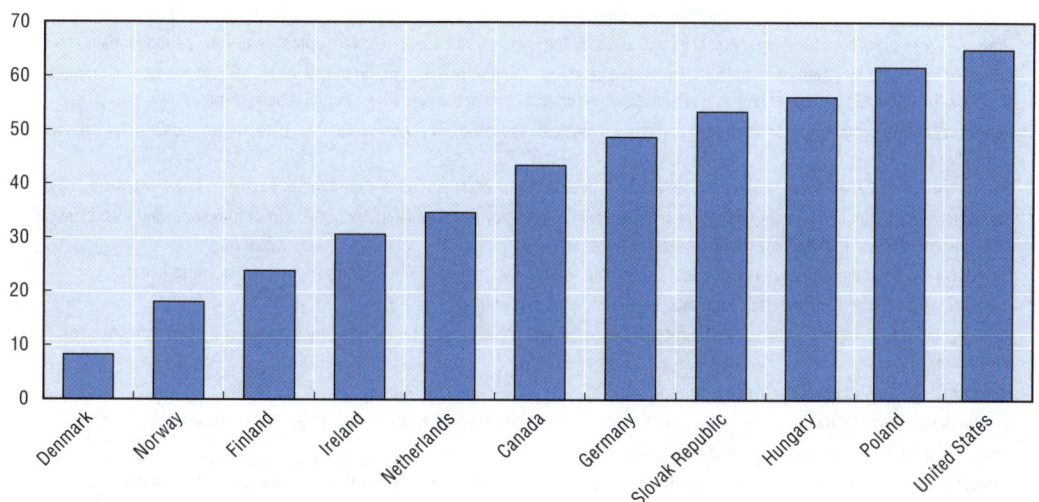

a) Data for Poland refer to 2003; 2004 for Canada, Ireland and Slovak Republic.

b) Data for Ireland refer to persons applying for the Illness benefit after two years; for Canada and Germany, the contributory pension only and for Poland to the KRUS pension scheme only.

Source: National submissions.

Temporary benefits and regular assessment of medical conditions

Temporary benefits with either fixed or flexible frequency of retesting

One of the reasons for disability benefit being regarded as more attractive than other working-age benefits is the more permanent beneficiary status which it brings with it. Very few people ever leave a disability benefit before reaching the statutory pension age, and even fewer move back into employment (Chapter 2). In aiming to prevent people from becoming permanently trapped on disability benefits, an increasing number of OECD countries are restricting new applicants to time-limited or temporary payments. This is done in different ways (Table 4.2).

Table 4.2. **More and more countries are providing disability benefits for a temporary period**

Regulations on benefit duration and re-testing of disability benefit entitlements

Australia	Risk-based profiling for medical reviews are irregular and uncommon, annual income and assets tests via a questionnaire.
Austria	Temporary for up to 2 years (repeated renewal), continuation of payment if no health improvement; permanent if 100% disabled (20-25% of the inflow).
Belgium	Granted indefinitely, with flexible examinations (in most cases, several control examinations); after three years usually permanent.
Canada	*De facto* permanent with regular earnings reviews.
Czech Republic	Temporary; reassessment is performed at regular intervals, depending on the condition.
Denmark	Permanent if rehabilitation failed (no re-tests).
Finland	Temporary subject to a rehabilitation plan and assessment.
France	Temporary subject to flexible re-evaluation.
Germany	Temporary for up to 3 years if reasonable prospect for improvement, with repeated renewal; partial entitlements that are paid as full benefits because of poor labour market are always temporary.
Greece	Temporary and reassessment should be at regular intervals but could become permanent.
Hungary	Temporary with renewable periods (necessity and time of the next examination is determined during the actual medical testing).
Ireland	*De facto* permanent.
Italy	Permanent for full permanent disability; temporary for up to 3 years for partial benefit *i.e.* partial disability (after 6 years benefit becomes permanent).
Japan	Temporary and reassessment should be at regular intervals.
Korea	Flexible; periodic review of not completed diseases.
Luxembourg	Retesting at irregular intervals in case of temporarily disability. No re-testing in case of permanent disability benefit or tide-over allowance.
Mexico	Temporary for renewable periods (periodical examinations in the first year) if there is recovery potential; usually permanent after two years.
Netherlands	Permanent payment for people with full and permanent disability. Temporary payment, up to five years, for partial and/or temporary disability. Ex officio reassessment always possible (and not unusual) when the assessment criteria have changed.
New Zealand	Regulated review procedure. Case managers can require medical reassessment at two years, five years, or never depending on medical information.
Norway	Either a temporary benefit if the situation is likely to improve (with reassessment upon expiration of payment) or a permanent benefit.
Poland	Strictly temporary; upon expiration (usually after three years) payments are terminated, individuals have to reapply and their case will be fully re-examined as if it was a new claim.
Portugal	Permanent but not definitive, *i.e.* a revision test is possible at any time (and common after three years on sickness benefit).
Slovak Republic	Reassessment is performed at certain intervals, depending on the conditions.
Spain	Permanent, but for temporary disability a long-term sickness benefit can be paid for up to 30 months (after that, benefit becomes permanent).
Sweden	Permanent; but subject to review every third year.
Switzerland	Granted for as long as conditions are fulfilled but re-test possible any time (either on request of the benefit recipient or *ex officio*).
Turkey	Subject to re-testing according to request by the Institution.
United Kingdom	Generally temporary as long as the Work Capability Assessment threshold is met; review frequency assessed at each new assessment.
United States	Periodic continuing disability eligibility reviews, conducted at 6-18 months intervals if medical improvement is expected; every 3 years if medical improvement possible; and every 7 years if medical improvement is not expected (authorities have to prove impairment has improved).

Note: Information relates to the main disability benefit programme.
Source: Information provided by national authorities.

In some countries, benefits are strictly granted for a fixed period unless the person is fully and permanently incapable of working. Disability benefits are initially granted for up to two years in Austria and up to three years in Germany and Italy, with repeated renewal; benefits can be turned into permanent ones after a certain period, *e.g.* in Italy usually after six years. Poland, following reform in the early 1990s, went a step further. Disability benefit is not only always granted temporarily, for no more than three years at a time, but recipients must reapply for a benefit every third year, thereby going through a full new assessment of their case each time to determine continued eligibility. Some countries use a similar but less binding approach, granting benefits permanently or indefinitely in principle but subject to review in regular intervals. This interval is also often three years, *e.g.* in Belgium or Sweden.

Other countries, including the Czech Republic, France, Hungary, the Slovak Republic, the United Kingdom and most non-European countries, use a more flexible system. Benefits are granted for a flexible period the length of which is determined at the time of the assessment; at each reassessment, the period until the next review is set. In the United States, for instance, this period ranges from 6-18 months if medical improvement is expected to every seven years if no such improvement is expected. Other countries do not set the review period initially but instead review entitlements at irregular intervals.

Three questions are critical: First, how seriously are reassessments taken; secondly, what are the criteria against which the person is being reassessed; and thirdly, what is the impact of having a temporary payment on the likelihood of granting such a benefit in the first place?

On the first question, evidence suggests that due to resource constraints, a very large group of people in many countries are not reassessed, or not thoroughly. Reassessment in such cases can, for example, be nothing more than asking the recipient whether his/her health condition has changed. On the second question, the criteria for reassessment, many countries use a very narrow definition according to which a benefit payment can only be reconsidered or withdrawn if the medical condition has improved. In addition, in most cases it is the benefit authority that would have to prove that such an improvement has occurred. This explains why in most cases having temporary disability payments with reassessments is a rather ineffective policy tool.[5]

The third question is difficult to evaluate. By and large, most temporary payments are renewed or turned into permanent ones at some stage.[6] In principle, therefore, if eligibility for a temporary benefit is less strict, such payment may contradict the stated purpose and in fact increase long-term inflow rates and, hence, reduce total labour supply. Norway is a good example to consider here because it introduced temporary payments only in 2004 and operates the temporary-benefit scheme (with benefits initially being granted for between one and four years) alongside the permanent-benefit scheme (with two-thirds of all new claims being permanent). Age-specific rates of annual new claims before and after reform, in 2003 and 2005, show a huge 40-60% rise in the inflow rate for applicants in the age group 20-39 years (OECD, 2006). This seems to indicate a significantly lower entry threshold for new benefit grants for these groups, posing a major problem given that the vast majority of temporary claims are turned into permanent ones after a certain time period has elapsed.

Reassessment versus tighter entry into benefit for young people

In view of the Norwegian experience, countries should not choose between either lower entry criteria combined with regular entitlement reassessment, or strict entry criteria without reassessment. The main question, however, is the criteria on which reassessments are being made. Overall, it appears that there is a mismatch in many countries between the increased focus at the application phase on remaining work capacity on the one hand, and the continued rather strong medical approach taken for reassessments on the other. Improved work capacity despite an unchanged medical condition could be quite frequent, for instance as a consequence of being better able to manage the condition – *e.g.* a mental health condition – and maybe also because of better knowledge on how best to handle conditions at the workplace.

This mismatch in reassessment criteria is of particular concern for young beneficiaries, who will often stay on disability benefit for several decades. Young beneficiaries usually lack work experience and have on average lower educational backgrounds, thus strong reintegration measures accompanied by participation requirements are fundamental to help them access the labour market. In this regard, there is increasing recognition that granting a disability too early in life is counterproductive. Denmark has recently discussed the option to replace disability benefit for young people by a more active regime. Recent reforms in the special disability scheme for young people in the Netherlands go in the same direction:

- In view of the fast increase in the number of young people entering into disability benefit, recent reform in the Netherlands aims to make better use of the work potential of many of these claimants. The scheme has now been split into two phases: 18-27 year-olds are given a mandatory "participation plan", either work or study with a wage or study subsidy, with intense job-seeking support and job coaching. Only at the age of 27 is a final assessment performed to establish their degree of disability (*i.e.* the degree of earnings capacity loss with respect to the minimum wage).

- As part of the 2010-11 budget, the Australian government is funding a two-year trial that enables young people with disability to enter disability employment services directly from a transition-to-work programme, or within 12 months of leaving school, without the need for any additional assessment or other intermediate interventions.

- A Qualification Programme and Benefit, introduced in Norway in 2009, aims to improve the qualification of young persons with very limited education and/or work experience.

Disability benefit grants at a very young age indeed seem to steer people with disability into benefit dependence. The differences across OECD countries in disability beneficiary rates of the 20-34 year-olds are stark, ranging from less than 0.5% of the corresponding population in countries which require labour force experience for their main disability programmes (*e.g.* Austria, Germany) to 3-4% in countries like the Netherlands or the United Kingdom.

Reassessment versus benefit suspension for long-term recipients

Not only are reassessments more medically-focused than initial assessments, but there is another problem: Most countries disallow reassessments on the basis of new entitlement criteria, such as a new minimum entry threshold or changed assessment procedures or criteria. Also, to win stakeholders over a more comprehensive reform, several countries (*e.g.* Australia) have chosen to grandfather existing entitlements, *i.e.* to apply new rules to new applicants only while leaving old entitlements untouched. This is unfortunate because it traps current recipients on long-term benefits and means missing out on opportunities. Only very few countries have ever done widespread reassessments of large parts of the beneficiary caseload. In Poland, in 2004, a comprehensive reform package was proposed which included a plan to reassess all claimants under age 50/55 (women/men); however, the package was adopted only partially, and the reassessment element was abolished by parliament. Lessons from large-scale reassessments in the Netherlands are telling:

- The Netherlands has frequently reassessed many of its recipients following comprehensive reform. In the years 2005-09 in the aftermath of a change in benefit eligibility rules, the entire caseload of beneficiaries under age 45 was reassessed according to the new rules. Almost 40% were found to be fit for work or have a lower disability level than before, younger recipients in particular. Cohort evaluation of reassessed beneficiaries suggests that about one-third moved into work within 18 months, partly with special reintegration support offered for this group.

While evidence shows that reassessment can be very effective, several other countries have instead made it easier for beneficiaries to try to work. To make this more attractive, benefit suspension rules (or linking rules, as they are called in the United Kingdom) are being implemented and extended which allow recipients to try out work without losing their benefit entitlement and without a need for reapplication. Benefit suspension is now possible for up to two years or more in countries like Australia, Canada, Finland, Norway, the United Kingdom and the United States. Canada also offers a fast-track reapplication process within five years. Denmark and Sweden have recently gone farthest, allowing recipients to cease work and resume their disability benefit at any time and without reassessment to help overcome any fears of entitlement loss as a consequence of attempting to work.

Given the large gains to the public purse to be made from benefit off-flows, there is no good argument for any time limits for such benefit suspension rules. However, there is an inherent contradiction with the move in many OECD countries towards temporary entitlements with comprehensive reassessment at periodic intervals. Countries cannot easily encourage people to try work while at the same time telling them they will be reassessed comprehensively at their return to benefit. This problem could be solved in two ways, both allowing for some inequality across beneficiary groups. One would be to move to temporary payments for new applicants while allowing unlimited benefit suspension without reassessment for those on benefit already. This might be the best approach for countries unwilling to retest the caseload comprehensively and along revised criteria. An alternative would be to strengthen reassessment for some groups closer to the labour market, for instance all recipients under age 45, while offering generous suspension rules for those less likely to ever return to employment.

4.3. Making work pay: reforming tax and benefit system

One of the biggest challenges facing governments is how best to reform tax and benefit systems for persons with disability with a view to providing them with appropriate financial incentives to take up jobs, to remain in work and to increase work effort. As a complement to changes in the way partial work capacity is assessed, reassessed and dealt with by the benefit and employment systems, work must pay. This section focuses on the financial incentives that the tax and benefit systems of OECD countries offer to workers with health problems to stay in employment or to increase their working hours.

Adequacy and generosity of disability benefits

An adverse health shock is a key driver of the transition from employment into disability, but the chances of remaining in employment after the onset of a health problem differ substantially across countries and socio-demographic groups. An argument brought forward repeatedly as an explanation for such differences, is the *generosity* of benefits systems. Generous and easily accessible payments can erode the willingness to work of individuals with health problems. They may also increase the likelihood, especially for the long-term unemployed, of seeking a benefit that is generally regarded as permanent (OECD, 2003). Similarly, disability benefits which are relatively more generous than other income support schemes may more generally attract people of working age who are facing labour market difficulties.

How much do people get when entitled to a disability benefit?

Low *net replacement rates* (NRRs) for people who become totally incapacitated for work in the midst of their professional career may raise concerns about poverty and social exclusion, especially if the person has caring obligations towards children.[7] However, a majority of persons with disability are not fully incapacitated for work but experience health-related problems which hinder their chances of staying in the labour market. In the case of NRRs approaching or even exceeding 100%, disability benefit schemes may become an attractive alternative to employment; not only for employees facing problems, but also for employers looking to adjust their workforce without causing labour discontent.

Across the reviewed countries, NRRs provided by the main disability benefit schemes are generally very high, especially for low-wage earners – with replacement rates in the range of 70% to 110% (Figure 4.2).[8] NRRs are typically 15-30 percentage points lower for average earners, ranging from just over 50% in Australia to 80% in Denmark and Switzerland. The higher NRRs for low-wage earners result from the interplay with other benefits, especially housing benefit and social assistance payments, income-test thresholds and tax rates. In two countries, the NRRs for low-wage earners even surpass 100%, owing to general family allowances and special child supplements within the disability benefit system in the case of Switzerland and social assistance and housing benefits in Denmark. Individualised monetary and in-kind benefits – such as the free medical care for disability beneficiaries in Ireland – are *not* taken into account in the model estimates presented in Figure 4.2 and may further increase the "net worth" of disability benefits for certain beneficiaries.

How does disability benefit compare with other working-age benefits?

In most countries a majority of those who take up a disability benefit (typically 50-90%) do so after a period on sickness benefit. Others first move into unemployment, often drifting into long-term unemployment, after the onset of a health problem before switching onto disability benefit. A relevant question is thus how disability benefits compare, in terms of income replacement rates, with other main income support schemes for the working-age population. Figure 4.3 compares NRRs for disability, unemployment and social-assistance benefit schemes. Again, a synthetic indicator is used to take into account different schemes and family situations.

Overall, disability benefits appear to be more generous than social assistance payments but by and large very similar to unemployment benefits. Except for former low-wage earners in Luxembourg, disability benefits always have higher NRRs than regular social assistance (*i.e.* the resulting ratio exceeds unity). The difference in compensation is particularly large for former average-wage earners, with disability benefit replacement rates in Spain, the Netherlands and the United Kingdom being more than 50% higher than

Figure 4.2. **Net replacement rates are often high, especially for previous low-wage earners**

Synthetic indices of NRRs of main disability schemes for six family types and two earnings levels[a, b, c]

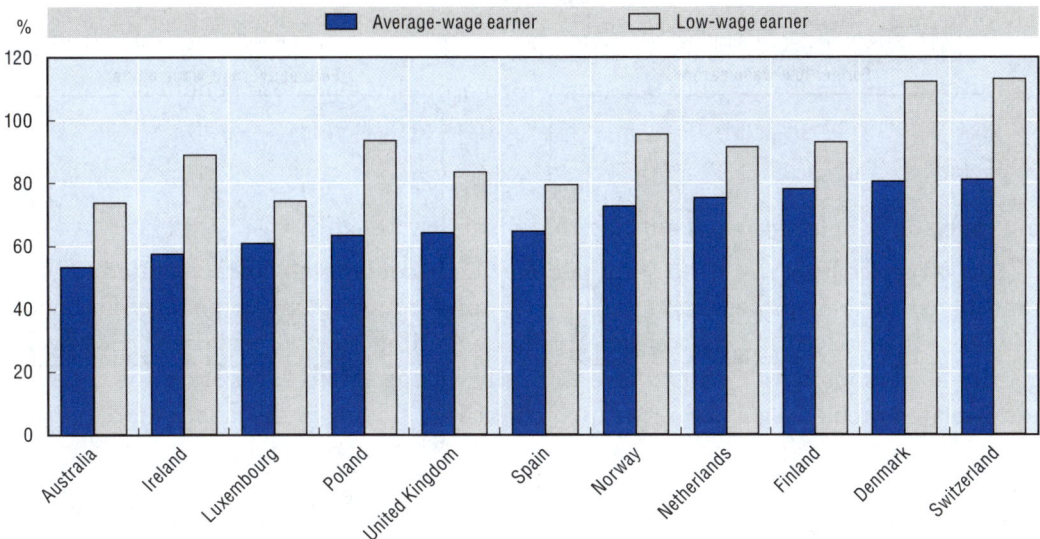

a) Data for Australia, Luxembourg, Spain, and United Kingdom refer to 2005; Denmark, Finland, Ireland and the Netherlands to 2006; Norway, Poland and Switzerland to 2008. Countries are ranked according to the synthetic NRR index for previous average-wage earners from lowest to highest.

b) Calculations consider cash incomes (such as social assistance, housing benefits and family benefits) as well as income taxes and mandatory social security contributions. The synthetic indices are calculated for a 40-year-old person with a full earnings history since age 18 and are unweighted averages over the main disability benefit scheme(s) in the country and six family types (single persons, one-earner married couples, two-earner married couples with spouse earning 67% of the average wage (average production worker wage in the case of Ireland); each time with and without children). Children are aged four and six, and neither childcare benefits nor childcare costs are considered. A low-wage earner is a person who previously earned 40% of the national average wage (or the national minimum wage, if the latter is higher; this is the case for Australia and Ireland, where the national minimum wage was respectively 49% and 44% in the year under consideration).

c) "Main" disability benefit schemes covered in the model results include Disability Support Pension for Australia; Invalidity Pension and Disability Allowance for Ireland; Disability Benefit for Luxembourg and Switzerland; Partial and Total Disability Benefit for Poland; Long-term Incapacity Benefit and Income Support with Disability Premium for the United Kingdom; Partial Incapacity Benefit for Spain; Permanent and Temporary Disability Benefit for Norway; Full Disability Benefit (WGA) for the Netherlands; and Disability Pension for Finland and Denmark.

Source: Special module of the OECD tax-benefit model. Information provided by national authorities.

those of social assistance. Unemployment benefits, on the other hand, are *higher* than disability benefits in about half of the investigated countries, but the difference is often negligible. Hence, the attractiveness of disability benefit in comparison with unemployment benefit does not, in general, result from higher benefit levels but rather from other features of the disability benefit system, such as the lack of work and activation requirements and thus the more permanent nature of payments.

Counteracting labour market traps

Disability benefit recipients who enter a job generally lose entitlement to part or all of their benefits. How these benefits are phased out can be decisive for whether or not it pays to work. High tax burdens on earnings are an additional factor limiting the financial gains from employment. For those with remaining work capacity, the net income effect, *i.e.* the extent to which earnings are "taxed away" through a combination of reduced benefits and higher taxes, will therefore be crucial when considering taking up a job or increasing working hours. Such financial incentives and disincentives in a country's tax/benefit

Figure 4.3. **Disability benefits are above social assistance but comparable with unemployment benefits**

Synthetic indices of net replacement rates for disability benefits, unemployment benefits and social assistance[a, b]

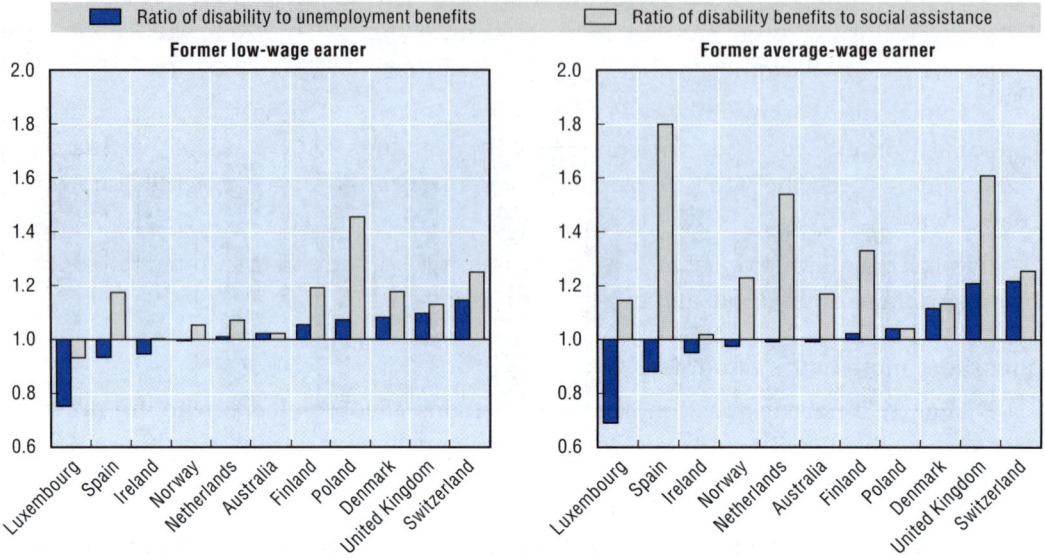

a) Data for Australia, Luxembourg, Spain, and United Kingdom refer to 2005; Denmark, Finland, Ireland and the Netherlands to 2006; Norway, Poland and Switzerland to 2008. In each graph, countries are ranked according to the ratio of disability benefits to unemployment benefits.

b) For technical specifications, see notes b and c for Figure 4.1.

Source: Special module of the OECD tax-benefit model. Information provided by national authorities.

scheme can be expressed as an average effective tax rate (AETR) – for entering a job – or as a marginal effective tax rate (METR) – for increasing hours of work.

Does it pay to work?

On average across the reviewed countries, a disability benefit recipient returning to a full-time job of 40 hours at the average wage loses almost 60 cents of each euro earned in the job as a result of both in-work taxes and benefit withdrawals. Spain has the lowest effective taxation throughout the entire earnings range – 24% for average earners – as earnings can be accumulated with disability benefits without limit or phasing out, and taxation on this combined income is low. AETRs are, however, much higher in a number of countries and for certain ranges of working hours, creating strong disincentives to take up employment. This is the case in Finland (if working more than 16 hours), Ireland (less than 20 hours), the Netherlands (irrespective of the hours worked) and the United Kingdom (for part-time employment), where AETRs are around 80% and higher (Figure 4.4).[9] Such high effective tax rates arise either because of the complete withdrawal of disability benefits once earnings or working hours exceed an allowed maximum, or because of high income taxes and social security contributions.

In-work benefits are one of the tools that have been used more recently in order to raise the financial returns to work. A number of countries introduced in-work payments which top up earnings for certain wage levels or a minimum number of hours. This can be a useful measure to reduce AETRs and to motivate groups with particularly poor work incentives or labour market opportunities:

● In Ireland, when disability benefit recipients take up work for at least 20 hours, their AETR drops from a level close to 100% to some 45% for former average earners (and as low as 20% for low-wage earners; not shown in the figure) thanks to the Back-to-Work Allowance. This allowance is phased out gradually over a four-year period.

● In Canada, the Working Income Tax Benefit, a general earnings supplement for low-income workers, together with the Disability Supplement for people with a severe disability reduced the METR by over 20% over an earnings range up to full-time work at lower wages.

In-work benefits also exist in other countries, *e.g.* Finland and the United Kingdom, but they play a more limited role and effective taxation remains high.[10]

Is working more hours rewarded?

A slightly different question arises for persons *already in work*, who are drawing a (partial) disability benefit, and considering increasing their weekly working hours. Analysis for 11 OECD countries of the financial consequences of increasing working hours in 10-hour steps suggests the following conclusions.

● There are several "zones" in most countries where working more does not pay, *i.e.* the resulting METRs exceed 100%. In such cases, persons are encouraged to stay in their current position despite their wish to become more active due to, for instance, improvements in their health condition. Such "low-wage traps" often occur when disability benefits are suspended, and they are generally more frequent and more pronounced for low-wage earners.

● In Ireland and the United Kingdom, on the contrary, it does not pay to take up work for one or two days a week since disability payments are suspended and in-work benefits are not yet available at this earnings range.[11] The substantial in-work benefits in Ireland generate a huge incentive for low-wage earners to take up part-time work, with a considerably negative METR.

● In Denmark, Luxembourg and Spain, effective tax rates are stable throughout the working hours range, reflecting the gradual phase-out of disability benefits in the former two countries and the unlimited possibility to combine disability benefits with earnings in Spain.

Overall, incentives to take up work or to increase the number of hours worked vary hugely both across countries and across (previous) income levels and working hours within countries. The interplay between (gradual) benefit withdrawal and increasing taxes produces, for most countries, a range of situations in which working or working more hardly pays.

Figure 4.4. **Taking up work does not always pay, but country differences are large**

Average effective tax rates for a 40-year-old single person on disability benefit, percentage of earnings[a, b]

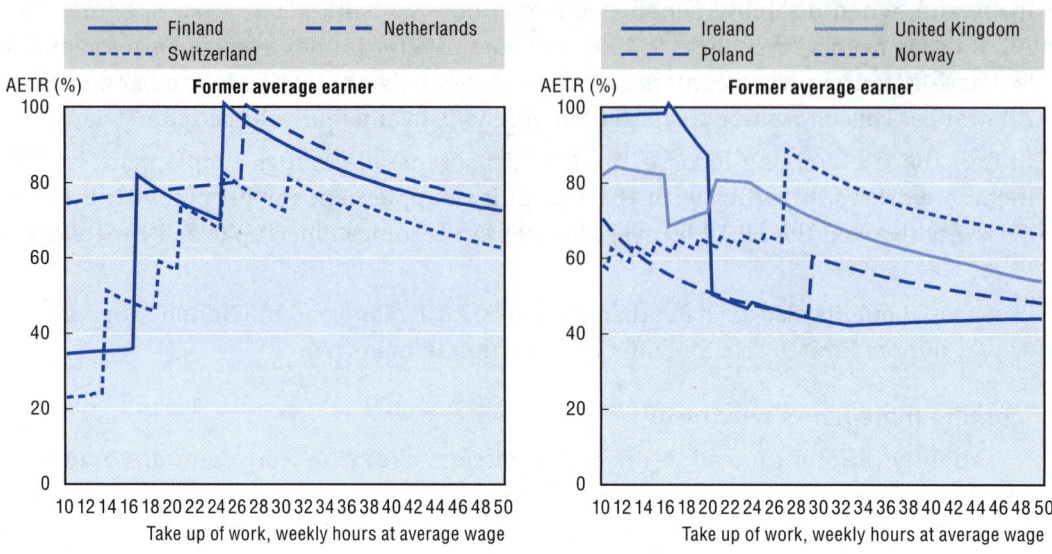

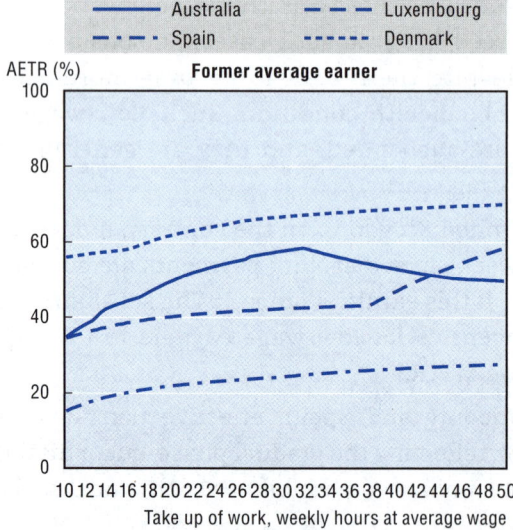

a) The average effective tax rate (AETR) is the percentage of earnings that is "taxed away" via increased taxes and reduced benefits when taking up work. The AETRs are estimated for a single 40-year-old person with a full earnings history since the age of 18, who was earning the average wage (average production worker wage in the case of Ireland) prior to acquiring a disability. The person is assumed to be on (partial) disability benefit, if such benefit exists, and returns to a job at the previous wage level but at working hours ranging from 10 to 50 hours per week.

b) Data for Australia, Luxembourg, Spain, and United Kingdom refer to 2005; Denmark, Finland, Ireland and the Netherlands to 2006; Norway, Poland and Switzerland to 2008.

Source: Special module of OECD tax/benefit model. Information provided by national authorities.

4.4. Conclusion

Countries have started to understand the disabling effect of the disability benefit system and to address some of the features responsible for the widespread granting of disability benefits. In particular, many countries are now making increasing efforts to look at the person's remaining work capacity when determining benefit eligibility, rather than putting all the focus on identifying disability. Moreover, more is being done in a range of OECD countries to support people in using their remaining capacity. However, much more will have to be done to transform what is still a rather passive benefit system in most cases into an employment-promoting instrument.

There are three main remaining weaknesses in many cases. First, the activation stance now applied in unemployment benefit systems differs drastically from the stance taken in disability benefit systems. Too low expectations on the part of (potential) beneficiaries and too lax or nonexistent participation requirements often counter the stronger employment and employability supports offered. Secondly, the change in entitlement criteria and assessment procedures is not yet reflected in a similar shift in the way reassessments are being done and continued eligibility is re-established. This is a missed opportunity and contributes to trapping people in long-term benefit dependency. Lastly, work does by no means pay for all people receiving (or applying for) a disability benefit, with huge differences in work incentives not only across countries but equally so within countries across different income groups.

Notes

1. However, this general rule has not always been enforced. Finland uses a different principle, giving people a *legal right* to vocational rehabilitation.

2. In some pilot areas, the Pathways-to-work process has been extended, on a mandatory basis, to some existing incapacity benefit customers; in a first stage to people whose benefit claim started in the two years prior to the rollout of Pathways and later on including those whose claim started up to six years before.

3. Disability employment services can be accessed by people with disability, injury or a health condition to support them to find employment that matches their work capacity. Moreover, depending on their earnings, they may continue to receive part-rate income support on an ongoing basis.

4. In Norway and other Nordic countries, those people will often have remained on rehabilitation benefits for an extended period, owing to the rehabilitation-before-benefit principle. With increasing period on such benefits, returning to the labour force is becoming more and more difficult.

5. The United States provide an interesting example in this regard. The implementation of mandated continuing disability reviews in the early 1980s on the basis of current medical evidence faced considerable challenges. The States were concerned about financial consequences because many terminated disability benefit recipients were likely to fall back on state-funded social assistance payments. Also, beneficiaries and administrative law judges were concerned that their prior disability decisions could be overturned. A 1981 court decision finally held that an individual's disability benefits could not be terminated on the basis of medical factors absent a finding of clear error in the previous determination of disability or evidence of medical improvement sufficient to establish that the individual was no longer disabled (Derthick, 1990).

6. Even in Poland, which on paper operates the most stringent temporary benefit scheme, less than 10% of all reassessed payments are ceased, corresponding to 2.5% of the caseload in any given year (OECD, 2006).

7. Net replacement rates compare the income situation when moving from paid work to inactivity. They thus provide indicators of both the adequacy and the generosity of disability benefit schemes. NRRs take account of income tax and social security contributions to be paid as well as other benefits the person or household may be entitled to, including *e.g.* family allowances and housing benefits.

8. To evaluate the generosity of disability benefits across countries, a synthetic index of net replacement rates is constructed considering different schemes and family situations. The index is not meant to take into account the relative frequency of the respective family types or schemes in a country, but should be seen as a policy indicator summarising the main disability benefit systems that exist.

9. Figure 4.4 shows the AETRs for the countries' main disability scheme for a single 40-year-old person who was earning the average wage. The person is assumed to return to a job at the previous wage but at varying working hours. High AETRs indicate that transitions into work result in small or no gain in net incomes.

10. Finland operates an employment-conditional "earned income allowance". While this benefit is available to all persons taking up work, there is special tax allowance and a tax credit for persons with disability.

11. In-work benefits come into play between 16 and 21 hours in the United Kingdom (Working Tax Credit and Return-to-Work Credit) and at 20 hours in Ireland (Back-to-Work Allowance).

Bibliography

Bewley, H., R. Dorsett and S. Salis (2009), "The Impact of Pathways to Work on Work, Earnings and Self-reported Health in the April 2006 Expansion Areas", *Research Report*, No. 601, Department for Work and Pension, London.

Blyth, B. (2006), "Incapacity Benefit Reforms – Pathways to Work Pilot Performance and Analysis", *Working Paper*, No. 26, Department for Work and Pensions, London.

Campbell, A. and J. Ogden (2006), "Why Do Doctors Issue Sick Notes? An Experimental Questionnaire Study in Primary Care", *Family Practice*, No. 23, pp. 125-130.

Derthick, M. (1990), *Agency Under Stress. The Social Security Administration in American Government*, Brookings Institution Press, Washington.

Hunt, D.G., O.A. Zuberbier *et al.* (2002), "Are Components of a Comprehensive Medical Assessment Predictive of Work Disability After an Episode of Occupational Low Back Trouble?", *Spine*, Vol. 27, No. 23, pp. 2715-2719.

Lalive, R. and J. Zweimüller (2002), "Benefit Entitlement and Unemployment Duration: The Role of Policy Endogeneity", *CEPR Discussion Paper*, No. 3363, London.

OECD (2003), *Transforming Disability into Ability*, OECD Publishing, Paris.

OECD (2006), *Sickness, Disability and Work: Breaking the Barriers. Vol. 1: Norway, Poland and Switzerland*, OECD Publishing, Paris.

OECD (2007), *Sickness, Disability and Work: Breaking the Barriers. Vol. 2: Australia, Luxembourg, Spain and the United Kingdom*, OECD Publishing, Paris.

OECD (2008), *Sickness, Disability and Work: Breaking the Barriers. Vol. 3: Denmark, Finland, Ireland and the Netherlands*, OECD Publishing, Paris.

OECD (2009), *Sickness, Disability and Work: Breaking the Barriers. Sweden: Will the Recent Reforms Make it?*, OECD Publishing, Paris.

Reijenga, F. A., T. J. Veerman and N. van den Berg (2004), *Onderzoek Evaluatie Wet verbetering Pootwachter*, Den Haag.

Chapter 5

Activating Employers and Medical Professionals

Employers are key players in preventing health problems at work and facilitating a swift return to work for people absent from work due to sickness. This chapter sets out examples of good practice across the OECD to provide an effective combination of responsibilities and supports for employers, including stronger financial incentives to retain workers. It also seeks answers to the question how to provide a balanced policy package so to promote employment of people with health problems or disability through both job retention and new recruitment. Finally it also addresses the key role general practitioners are playing in the early phase of a sickness absence and ways to strengthen the employment orientation of doctors' sick-listing practices.

To raise labour demand for workers with health problems or disability is a major challenge for policy makers. Good incentives to work for those workers and good incentives for public authorities to provide the necessary employment support and enhance these workers' employability will not be enough. Employers are key players too. Employers, together with medical professionals and workers' representatives, are critically positioned to influence the trajectory of workers with health problems before labour market detachment has occurred. However, significant obligations for employers towards people with a chronic illness or disability, together with concerns about the implications in terms of the company's productivity and costs, can act as deterrents to employment.

A key challenge facing policy makers is to implement measures that promote job retention among people with reduced work capacity, but not to the extent that they simultaneously discourages the hiring of new workers with reduced work capacity, a chronic health problem or a disability. A flexible labour market is needed that accommodates the needs of these persons, together with strong responsibilities for employers to offer safe and healthy workplaces and to prevent sickness and work incapacity leading to entry into disability benefits. To this end, medical professionals who assess sickness and work incapacity act as gatekeepers for the benefit system and also need clearer responsibilities and directions.

5.1. Strengthen incentives for employers to keep workers with health problems

For workers with health problems who still hold a job, irrespective of whether they are on sick leave or not, preventative measures at work will help to retain employment and avoid transfers onto disability benefits. Employers, supported by workers' representatives, are uniquely well placed to help prevent such illness leading to deterioration of health and work readiness, and ultimately labour market detachment, because they are among the first to see the early signs and, knowing the worker's abilities and strengths, better able to respond adequately.

Obligations and financial incentives for employers are needed because they are very sensitive to the costs of employment. Employers will often think it would be in their interest to allow a worker with a history of sickness absence to quit work and take up publicly-funded income support, so the worker can be replaced by a worker in better health. Many employers perceive the costs of new recruitment and training to be lower than the costs of retention, adjustment and accommodation needed to maintain productivity with existing workers with health problems. In response, a number of OECD countries have set out to adjust the balance of carrots and sticks such that it is in an employer's financial interest to retain sick workers.

Health-enhancing work environments

The range of involvement of employers in the sickness and rehabilitation phase, their responsibilities towards their workers and the support given to them to fulfil these differ widely across countries (Table 5.1). In short, the following picture emerges. First, in most countries today employers have an obligation to accommodate work or the workplace up to the point of accommodation reaching unreasonable or disproportionate expenses, though with rather different degrees of enforcement of this requirement. Secondly, most employers across the OECD are obliged, by law or through collective or individual agreements, to cover sick-pay costs for a sick worker for a certain period; this period, however, and the share of the wage to be paid, differ drastically across countries. Thirdly, in only a few countries do employers have any particular obligation in relation to a sick worker's rehabilitation, though in those few countries this obligation is considerable. Finally, there are big differences across countries in dismissal regulations, which are much tighter for workers who are sick than for other workers in some countries (making dismissal of a sick worker very difficult), but lower – though sometimes requiring the consent of the authority – in other cases (explicitly allowing dismissal because of sickness).

Strengthened employer obligations

A few countries stand out as having legislated obligations for employers that are more specific than elsewhere and go beyond the more general work or workplace accommodation obligation, which is difficult to enforce in practice. Although no evaluation exists of such specific regulations, they should make it more likely for workers with health problems or disability to be able to benefit from legislation and to improve their workplace skills and qualifications. Such regulations also take into consideration the wider benefits for both employers and society in terms of human capital improvements:

- Employers in Germany have to offer preferential selection for within-company training to workers with health problems and support them in attending training elsewhere. Moreover, these workers have not only a right to work assistance and an adapted workplace but they are also entitled to part-time employment.

- Larger employers in Luxembourg (25+ workers) are obliged to find an appropriate job for their sick workers, be it the same job at reduced hours or a different job.

- Employers in Spain must keep a post open for a worker with health problems for up to two years in case of a rehabilitation process that is projected to be successful. Moreover, former employees on disability benefit, once having recovered, have absolute priority for filling a suitable vacancy or must be offered a similar job (possibly with a reduced wage) when returning from a partial disability benefit.

The key challenge for all these employer obligations is their enforcement. Successful enforcement will also require the timely involvement of workers' representatives and trade unions. This is particularly so in countries where the social partners have traditionally been central players in social and labour market policy, *e.g.* the Nordic countries or Austria. Social partners can play an active role in supporting job retention and reintegration of workers with chronic health problems or disability through initiatives facilitating labour market mobility and flexibility. In Sweden, for example, recent bargaining includes efforts to introduce employer-paid rehabilitation in exchange for loosening employment protection. More generally, more flexibility in wage setting in collective agreements can also be useful to allow payment of a reduced hourly wage in cases where a workers' productivity fluctuates or is reduced due to a disability. Such reduced wages can be agreed for instance in Australia.

Table 5.1. **Obligations for the employer are generally weak in regard to vocational rehabilitation**

Employer obligations in three areas: work accommodation, vocational rehabilitation and sick pay

	Regarding work	Regarding rehabilitation	Regarding sick pay
Australia	Obliged to accommodate work or workplace, unless this would impose unjustifiable hardship (rigid interpretation of the term "unjustifiable").	Responsible for assisting in the occupational rehabilitation and return to work of their workers, as well as keeping the job available for a reasonable time.	The National Employment Standards provides for ten days of paid leave for each year of service for employees engaged on a full-time and part-time basis.
Austria	Obliged to provide reasonable accommodation, unless this would pose a disproportionate burden on the employer (when taking public aid funds into account).	No employer obligations.	Continued full wage payment for 6-12 weeks (depending on length of employment); thereafter half the wage for a period of four weeks (which is topped up by sickness benefit).
Belgium	Only for some high-risk sectors of the economy: reassign or adapt job after absence of four weeks due to illness or accident.	No employer obligations.	Continued wage payment for one month: 100% of earnings for white-collar workers; for manual workers 100% in 1st week, 60% thereafter.
Canada	Duty to accommodate workplace conditions (eliminate discrimination resulting from a rule, practice or barrier) except for cases of undue hardship (with fines in case of non-compliance).	For work-related injuries and illnesses, where reasonably practicable, duty to return an employee to work, possibly in a different position with different conditions.	No period of continued wage payment.
Czech Republic	Accommodate work conditions in response to the worker's abilities and health competence or offer a different job in case of long-term disability as proven by a medical certificate.	No employer obligations.	60% of average salary from the 4th-14th day, based on hourly salary and working hours.
Denmark	Emphasis on encouraging social responsibility of employers (social index, social accounting); duty for the employer to make appropriate adaptations which are not unreasonable. Dismissal during illness possible if established that the employee will not get well.	No employer obligations.	Collective agreements provide for continued wage payment in case of sickness for certain groups of employees (employer entitled to receive the worker's sickness cash benefit).
Finland	Reasonable accommodation related to work conditions, work organisation, working hours, work methods, facilities, training and arrangement of work, and work guidance.	No employer obligations but disability benefit premiums are experience-rated and employers have occupational safety and health obligations.	Continued wage payment for first nine days of sickness (50% if employed less than one month). By collective agreements most employers pay full salary during the first 1-2 months.
France	Duty to take measures to give access to, or to keep, a position corresponding to qualifications and to give access to professional training (unless costs are "disproportionate").	No employer obligations.	Full or part of the difference between the salary and the sickness cash benefits, in accordance with either national inter-professional agreement or the collective agreement conditions.
Germany	Provide employment according to skills and abilities, preferential selection for training within company, support to attend training elsewhere, examine vacancies for potential for disabled persons, right to work assistance, right to part-time employment, right to adapted workplace.	No employer obligations.	Continued wage payment for first six weeks; without re-insurance possibility.
Greece	Reasonable adjustments to have access to employment, work and participate in vocational training, without causing disproportionate expenses for the employer.	No employer obligations.	No statutory continuation of payment. Leave of absence may be increased by six working days for workers with an assessed disability of at least 50%.
Hungary	Ensure the provision of appropriate working environment to perform the job.	No employer obligations.	80 % of the "absentee pay" for up to 15 days. Can but is rarely supplemented by collective bargaining agreements (up to 100%).
Iceland	A new obligation to provide reasonable accommodation is in preparation.	No employer obligations.	Continued wage payment for at least one month after 12 months of consecutive employment. Collective agreements often more generous.
Ireland	Obligation of reasonable accommodation, including adjustment to provide access to the workplace, modifying the job content, working time and work organisation; dismissal possible during absence and because of the illness.	No employer obligations.	No statutory sick pay but many organisations operate sick-pay schemes: public sector, full wage for six months and a half wage for another six; private sector, full wage for 4-26 weeks.
Italy	Assign equivalent tasks or lower-graded tasks but under old conditions, make necessary adaptations to work organisation.	No employer obligations.	Statutory continuation of payment of wage for a maximum of 180 days per year (and in some specific cases 180 days again in the next year).
Japan	Take measures following a doctor's advice to change the nature of work, working hours or adapt the workplace of an employee.	No employer obligations.	Wage payment for three days.

Table 5.1. **Obligations for the employer are generally weak in regard to vocational rehabilitation**
(cont.)

Employer obligations in three areas: work accommodation, vocational rehabilitation and sick pay

	Regarding work	Regarding rehabilitation	Regarding sick pay
Korea	With technical guidance, offer employment in line with abilities (but no sanctions).	No employer obligations.	No sick-pay scheme. Collective agreements can include regulations on sickness-related payments (*e.g.* for government officials).
Luxembourg	Companies with 25+ employees obliged to find an appropriate job for their worker, same job at reduced working hours or a different job (internal redeployment). If not possible or at excessive cost, external redeployment is sought.	No employer obligations.	Employees in the private sector continue to receive pay by the employer for 13 weeks (system for public sector is more generous).
Mexico	No employer obligations.	No employer obligations.	No period of continued wage payment.
Netherlands	Rehabilitation obligation can include work accommodation and working hours reduction, as well as training.	Duty to prepare a reintegration approach within eight weeks, submit a plan on rehabilitation measures after 42 weeks and a report after first year of sick leave; sanction: continued wage payment for up to a further year.	Continued wage payment – at least 70% of the salary, in practice up to 100% – for two years (except for work disabled persons for first five years of employment), but employers can take out private insurance; obligation to contract with sickness absenteeism management service.
New Zealand	Obligation to provide reasonable accommodation (employees and new applicants); employers are allowed to discriminate in case of risk of harm to that person or to others.	No employer obligations.	Five days' of paid sick leave after six months of continuous employment; plus five days for each subsequent 12-month period. Agreements can provide for more generous sick leave provisions.
Norway	Ensure suitable work (but dismissal possible after 6-12 months), arrange work conditions in general so as to enable employment of people with disabilities.	No employer obligations.	Continued wage payment during the first 16 days. Where the employer continues to pay the salary beyond this period, the sickness cash benefit is paid to the employer.
Poland	Ensure workplace accommodation and access; for work injuries: arrange for suitable workplace if employee declares readiness to return to work.	Disabled employees have a right to special breaks for rehabilitation exercises.	80% of gross earnings during past 12 months, paid for first 33 calendar days of illness.
Portugal	Only for work injured: adapt workplace, offer compatible job and part-time work.	Again, only for work injured: offer vocational training and leave to train for other employment.	No obligation; moreover, topping up sickness benefits is not permitted.
Slovak Republic	Provide training or study to acquire the requisite qualification to facilitate employment. Improve the equipment of the workplace to enable the worker to achieve, if possible, the same work or set up a sheltered workplace.	Some obligations to provide qualifications upgrading.	For first three calendar days, 25% of the daily earnings in the previous year; from 4th to 10th calendar day of incapacity for work, 55%.
Spain	Former employees on disability benefit who recover have absolute priority for filling a suitable vacancy; or (after partial benefit) must be offered similar job, with up to 25% reduced wage.	During promising rehabilitation process, employer must keep post open for two years.	Sickness benefit payment from 4th to 15th day of illness, at 60% of wages.
Sweden	Provide reasonable suitable accommodation if the employee or job applicant is sufficiently qualified (*e.g.* purchase tools and change working environment, work organisation, work tasks and working hours); provide, if possible, a different job in the company.	If sick employee is not eligible to disability benefit, employer needs to find suitable work or is responsible for taking rehabilitative measures that can be conducted in the company.	Continued wage payment during the first 14 days (except for first day) at 80% of wages.
Switzerland	Anti-discrimination regulations do not include hiring and firing practice; dismissal protection during period of continued wage payment.	No employer obligations.	Continued wage payment at 100% for three weeks. Generally, employers pay full salary for three to six months, then 80% for up to two years.
Turkey	Work-injured workers are given priority; civil servants have the right to ask for a suitable job.	No employer obligations.	Continued wage payment for civil servants borne by state as employer.
United Kingdom	Must make reasonable adjustments, *e.g.* adjust premises, reallocate duties, alter working hours, modify equipment; advice and financial support available in certain circumstances.	No employer obligations except for allowing rehabilitation absences if this would be a reasonable adjustment.	Sickness benefit payment during entire 28-week period (reimbursement possible where costs exceed 13% of social security contributions); employers can re-insure with a private insurer.
United States	Provide reasonable accommodation, *e.g.* adjust equipment, make facilities accessible, modify work schedules, unless this would result in an undue financial hardship (sanctions include, *e.g.* back and front pay, attorney fees, accommodation, re-instatement, job offers).	No employer obligations.	Voluntary employer-paid benefits like leave accrual plans (paid sick leave up to 12 days per year or balance of 6-12 weeks, paid time off up to 20 days per year or balance of 4-6 weeks) or short-term disability benefits (which cover first 13-52 weeks).

Source: Information provided by national authorities.

Occupational health services

In many countries, prevention policy is still predominantly focused on preventing work injuries and occupational accidents and diseases. Occupational health and safety regulations are well developed throughout most of the OECD, and they have contributed to a decline in work accidents in most countries. However, several countries have gone a step further and put in place regulations to help prevent unnecessary labour market detachment arising from poor working conditions. Occupational health services (OHS) are often used as a tool for achieving this:

● Regulations in Finland ensure that employers have access to information, advice and support. Employers are legally obliged to purchase private or community-run preventive OHS to monitor workplace practices on a regular basis, through active programmes assessing and minimising workplace risks, early detection of reduced work capacity and other strategies to prevent disability. Public subsidies are available to support employers in these tasks.

● Also in the Netherlands, until recently employers were obliged to contract an OHS company. This strict obligation was introduced in 1996 when employers became responsible for sick-pay for a whole year. The formal obligation was alleviated recently because the system is now well embedded. The role of the OHS is broader than in Finland and includes advice on prevention, but also management of sickness absenteeism and prescriptions for rehabilitative health treatment.

● Sweden is putting considerable new resources recently into re-establishing its OHS system, with generous financial support to companies contracting services approved by the National Social Insurance Agency. Although contracting is voluntary, OHS covers nearly half of the workforce. The function of OHS is to facilitate early and co-ordinated medical and vocational rehabilitation and work accommodation actions, including – where needed – background assessments of the employee's work capacity, according to the Social Insurance Agency's recommendations.

Other countries are strengthening their systems in similar ways, without necessarily using OHS. Denmark, through its Working Environment Act, has put in place similar requirements on employers to monitor and address issues in the work environment, including risk assessment and the effects of the work environment on sickness absence. The Working Environment Authority visits employers unannounced and require them to address hazards. If violations are not attended to within six months, fines can be imposed. In addition, assessments are published, including all violations, on the authority's website as a further incentive to employers to address this issue. The effects of all these developments have not been evaluated rigorously. However, it appears that such changes are a useful complement to more far-reaching changes to employer incentives.

Dealing with arduous work

A particular issue is how best to tackle deteriorating health of people working in arduous jobs or occupations for many years or decades. Early retirement schemes were introduced during the 1980s in most OECD countries with an eye on jobs which cannot realistically be maintained all through the working life until the legal retirement age of around 65 years. With the phasing-out or abolition of early-retirement schemes in many OECD countries in the course of comprehensive pension reform and the (planned) increase in several cases of the legal retirement age (often to around 67 years), the issue of how to address arduous work is back on the policy agenda again in several countries. Some countries, including *e.g.* Austria and Poland, have introduced special retirement schemes for arduous work, allowing earlier retirement with no or lesser benefit cuts for certain workers. These schemes are narrowly defined (*e.g.* in terms of far-above-average calorie usage for large parts of the career) to avoid misuse; as a result, take-up is very low.

In most countries, arduous work is treated within the existing systems and will often lead to premature retirement through a disability benefit. Countries have done very little to prevent or address this issue directly. A notable exception is the planned Dutch regulation on arduous work. In essence, arduous work should not last more than 30 years. After this period, the employer is requested to move the employee into a different, not arduous job. If the employers fail to find new employment for their workers in question, they will have to start paying into a fund for each individual employee. The worker can draw upon this fund, thus in essence allowing retirement some two years before the regular age (which is now 65 and will be raised to 66 in 2020 and 67 in 2025). In this way, earlier labour market exit – of up to two years – would be fully funded by employer premiums. This is an innovative approach making employers more responsible, although the resulting buffer fund for two years may not be large enough to address the problem fully. Moreover, problems could also arise for workers moving to arduous jobs with *other* employers.

Sickness monitoring and management responsibilities to shorten sickness absence

The majority of people ending up on a long-term disability benefit initially go through a period of employment and sick-pay of varying length. Pathways into disability benefit show considerable variation across the OECD, but in all countries between one-half and three-quarters of all new disability benefit claimants were previously employed or drew a sickness benefit (Table 5.2).[1] These shares refer to the status *immediately* before the claim; many of those claiming a disability benefit from unemployment or social assistance will also have had interim periods of sickness absence beforehand. This is the major reason for why tackling sickness absence early on can be a very effective strategy for minimising the likelihood of eventual long-term labour market detachment. Employers are critically positioned to monitor absences, which in and of itself can reduce inappropriately long sick leave (*e.g.* Puhani and Sonderhof, 2009), and to support an employee in recovering or learning to manage their condition such that they remain in work.

Procedures for assessing and monitoring sickness absence

Several countries, in an attempt to curb high absence rates, have put in place a process of early intervention and absence monitoring involving employers in various ways. Norway and the Netherlands provide two good examples:

● In Norway (where sickness benefit can be received for up to one year), within the first eight weeks of absence the employer together with the employee has to draw up a follow-up plan describing the return to work and including relevant documentation. Employers are obliged to submit this plan to the national insurance office on request. Measures to prevent long-term absence and test the worker's functional ability must be carried out at the workplace.

● In the Netherlands (where sickness benefit can be received for up to two years), employers need to inform the company doctor during the first week of absence. By week eight, the employer and the employee must prepare a reintegration plan with concrete steps to be taken to achieve reintegration and arrangements for evaluating progress.

Table 5.2. **Pathways into disability benefit are manifold but sickness is a major precursor everywhere**

Origin of new disability benefit claimants as a percentage of all new claims, most recent available year

Australia[a]	2008	Denmark	2006	Finland[b]	2004	Luxembourg[c]	2005
Employed	44	Employed	7	Employed	4	Employed or sickness benefits	67
Sickness benefit	1	Sickness benefit	39	Sickness allowance	60	Unemployed/Redeployed	23
Unemployment benefit	36	Flex job	3	Unemployed	26	Social assistance	2
Other	18	Waiting benefit	9	Study grant	1	Other inactives	7
		Rehabilitation	3	Rehabilitation allowance	8		
		Social assistance	34	Parenthood allowance	1		
		Other	4				
Total	100	Total	100	Total	100	Total	100

Netherlands	2006	Norway	2004	Sweden	2007	United Kingdom[d]	2002
Employer paid sick leave	62	Unemployment	2			Employed	40
UWV sickness benefit	38	Sickness benefit	42	Sickness benefit	76	Statutory sick pay	17
Of which:		Medical rehab benefit	34	Other	24	Unemployed	26
Temping agency workers	4	Vocational rehab benefit	22			Income support	12
Temporary contracts	17					Other inactives	5
Unemployed	15						
Other	3						
Total	100	Total	100	Total	100	Total	100

a) Based on people entering onto Disability support pension between mid-2007 and mid-2008.
b) Based on KELA social insurance benefits only.
c) Based on people entering into either temporary or permanent disability benefit or the tide-over allowance in 2005.
d) Data refer to 2001/02. Previous benefit status is defined as statutory sick-pay receipt *immediately* before staring an incapacity benefit claim, and refers to the *90-day period* before starting a claim in case of previous unemployment or income support status.

Source: National submissions.

Steps need to be re-evaluated at six-week intervals. After the first year of illness, an evaluation report has to be drawn up to summarise the efforts during the first year and set out the steps planned for the second year. A final reintegration report has to be prepared by week 87-91, upon filing a disability benefit claim.

These strengthened sickness monitoring obligations had a major impact on sickness absence rates in the Netherlands (*e.g.* de Jong *et al.*, 2006) but not in Norway. Significant drops in absence rates will only occur if changes are implemented rigorously and in combination with much stronger financial incentives for employers to follow these regulations, and sanctions for those who do not. For example, sanctions are legally possible in both Norway and the Netherlands but while sanctioning employers is not done in Norway, 13% of all Dutch employers face the major sanction of having to continue sickness benefit payment for a third year because of failure in making sufficient efforts to retain a sick worker. In addition, especially for countries hesitant to strengthen employer incentives, absence monitoring cannot be left in the hands of employers alone but will also have to involve the responsible public authorities in various ways, not only to monitor and support employers' actions. This issue is addressed in Chapter 6. The critical role in this context of general practitioners is the topic of Section 5.3.

Financial liability for sick pay

Research for Sweden, which has changed sickness benefit payment rates repeatedly over the past two decades, has shown that workers react very sensitively to changes in payment rates (*e.g.* Henrekson and Persson, 2004, Hesselius and Persson, 2007). Evidence on the impact of stronger employer incentives is scarce because few countries have ever changed these significantly. Those which have, like the Netherlands and the United Kingdom, have seen considerable falls in sickness absence rates (Chapter 2):

- The Netherlands went furthest in this regard. Starting with a fully public sickness benefit system until the mid-1980s, step by step a larger share of the financial liability for sickness benefits was transferred to employers – initially for a few weeks, later for a full year and now employers pay the costs of sickness benefits for as long as two years during which workers usually cannot be dismissed (unless they fail to comply with their co-operation obligation and refuse to accept another position or role in the company). Employers can reinsure their risk with a private insurer, as most of the small but only a few of the large companies do.

- In a similar way in the United Kingdom, employers are now responsible for statutory sick-pay for a period of six months, again with reinsurance possibility. However, not only is the period shorter than in the Netherlands but also benefit payment rates are lower and other obligations in terms of monitoring and managing sickness absence largely non-existent.

The extent of employer co-payment differs drastically across OECD countries (Table 5.1). Some countries have long had a period of continued wage-payment by the employer of several months, without a reinsurance possibility, including Austria (6-12 weeks), Germany (six weeks), Italy (up to 180 days), Luxembourg (13 weeks for white-collar workers) and Switzerland (up to six months, varying with tenure). None of these countries have particularly high absence rates, while those countries with the highest absence rates (like the Nordic countries) tend to have a very short employer-provided wage-payment period. There is no "ideal" period, but increasing employer co-payments can be an effective strategy in tackling high absence rates.

Absence trends in the Netherlands and the United Kingdom suggest that strengthened employer co-payments will initially lead to a significant fall in short-term absences. To reduce long-term absences, considerable financial incentives will be needed: In the Netherlands, for example, increasing the employer-paid period from one year to two years was apparently more effective in lowering long-term absence than increasing this period to one year (OECD, 2008). However, it is difficult to disentangle the various independent effects of the incentives shift on the one hand and the much stronger monitoring obligations on the other.

Financial liability for disability benefit costs

While employer-provided sick pay of varying duration is common across the OECD with a trend in some cases towards extending this period, only a few countries go a step further and mandate an employer contribution to longer-term disability benefit costs via experience-rating of premiums, whereby employers pay more if their workers make above-average claims. In the Netherlands, experience-rating of public disability insurance was first introduced in 1998; since 2003, employers have to pay for most of the costs of the first five years of disability benefit receipt by their former workers. With the latest benefit reform the system was changed yet again, so that now employers are *de facto* paying for as much as ten years for those with a partial earnings incapacity but no longer for those with full and permanent incapacity. A similar system in Finland, affecting large firms only, implies that companies may have to pay up to 80% of the total disability benefit bill of their workers in case of job loss as a result of disability. Switzerland and Canada are seeing similar trends but in this case they are being driven by the private insurance sector which is very important in both countries (OECD, 2006 and OECD, 2010).[2]

What was the impact of these changes? In the Netherlands, this particular feature of reform was one of the key factors explaining the recent and very sharp fall in the rates of inflow into disability benefits (Koning, 2005). For Finland, it was shown that experience-rating reduces the flow from sickness benefit to disability benefit, while not affecting the flow into sick leave (Korkeamäki and Kyyrä, 2009). The recent development of experience-rating in the private insurance market in Canada and Switzerland has never been evaluated but this change is likely to have contributed to the very large and somewhat unexpected drop in the inflow into disability benefits in Switzerland (partly via falling levels of sickness absence) and the small drop from an already rather low level of annual disability benefit claims in Canada.

5.2. Supporting measures to ensure employers can fulfil their responsibilities

Financial incentives are the most effective means to ensure enforcement of employer responsibilities because failure to fulfil obligations automatically leads to a sanction in the form of *e.g.* higher benefit co-payment. Without adequate financial incentives it is difficult to enforce strengthened employer responsibilities. Moreover, incentives or sanctions are often not strong enough, as is for example the case for mandatory employment quota schemes in most countries which impose a penalty (OECD, 2003) which many employers just see as a minor additional non-wage cost.

Stronger responsibilities and financial incentives for employers also need to be matched by better supports to help them fulfil their obligations. This includes making employers aware of the extent to which their management practices affect the health of workers and their ability to remain attached to the labour market despite an illness (*e.g.* Tepper, 2007; Fjell *et al.*, 2007). Awareness-raising is also important with regard to false beliefs on the costs of workplace accommodation: Evidence suggests that accommodation costs are close to zero in around one-third of all cases, and substantial in only a few cases.

Employers vary in their expertise and experience in managing sick workers and it is impractical to expect them to fulfil their responsibilities to a high standard without quality supports, and backup. Better supports need to be provided by public employment agencies in particular. Employers also typically shy away from cumbersome administrative procedures and contacts, so the challenge for operational policy makers is to provide support in a form that fits with the needs of employers.

Job retention versus new hiring: the inherent challenge

Adequate support for employers is particularly important with the aim of providing a level playing field for job retention and job hires so as to help both insiders and outsiders – the inherent challenge for all labour market policies and institutions. Policy can influence the retention-hiring challenge, as research comparing the situation in the Netherlands, with its strong focus on job retention, and Denmark, with its flexicurity model with easy dismissal has shown. According to Veerman (2001), a much larger proportion of sick workers return to work with their employers in the Netherlands (72%) than in Denmark (40%). On the contrary, the dismissal of a sick employee does not seem to have any negative impact on the likelihood of return to work in Denmark but has a strong negative impact in the Netherlands (Høgelund, 2004).

As noted in Chapter 3, there are a range of employment measures that countries can use to support either job retention or hiring of new workers. However, evidence on the effectiveness of some of these measures is generally poor and sometimes inconclusive. Moreover, the limited available evidence suggests that most measures including employment quotas, anti-discrimination legislation and regulations which create strong financial incentives to keep people with health problems in work will often serve to protect the jobs of *existing* workers. At the same time, these measures can inadvertently reduce hiring opportunities for jobseekers with health problems or disability because employers form a view that the various imposed responsibilities (including accommodations costs but also costs arising from increased chances of a lawsuit) are collectively so onerous and contracts with those workers legally so difficult to terminate, that it is safer not to take on any workers with (potential) health issues.

For example, a number of empirical studies on the impact of anti-discrimination regulations in the United States have suggested that new legislation had resulted in lower employment rates for people with disability (*e.g.* DeLeire, 2000; Acemoglu and Angrist, 2001), even though the gradual fall in employment rates of people with disability since the mid-1990s cannot be *causally* linked to the introduction of such legislation (*e.g.* Begle and Stock, 2003).

Mandatory employment quotas, which are generally better enforced than anti-discrimination legislation though not better evaluated, seem to suffer from the same problem. Evaluation of the impact of the quota scheme in Austria, one of the countries with relatively high quota enforcement and fulfilment (OECD, 2003), suggests that the quota helps some workers developing a disability to stay in work, but at the expense of keeping jobseekers with disability further away from the labour market, with the net employment effect being *negative* on balance (Humer *et al.*, 2007). The problem may be one of incentives and enforcement insofar as there is no practical way of preventing an employer from filling their quota with existing staff who have low productivity because of existing health issues, rather than taking on new workers with reduced work capacity who are perceived to be less productive.

There is no obvious solution to this problem but governments need to be aware of the risks and fallacies, try to provide a balanced set of supports to stimulate labour demand through both job retention and new hiring, and to adjust the balance in line with measured outcomes. For instance, improvements of a quota system, even if far-reaching and including *e.g.* an increase in the levy to be paid for non-fulfilment, may not be enough to stimulate employment prospects for workers with health problems unless overall labour demand is buoyant.[3]

Provide adequate support for employers to match responsibirlities

Financial supports for employers

Subsidies are the most commonly employed policy measure in OECD countries for promoting employment opportunities for people with disability. Subsidies are typically available in two different forms: *i) accommodation subsidies* supporting the costs associated with making accommodations to a workplace; and *ii) wage subsidies* contributing to the costs of employing a worker with a chronic health problem or disability. The former will often be used to retain workers and the latter for stimulating new job hires. However, there is considerable overlap and a scheme providing a generous and permanent wage subsidy – like the Danish flex-job scheme – can easily encourage employers and employees alike to transform a full-time job into a subsidised part-time position.

Workplace accommodation subsidies have gained in importance in the course of the spreading of anti-discrimination legislation across OECD countries. A recent EU study concluded that workplace accommodation tends to be too limited in focus – *i.e.* too much centred on the reimbursement of direct costs – and that effective workplace accommodation should combine technical solutions to accommodate a particular health problem with training measures (before and after recruitment), on-the-job assistance and awareness-raising measures targeting managers and co-workers (Heckl, 2009).

As far as wage subsidies are concerned, systems that are well targeted to the needs of the employer and the employee and flexible over time and in relation to the person's work capacity (which might be changing over time) so to allow the employer to test a worker and the PES to lower or cut-off the subsidy quickly when the worker's productivity has increased seem to be most efficient. Several countries have interesting systems in place, although evaluations of these are often lacking:

- The Swedish employment agency offers a flexible wage subsidy mainly for new recruitments. The subsidy can cover up to 80% of the wage cost for a period of up to four years. The level of the subsidy is determined by the degree of work capacity, as assessed by the agency, and adjusted regularly in line with changes in the person's capacity level.

- The PES in Luxembourg operates a wage subsidy that is temporary, though usually lasting for three years; to extend the subsidy an employer must re-apply and prove that the productivity of the person continues to be reduced.

- The Finnish PES uses a flat-rate wage subsidy paid at a level below the minimum wage which is granted for up to 24 months at a time (social enterprises can receive a more generous subsidy).

One major issue for wage-subsidy schemes is to avoid deadweight, substitution and displacement effects.[4] If it is very easy for an employer to claim such subsidy for a worker with disability, this is likely, *ceteris paribus*, to raise deadweight. To avoid deadweight, the Finnish system is very strict in terms of conditions to be fulfilled by the employer who would, for instance, not be entitled to a subsidy if the vacancy could be filled without such subsidy. Indeed, the well-targeted Finnish scheme was shown to have stimulated employment in subsidised firms without distorted competition or crowding out of employment in non-subsidised firms (Kangasharju, 2005). This contrasts with findings for the very generous Danish flex-job subsidy which has produced only modest employment effects, with an estimated 52% deadweight loss (Datta Gupta and Larsen, 2007).

Notwithstanding the risk of deadweight loss, a key issue in increasing the effectiveness of wage subsidies is to increase their use. Take-up of such programmes tends to be low (see Chapter 6), be it because of a relative short payment period and/or a low and inflexible payment level, or because of a narrow target group and/or a burdensome procedure to justify eligibility, or a combination of both.

Accessible information and guidance when it is needed

Two key issues in relation to the limited use of tools designed to stimulate labour demand are a lack of awareness among employers of the availability of these schemes and the onerous procedure in many cases for applying for support. Employers in many countries have indicated their willingness to try to employ a person with reduced work capacity and productivity with financial support compensating this disadvantage if only this would be easier to apply for and not require much time investment. In response to this, several countries have put in place easily accessible information systems for employers:

- In Norway, mirroring the one-stop-shop idea for people with disability, employers have a personal contact officer in the nearby local workplace centre who will provide timely advice on all sickness and disability-related matters including sickness management and job retention as well as information in regard to challenges and available services for new job hires.

- The JobAccess initiative in Australia includes a comprehensive internet website (*www.jobaccess.gov.au*), a free telephone advice service (handled by trained advisers), an online workplace adjustment tool giving a range of practical ideas and solutions for workplace modifications and adjustments, and an online claims process for the payment of workplace modifications and other services.

- Spain's National Centre for Personal Autonomy and Technical Aids operates a comprehensive website on assistive technology and accessibility (*www.ceapat.org*). Services offered include assessment and advice for workplace adaptations, adaptation of technical tools, training activities and information and advice on universal accessibility.

- In the Netherlands, following new legislation in 2010, 30 new service institutions were established for employers to reduce cumbersome administrative procedures.

A key factor in stimulating labour demand and the use of corresponding support schemes is the *business case* for employing people with health problems or disability. Especially for smaller companies, it is often difficult to make a business case based on hard evidence, even though anecdotal evidence suggests that workers with disability tend to be sick less often, extremely reliable and loyal to their employer and thus have a high retention rate. A key challenge therefore is to convince employers to hire *one* worker with disability: Once employers have their first positive experience, they are far more likely to hire another worker with disability.

A special issue in this regard is the need for the Public Employment Service to lead by example. The PES will have to be a model employer so to be able to make a convincing business case and place people with health problems into work successfully. Along these lines, the PES in Germany has made great efforts in recent years; today, 9% of its workforce has a disability.

Facilitating employer networks

What has been found to be of particular importance in motivating employers to hire a worker with disability is information based on experiences from *other* employers. To collect and share experience is one of the main aims of the United Kingdom's Employers' Forum on Disability, a charity organisation funded by voluntary contributions from its members (mainly large private companies). The Forum advises employers through regular exchange and conferences, produces relevant publications, such as a guidebook on sickness management, and benchmarks its members against other members.

Information and good-practice sharing organised by employer-funded networks is important. Governments cannot do everything and encouragement is needed for initiatives that arise from the private sector. In this regard, employer-run circles or networks have developed in a number of OECD countries, either at the behest of government initiatives or by groups of employers in certain branches or regions directly. These employer collectives may play an important role in helping employers redeploy workers who are no longer suited to a particular job because of illness or injury to other firms, without the involvement of public authorities. Such networks have grown in those countries which have recently shifted considerable responsibilities onto employers:

- In the Netherlands, in response to the extension of employer-provided sick-pay to two years, during which dismissal is almost impossible, employer networks have mushroomed. These networks are organised on a regional level.

- Also in Sweden, in response to the recent requirement for employers to seek alternative jobs in their company for a worker who has been sick for over three months, employer circles have arisen to help place in other jobs or companies workers no longer suited to their own job. There are two lessons from these examples. First, the strengthened employer responsibilities created a stronger mutual interest and willingness to hire workers from other companies in exchange for the possibility of redeploying their own workers who develop problems that may leave the employer with a large wage bill. Secondly, there is great potential in organising such networks on a regional level so to stimulate transfers *across* sectors where it is less likely for a worker to experience the same workplace factors that may have contributed to their sickness absence.

Mitigating employer risks associated with hiring disabled persons

With strengthened employer responsibilities like those in Sweden or the Netherlands, there is also a strong case for measures directly addressing the retention-hiring challenge. Obligations for employers to offer sick workers another job in the company, or even help them find another job elsewhere, and financial incentives like experience-rating of disability insurance premiums, as discussed above, include the risk that employers will actively seek to avoid hiring persons who they perceive to be at higher risk of sickness or disability. Measures are needed to mitigate these risks in order to avoid that better employment outcomes resulting from the new tools stimulating job retention are countered by falling recruitment of workers with disability.

The Netherlands – where policy development over the past 15 years was driven by the aim to straighten incentives for employers and workers – has gone furthest in addressing this goal. The Dutch *no-risk policy and premium discount* effectively absolves employers of a significant part or all of the risks that arise when taking on a person at higher risk of sickness. The no-risk policy, introduced in 2003 and extended in 2005, removes the usual obligation of employers in the Netherlands of paying sickness benefits for up to two years of illness for employees with a disability.[5] Instead, the employee insurance covers these costs. Disability premium discounts are also available when employers hire these types of workers. In addition, hiring a person aged at least 50 years or keeping an employee older than 54.5 (that is, older persons at high risk of entering disability schemes as a form of early retirement) earns employers an additional financial advantage: They do not pay the basic disability premium for these workers. To date, no evaluation of these measures is available.

Finland has also recently introduced regulations mitigating somewhat the hiring disincentive arising from the experience-rating of employer premiums to its disability benefit scheme. With lesser employer obligations, it seems less urgent at this very moment for several other countries to introduce balancing measures like these.

5.3. Stronger employment focus by medical professionals

Like employers, medical professionals who assess sickness and disability claims are key actors in determining the take-up of sickness and disability benefits. The decisions they make about a person's fitness for work determine how long that person can remain detached from their workplace and claim benefits. This is crucial because allowing a person to stay out of work for an extended period of time is a known route to disability benefit schemes and permanent detachment from the labour market.

The formal justification for allowing such extended periods of work absence is that the medical practitioner has found robust evidence to conclude that being away from work is necessary for recuperation, and that to do otherwise would be to jeopardise the individual's health. However, given the prohibitive cost of comprehensive medical testing and the absence of objective tests for a range of health problems, practitioners must often base their decisions on the self-reported symptoms of the patient. Work by the National Board of Health and Welfare in Sweden suggests that practitioners may unwittingly authorise more sick leave than is necessary, in cases actually diminishing health outcomes.[6]

In view of the large and increasing body of literature concluding that work is generally good for health, especially mental health (Waddel and Burton, 2006, OECD, 2008a), more efforts will need to be made to keep sickness absence periods no longer than necessary. General practitioners (GPs) are typically the first contact for a person whose health is deteriorating. The doctor's reaction and advice will be crucial in terms of guiding the sick worker back to work quickly, or allowing the worker to become sick on a persistent basis.

Recognising that inappropriately long sick leave incurs costs for employers and the public purse and risks labour market detachment, countries are exploring ways of improving sick-listing practices. In regard to medical assessments for disability benefit entitlement, a general trend across the OECD is to raise the medical powers of the benefit-granting institution, thereby reducing the relevance of the practitioner's assessment. The introduction of regional medical services of the disability insurance in Switzerland, a country which used to rely heavily on GPs' assessment in determining disability benefit eligibility, is an example in case: Medical assessments have become easier and more homogenous across the country, and the new medical gate-keeping role assigned to the disability insurance system is also a factor in the recent large drop in disability benefit inflow rates.

There is no such shift towards an increased medical role on the part of the social insurance authority in certifying sick leave. Across the OECD, such certificates continue to be provided by GPs and form the basis for paying a sickness benefit. However, a number of promising reforms have been implemented addressing sick-listing practices of medical professionals, including one or a combination of the following three elements: i) provision of medical guidelines for doctors; ii) clearer administrative procedures; and iii) systematic control of sickness certificates.

Providing medical guidelines

In the first place, it is important to provide sufficient information to medical professionals about the "ideal duration" of absence from work for the most frequent health problems; ideal in terms of ensuring a fast recovery as well as enabling a return to work as quickly and fully as possible, recognising the negative longer-term effect of enduring periods of inactivity for the worker. Several countries have started to realise the need for better medical guidelines for GPs, in particular in view of the large share of mental and muscular-skeletal health problems reported:

- In Sweden, medical guidelines introduced in 2007 prescribe appropriate periods of sickness absence that are likely to produce a good outcome for the 90 most frequent medical conditions, which together account for three-quarters of all sick leaves taken. Recommendations also include information on treatment, prognosis and expected recovery time. The recommended period of absence was developed on the basis of empirical data on the typical absence period, and in consultation with medical experts. The development process itself has helped to generate awareness among GPs and the public alike of the forthcoming change in sick-listing practice.

- Similarly, in Ireland and the Netherlands, medical guidelines and protocols are currently being developed to encourage earlier return from sick leave. Guidelines in the Netherlands aim at improved co-operation between GPs and occupational health doctors by making the former more aware of the importance of the concept of work capacity and the advantages of resuming work. Protocols provide scientific evidence about the relation between a particular illness, treatment and work capacity to promote more uniform medical assessment.

Rigorous evaluation of the impact of the guidelines is unavailable but it is likely they are a contributing factor to the sharp decline in sickness absence rates in both the Netherlands and Sweden. It will be important to ensure that medical professionals fully understand and make use of these guidelines. Therefore, it is essential to develop them on the basis of medical but also occupational evidence, ideally produced and agreed upon by the medical sector itself. It is also important to spread the general principles of the guidelines including the need for GPs to use sickness certificates as yet another tool for care and treatment so to speed up recovery, not as a bridge into inactivity (OECD, 2009).[7]

Clear procedures for medical professionals

A second way to harmonise sick-listing practices and avoid unnecessarily long sick leave is by setting clearer and pre-defined administrative procedures which doctors ought to follow. Again, several countries have taken steps into this direction:

- In Norway, GPs are obliged to guide sick workers in a manner that strengthens their work motivation and base sickness certificates on the question of whether or not there are sufficient medical grounds for an absence from work. After six weeks of absence, an extended medical certificate must be completed and sent to the insurance authority. GPs who fail to follow the regulations could lose their entitlement to issue medical certificates.

- In Luxembourg, since 2005, after an extended period of sickness absence (six weeks in the past sixteen weeks) a special form has to be completed by the attending GP and forwarded to the Administration of Medical Control. Information on the form allows the public administration to judge the justification of the extended sick leave. If the form is not returned within four weeks (following a reminder after two weeks), benefit payments will be stopped. As this form and also the reminder are sent to the sick person rather than the doctor, the patient and the doctor jointly carry responsible for explaining extended periods of sick leave.

Administratively prescribed procedures often go far beyond merely requesting GPs to provide regular updates of the sickness certificate. Frequent certificate updates can be a useful first step but only if this information is used in a productive way. For instance, in Ireland sickness certificates have to be renewed on a weekly basis but there is no limit to the number of renewals and no particular intervention in case of frequent renewal. Along these lines, the potential of stricter administrative procedures for doctors will only be harvested if compliance is monitored and non-compliance sanctioned.

Systematic control of sickness certificates

Medical guidelines and clear procedures form the basis for more harmonised and less subjective sick-listing practice, but their impact hinges on the degree of compliance monitoring. Again, several countries have in place, or recently strengthened, monitoring and control systems:

- In Spain, in 2004, the national social security institute (INSS) established a special directorate responsible for absence controls. INSS employs over 500 doctors who monitor and reassess ongoing sickness cases. Selection for reassessment is based on a rich administrative database with complete sickness absence histories of the entire workforce, including information on the employee, the employer, the cause of absence and the full medical history. Information is automatically registered through mandatory reporting of every case by both the employer and the GP. The INSS controls people with absences which are longer than the average duration for a specific sickness, as specified by very detailed lists for almost all possible illnesses.

The Spanish case is probably not easily transferable to other countries because of privacy and confidentiality issues. The database includes *individual* information for every employee and information is automatically updated on a daily basis (OECD, 2007). However, better controls are possible in many different ways often requiring far less detailed and transparent information. For instance, monitoring can simply include regular controls of randomly selected sickness certificates by a higher authority, *i.e.* by controlling doctors employed or authorised by the benefit agency or the sickness insurance.

Several OECD countries, including Austria and France, have such control systems in place. In Austria, for instance, sickness certificates are regularly verified on a random basis, starting as early as after around one week of absence. Many of those absent from work who are called in for a control visit will have returned to work before attending the control visit – in itself indicating the effectiveness of this approach. Notably, in Austria such controls by social insurance doctors start so early despite an extended period during which sick pay is provided by the employer (6-12 weeks), recognising the long-run cost for the public purse of any long-term absence. This is only possible, of course, because of the strict duty of notification of absences by the employer from very early on.

Financial incentives for doctors

Ultimately, the effectiveness of these tools and interventions – guidelines, procedures, controls and combinations of those – in terms of actually changing sick-listing practices of medical professionals will depend on the sanctions subsequently imposed on them. This could in the extreme include a (presumably initially temporary) suspension of sick-listing authorisation which, in turn, would have a negative impact on GPs' incomes. However, this is rarely ever done even if it is legally possible, as is the case in Norway.

Instead, encouragement is used in other ways. A promising development recently in the Nordic countries is the move towards partial return to work from sick leave. For many illnesses, the question is not one of full temporary incapacity for work. Rather, especially for many of the growing number of absences due to mental health problems, it would often be possible for the patient to return to work in a partial capacity, thereby significantly reducing the duration of inactivity. Recent research from Norway has shown that more frequent granting of partial absence by doctors leads to less frequent slips into disability benefit of their patients three years down the road (ongoing research at the University of Bergen). In one way or another, all Nordic countries today have regulations in place so to increase the use of partial sickness leave – which is legally not possible in most OECD countries. In Norway, for example, partial sickness always has to be considered before a full absence can be granted.

At the broader systems level, the authorities who administer the national (or sometimes regional) health care entities that licence, employ or in some other way reimburse the GPs who issue sickness certificates, should have an intrinsic financial interest in managing their system in ways that promote employment. This issue goes beyond the scope of this report but one avenue to this may be through transferring a component of the liability for public expenditure on sick leave from social protection budgets to the health sector. In doing so, health system authorities who manage medical practitioners would have an incentive to encourage them to keep the duration and corresponding cost of sick leave to the minimum necessary for good health and good employment outcomes.

5.4. Conclusion

Many countries have started to realise the important role employers are playing in preventing, monitoring and managing sickness absence so to prevent longer-term labour market exit of their workers. Employers are best placed to ensure health-enhancing work environments and react at an early stage. Similarly, general practitioners have a key role to play in minimising sickness absence to the necessary length and setting people's mindset early on to a swift return to work rather than a continued sick role. In different ways, countries are seeking to engage better both employers and general practitioners.

For employers, the key issues will be to fortify, extend, monitor and enforce responsibilities and corresponding financial incentives, especially in regard to sickness absence, while at the same time providing sufficient supports for them to fulfil their strengthened obligations. For general practitioners, a combination of medical guidelines, clear procedural structures and systematic control will be needed.

A key challenge in stimulating labour demand is how to promote job retention of workers with chronic health problems or disability without jeopardising recruitment chances for those without a job. This will require a flexible labour market and a well-balanced mix of responsibilities and supports, and occasionally specific measures addressing any imbalances, thereby also requiring the involvement of the social partners.

Notes

1. Australia is an exception because of the particular sickness benefit eligibility criteria. After ten days of continued wage payment by the employer, sick employees can be laid off, and without a valid employment contract they will not be entitled to a sickness benefit. Instead, they will be directed to the unemployment benefit scheme. Unemployment benefit recipients with temporary work incapacity are not transferred to sickness benefit. Moreover, casual workers who make up for around one-quarter of the workforce and one-third of all workers with disability are not covered by sickness benefit.

2. For Canada, this statement refers to voluntary long-term disability insurance which covers roughly half of the employed workforce and makes up around one-fifth of total disability benefit spending. For Switzerland, this refers to both the mandatory second-pillar occupational disability benefit plans and the equally mandatory sickness cash benefit insurance, which is integrated in private health insurance.

3. Employment quotas are also only mildly effective for another reason: quotas across the OECD cover people with a legally registered disability status. This administrative legal status is yet again different from the definition used by disability benefit systems and defines disability in a rather narrow way. Hence, even in countries with relatively high quota fulfilment rates of around 60% (e.g. Austria, France and Germany), the quota will not make a difference for the much larger group of people with milder chronic health problems.

4. Deadweight losses arise when hiring would also have occurred in the absence of the wage subsidy. Substitution and displacement effects occur when the jobs created by the wage subsidy replace jobs for other categories of workers (substitution) or displace jobs elsewhere in the economy as a result of a distortion in competition (displacement).

5. Workers counting towards the no-risk group include persons who are entitled to a disability benefit (implying an earnings-capacity reduction of 35% or more); people whose earnings capacity after two years of illness is reduced by 15-34% (i.e. not enough to be entitled to a disability benefit); and individuals entitled to sheltered employment. It is applicable to new as well as own employees. Entitlement holds for five years initially, with the possibility of extension.

6. For example, it was found that workers meeting the criteria for Generalised Anxiety Disorder have a better prognosis if they stay at work rather than at home because, in isolation, they are more likely to ruminate excessively and further deteriorate. Likewise, four weeks recuperative leave following coronary surgery tends to have a better prognosis because becoming active (within prescribed limits) after this time supports healing and adjustment.

7. Notwithstanding the new guidelines, GPs in Sweden can award absence periods that are longer than recommended; however, they are required to provide written justification for why the extra time off work is necessary in a particular case.

Bibliography

Acemoglu, D. and J.D. Angrist (2001), "Consequences of Employment Protection? The Case of Americans with Disabilities Act", *Journal of Political Economy*, Vol. 19, No. 5, pp. 915-950.

Begle, K. and A. Stock (2003), "The Labour Market Effects of Disability Discrimination Laws", *Journal of Human Resources*, Vol. 38, pp. 806-859.

Datta Gupta, N. and M. Larsen (2007), "Evaluating Employment Effects of Wage Subsidies for Disabled Individuals – The Danish Flex-Jobs Scheme", Danish National Institute of Social Research, Copenhagen.

De Jong, P.R., M. Lindeboom and B. van der Klaauw (2006), "Screening Disability Insurance Applications", *IZA Discussion Paper*, No. 1981, Bonn.

DeLeire, T. (2000), "The Wage and Employment Effects of the Americans with Disabilities Act", *Journal of Human Resources*, Vol. 35, No. 4, pp. 693-715.

Fjell, Y., M. Österberg et al. (2007), "Appraised Leadership Styles, Psychosocial Work Factors, and Musculoskeletal Pain Among Public Employees", *Journal International Archives of Occupational and Environmental Health*.

Heckl, E. (2009), "Providing Reasonable Accommodation for Persons with Disabilities in the EU – Best Practices and Financial Schemes", Report of the Austrian Institute for SME Research on behalf of the European Commission.

143

Henrekson, M. and M. Persson (2004) "The Effects on Sick Leave of Changes in the Sickness Insurance System", *Journal of Labour Economics*, Vol. 22, No. 1, pp. 87-113.

Hesselius, P. and M. Persson (2007), "Incentive and Spill-over Effects of Supplementary Sickness Compensation", *IFAU Working Paper*, No. 16, Institute for Labour Market Policy Evaluation, Uppsala.

Høgelund, J. and A. Holm (2004), "Case Management and Returns to Work of Disabled Employees", Centre for Applied Microeconometrics, University of Copenhagen.

Humer, B., J.P. Wuellrich and J. Zweimüller (2007), "Integrating Severely Disabled Individuals into the Labour Market: The Austrian Case", *IZA Discussion Paper*, No. 2649, Bonn.

Kangasharju, A. (2007), "Do Wage Subsidies Increase Employment in Subsidised Firms?", *Economica*, Vol. 74, No. 293, pp. 51-67.

Koning, P. (2005), "Estimating the Impact of Experience Rating on the Inflow into Disability Insurance in the Netherlands", *CPB Discussion Paper*, No. 37, The Hague.

Korkeamäki, O. and T. Kyyrä (2009), "Institutional Rules, Labour Demand and Disability Programme Participation", *Working Paper*, No. 2009:5, Finnish Centre for Pensions, Helsinki.

OECD (2003), *Transforming Disability into Ability*, OECD Publishing, Paris.

OECD (2006), *Sickness, Disability and Work: Breaking the Barriers. Vol. 1: Norway, Poland and Switzerland*, OECD Publishing, Paris.

OECD (2007), *Sickness, Disability and Work: Breaking the Barriers. Vol. 2: Australia, Luxembourg, Spain and the United Kingdom*, OECD publishing, Paris.

OECD (2008), *Sickness, Disability and Work: Breaking the Barriers. Vol. 3: Denmark, Finland, Ireland and the Netherlands*, OECD Publishing, Paris.

OECD (2008a), *OECD Employment Outlook*, Chapter 4, OECD Publishing, Paris.

OECD (2009), *Sickness, Disability and Work: Breaking the Barriers. Sweden: Will the Recent Reforms Make it?*, OECD Publishing, Paris.

OECD (2010), *Sickness, Disability and Work: Breaking the Barriers. Canada: Opportunities for Collaboration*, OECD Publishing, Paris.

Puhani, P.A. and K. Sonderhof (2009), "The Effects of a Sick Pay Reform on Absence and on Health-Related Outcomes", *IZA Discussion Paper*, No. 4607, Bonn.

Tepper, B.J. (2007), "Abusive Supervision in Work Organizations: Review, Synthesis, and Research Agenda", *Journal of Management*, Vol. 33, No. 3, pp. 261-289.

Veerman, T.J (2001), "Work Status and Benefit Status", in F.S. Bloch and R. Prins (eds.), *Who Returns to Work and Why?*, International Social Security Series, Vol. 5, Transaction Publishers, New Jersey.

Waddel, G. and A.K. Burton (2006), *Is Work Good for Your Health and Well-Being?*, Report commissioned by the Department for Work and Pensions, TSO: London.

Chapter 6

Getting the Right Services to the Right People at the Right Time

More people with disability could work if they were helped with the right supports at the right time. The chapter argues that much can be gained from improvements in three areas: better cross-agency co-operation; systematic and tailored engagement with clients; and improved institutional incentives. Currently, in many countries too many actors and agencies are involved in benefit and service provision; they do not co-operate effectively; they do not have sufficient incentives to promote the new employment focus of policy; and they lack the tools and resources to provide timely services in the mix needed by the client. In seeking to improve their systems and measures, most countries face barriers stemming from the lack of data and evaluation of programmes currently in place.

Many people with chronic health problems or disability can and want to work, yet they often lack the employment and rehabilitation supports which would make it possible for them to stay in or enter the workforce. Services should fit peoples' (and employers') needs; they should be provided as timely as possible; and they should be easily accessible. This is true for all people seeking a job but fine-tuned services are more critical for persons with disability especially given the large heterogeneity of needs.

Most OECD countries have made considerable efforts to expand the available array of services and to modify the provision of services. However, these changes, albeit significant in many countries, have not changed outcomes very much. In brief, the following *status quo* emerges:

- The take-up of any single employment measure is very low, often just a few hundred of people; most people entering disability benefits have never received any such measure.

- The take-up of employment measures is particularly low among older workers, who in most cases still make up the bulk of all new disability beneficiaries.

- Employment supports are in most cases offered at a very late stage in the process, often many years after the onset of a health problem or sickness absence. In some countries, the target group for services is people on disability benefit – by definition implying a very late intervention.

- For those obtaining an employment measure, per-capita spending is in most cases very low, compared with the average disability benefit being paid.

- Programme outcomes are rarely measured and, if they are, tend to be highly variable. Often the only outcome measure available is whether or not a new benefit claim was avoided. Where employment is used as an outcome measure, usually very little is known about the persistence of work.

- In several OECD countries with above-average vocational rehabilitation spending, spending is predominantly on rehabilitation benefits (this benefit is often higher than a disability benefit) while only a minority of the total is direct costs for services.

- In several countries with relatively high overall spending on employment measures, this is predominantly covering the costs of subsidies for sheltered workplaces, from which there is very little transition into the open labour market.

This is not a satisfactory picture. Many of the institutions and agencies involved in implementing and delivering employment, training and welfare programmes are arranged in an unco-ordinated and unsystematic way that may contribute to such poor outcomes of sickness and disability policies. Thus, incentives for system administrators and service providers and the way their actions are monitored and financed can heavily influence the ultimate effectiveness of policies. In addition, labour market authorities have often failed to assess the impact of their employment programmes, as a result of which lack of data in virtually all OECD countries on the take-up and impact of employment and vocational rehabilitation measures is a major cause for concern.

This chapter addresses the main remaining issues in relation to institutional structures and employment programme delivery that need to be tackled in order to progress faster and more effectively to a situation that allows people willing and able to work to get the services they require at the time they need them.

6.1. Improving cross-agency co-ordination and co-operation

Smooth co-ordination and active co-operation between relevant agencies is particularly important because of the interdisciplinary nature of disability policy. The health system (treating people if needed and helping them manage their condition through medical rehabilitation), the benefits system (providing income support when necessary) and the national employment services (helping those with sufficient remaining work capacity to find a job) all play a key role, but they do not always follow the same objectives.

Historically, most OECD countries have developed fragmented welfare and employment institutions delivering programmes focused on different groups and often delivered by different agencies by drawing on diverse funding streams. This meant that the different institutions involved – like the benefit administration authorities, the local social assistance agencies and the public employment services (PES) – have developed diverging objectives and practices which have given rise to a number of problems. For example, disability benefits and employment services are often financed at national (or in some cases, regional, state or provincial) level. However, employment services are generally implemented at local level. The national government needs to maintain some control over local policy administration and implementation, because local employment services do not necessarily have a strong incentive to enforce eligibility criteria against individuals capable of working. Secondly, the setup of different agencies means that some local PES offices try to shift difficult-to-place unemployed workers with health problems from their own caseloads to other institutions and benefits.

Better co-ordination and co-operation between government agencies can be hard to achieve, for a number of reasons. In many cases fragmented systems are statutorily codified, making reform efforts all the more difficult, complicated and vulnerable to political interests. Especially in federal countries like Canada and Switzerland where the roles of governmental entities are demarked in the constitution, steadier and more tenacious political leadership may be required. In particular, it is important for public authorities to have sufficient incentives to invest in active labour market strategies with clients who will often need special support, rather than merely doing what they used to do and what seems easiest for the authority – and might often seem attractive to the client as well, namely to grant a benefit.

Towards an integrated gateway to benefits and services

Governments have recognised the need to couple policy with organisational reform and have linked the transition to active benefit regimes with fundamental changes in the bureaucracies and institutions charged with delivering and administering programmes. A radical way to induce better co-ordination and co-operation between public entities is to merge the relevant agencies into so-called "one-stop-shop" services. The one-stop-shop principle in labour market policy provides for access to labour market programmes as well as social benefits, where needed, through provision of joint services, even where the various programmes and benefits are operated by different agencies that maintain legal and financial autonomy from one another. Various OECD countries have followed such a trend in a range of different ways:

- One such case is the United Kingdom, where from 2002 onwards the Benefits Agency and the Employment Service were merged to form Job Centre Plus. This new agency provides a single point of delivery for jobs, benefits advice and support for people of working age. As a result, the practice of shifting people around – e.g. from unemployment to incapacity benefit and vice versa – has become less common.

- Norway has recently merged the National Insurance Administration (in charge of disability benefits) and the National Employment Service (responsible for all employment and rehabilitation programmes) into one national agency, the Labour and Welfare Administration, which co-operates closely with the local welfare offices. The main objective of this reform was to provide services in accordance with user needs, and for that purpose it aims at offering "one door" for all of its services by fortifying the partnership between central and municipal authorities.

- Australia has established Centrelink as a one-stop-shop statutory agency responsible for benefit payments and the delivering of a range of Commonwealth services and, if appropriate, referrals to a service provider. The decision to grant a disability benefit is also taken by Centrelink, not the work capacity assessor.

- In the Netherlands, when the PES was dismantled, most employment services were integrated into the Employee Insurance. Initially the two agencies operated with a shared one-stop-shop front office; later they operated on shared premises so to improve further service integration and client orientation; and in 2009 the two entities were merged.

In some cases, including Norway, it is too early to tell whether the ambitious reform effort has been successful. However, the UK example suggests that merging the employment and benefit authorities has not only helped to streamline services for the clients, but also influenced subsequent reform in benefits and employment services (OECD, 2007).

Similarly, gathering under one roof all case-managers and agencies handling income and employment policies for persons with disability can equally help to streamline the benefit mix and establish a system that procures more appropriate employment services in a timely manner:

- In Finland, separate labour force service centres were introduced with staff detached from local employment offices and municipal services, and in some cases also from the national social security institution, to provide specialised assistance for hard-to-place jobseekers. This new institutionalised co-operation has its limits; largely because of restricted funding, it targets the long-term unemployed and highly disadvantaged jobseekers. However, it has generated good-practice models for the establishment of one-stop-shop services and cost-sharing schemes (OECD, 2009).

To conclude, better co-ordination of policies and co-operation of agencies is a huge undertaking and merging government entities is one but not the only solution. Such change is only possible with very strong leadership at all levels to overcome genuine resistance from public servants, caseworkers and others to a comprehensive system overhaul. Change needs to be carried through by all actors in a transparent manner with effective information sharing to make sure potential synergy effects can be harvested.

Streamlining fragmented systems

Greater co-ordination and co-operation between different institutions is one way of simplifying current complex and fragmented systems. Too many different benefits, administered by different entities, and too many different types of employment services, offered by different providers and institutions, also make for a very complicated and non-transparent starting position. Some countries will further need to make efforts to simplify their systems, in order to make services more accessible for clients, outcomes more predictable and the overall system more efficient. Countries with fragmented systems are generally already acknowledging the problem and undertaking steps to achieve a simpler and better-structured benefits and services scheme.

Ireland has been such a case. Various long-term health-related benefits are available for persons with health problems. They are assigned based on the type of disability, claimants' insurance records, the nature of health conditions, or a combination of these, but not necessarily the claimants' work capacity. Ireland is now taking steps to streamline the benefit portfolio, merging the benefit responsibilities that were remaining under the Department of Health and Children into the Department of Social Protection for example.

In the case of Canada, benefit complexity remains an issue. The federal disability insurance programme and provincial workers' compensation programmes usually play the role of the first payers, with other benefits – including provincial social assistance, tax credits and private disability insurance – existing alongside. Benefit-stacking is allowed, usually with off-setting of other entitlements, but not explicitly encouraged (except by private insurers). Overall, one in four beneficiaries receives two or more benefits.

Spain has successfully integrated the benefit structure into one national agency while devolving the authority for labour market policy implementation to the regional headquarters which in turn direct their local agencies. The centralised benefit structure in combination with decentralised employment services does not lead to the level of co-ordination of benefits and services needed to help more persons with disability into the labour market.

In Finland, the problem of fragmented policy structure is most apparent in its vocational rehabilitation system, with too many actors being involved. The PES, the health care system, various insurance institutions and the municipalities all have their own roles, which make it almost impossible to identify the right path not only for potential users but also for the authorities involved. This situation is not atypical. Countries could follow the example of Germany which, in 2001, has streamlined its well-developed but rather complex system of vocational rehabilitation by harmonising the legal basis of service provision, thereby also granting more choice to rehabilitees.

Matching and sharing funding responsibilities

Methods of promoting cross-agency co-ordination and co-operation will differ subject to the country context and political choices and will include a physical merger or co-location in some cases but not in others. In any case, however, it will be important to identify and ensure the right role for the right agency and to match resources and funding responsibilities accordingly, especially when countries shy away from reshuffling or merging government bodies.

Matching funding mechanisms with responsibilities is even more difficult in cases where the roles and power are distributed not just horizontally between ministries or their agencies but also vertically between central and local government bodies. Ideally, the responsibility for a specific policy should be closely matched by the budget and the required expertise. To give an example illustrating the challenge, the Netherlands has experienced a sharp increase in the number of beneficiaries of its "Wajong" scheme, a nationally-funded disability benefit programme targeting persons who *acquired* a disability at a young age.[1] A big part of the reason for the increase has been the municipalities' incentive to encourage people on their own caseloads to apply for such a nationally-paid benefit instead of municipal social assistance so as to lower their own spending.

Trends in countries that have changed their financing arrangements in the case of long-term unemployment support the idea that local and regional co-financing can reduce caseloads. For example, in 2006 Finland introduced 50% municipal financial responsibility for spending on long-term unemployment, in addition to previously introduced national-municipal co-sharing of the costs of social assistance. After these changes, the relevant caseloads fell for several years (OECD, 2008) partly because local co-financing encouraged the introduction and implementation of activation measures.

Direct financial incentives are still relatively rare and mostly found across levels of government. In the Netherlands, for instance, although this is not directly related to disability, municipalities are now receiving a two-tiered budget, with one part of the transfer reserved for benefit payments and the other part for work-related measures. Unused spending on the latter has to be returned to the central government so as to stimulate a more active approach. Denmark is the most suggestive example of a country experimenting with financial incentives for its main public body, the municipalities:

- Through 16 years of continuous adaptation, Denmark has established a unique incentive system by reimbursing more favourably from central government funds work-related measures like wage subsidies and vocational rehabilitation than sickness or disability benefit payments. More precisely, the central government reimburses only 35% of the costs for short-term benefits (sickness benefit) and none of the costs for disability benefits, whereas the rate of reimbursement is 65%, for instance, for vocational rehabilitation spending. Furthermore, this system is matched by municipal tax collection accounting for almost 60% of total income tax revenues. Experience over the years has shown how strong the incentives need to be for municipalities to react in line with the federal government's goal to increase employment of persons with disability, and how important it is to close all loopholes (OECD, 2008).

- Another example of well-conceived funding, though on a much smaller scale, is the strategy in Sweden to enhance co-ordination between the Social Insurance Agency (SIA) and the PES. To help activate more persons with disability, the government opted to allocate funding to the SIA for the special purpose of working more closely with the PES, instead of the SIA just sending clients who are capable of engaging in vocational rehabilitation to the PES. This funding articulation helped to overcome the problem of funding in silos and to build a more positive relationship between the two government bodies, also at the local level (*e.g.* with staff from both agencies planning together the best use of the resources).

Setting direct financial incentives for public entities is often difficult, and more difficult than doing so for their private counterparts (see Section 5.3). Some countries have chosen to go for a "naming and shaming" approach, whereby results of regional (*e.g.*

Switzerland) or even local offices (*e.g.* Denmark) are being shared across offices, in the hope to stimulate a race to the top. Anecdotal evidence from those offices suggests that this approach can lead results.

Governance: monitoring regional and local authorities

Monitoring regional and local authorities is another way to ensure policy at the local level is being implemented as intended. Monitoring requirements for the national government are a direct function of the structure of a system. The more institutions and government levels involved, the more difficult it is to scrutinise and control actions and outcomes. Conversely, a concentration of benefit and employment matters in a single ministry and only a few agencies not only facilitates processes and cross-agency co-operation, but also secures better accountability of regional bodies and, thus, reduces considerably the need for supervision, especially when financial liability for revenues and spending also match. Accordingly, the challenges in supervising local administrations and encouraging them to follow the new policy line differ widely across countries.

Key players involved in many OECD countries are the PES, often under the auspices of the labour ministry, responsible for administering employment services, and the Social Insurance or a corresponding Benefit Authority, often under the auspices of the social ministry. Yet, in many cases several other agencies are also involved, and in some countries, municipalities are taking much of the responsibility. The PES in many countries has considerable experience in monitoring its regional and local entities, typically with more or less binding performance targets at various levels of the administration, including country-wide and regional targets and sometimes even targets for each office and caseworker. Targets are frequently modulated on an annual basis and do include in some countries, *e.g.* Norway, targets related to *e.g.* the share of people with disability participating in employment measures. However, in many cases (again including Norway) these operational targets are process-oriented rather than outcome-related, and financial transfers to local offices are not linked to the fulfilment of targets.

Such target-setting has yet to be introduced in most countries for the benefit authorities but a few promising examples exist:

- In Switzerland, where the cantonal disability offices are the key players in policy administration, the harmonisation of large cantonal differences through improved monitoring by the national supervisory body has become a driving force for policy change in the past few years. A better reporting and monitoring system and more frequent controls (on an annual rather than three-yearly basis) have strengthened competition between cantons. This is complemented by target agreements with each cantonal office, similar to those existing for a number of years between the PES and its supervisory body. Such type of management-by-objectives is still quite innovative for disability benefit or insurance authorities.

- Denmark also uses targets for its municipalities which run the benefit system and, through its job centres, also the employment system, with one of the three targets in 2009 for example being that "each job centre must ensure that the number of sickness benefit cases exceeding 26 weeks is lower than in the previous year".

An example showing the difficulty of designing a well-working funding and monitoring scheme is Canada, where the responsibilities for income supports and employment services are split between the federal and provincial governments. The federal government allocates considerable budgets to provinces to help improve employment of persons with disability, with limited control over the use of funds and modest reporting requirements for provincial governments. Such mismatch between funding responsibility and service programming is not ideal. This discrepancy can be solved in different ways, including by handing over to the regional jurisdiction, the provinces in the case of Canada, the entire funding and tax-raising responsibility.

In most countries where regional or local governments, or local offices of public agencies which accord considerable influence to local governments, have authority for employment services and/or benefit schemes while relying upon the central government for the budget to administer it, central governments stay away from using their disbursement and monitoring powers due to the heavily political nature of such distribution. The size of transfers to the local authority, or government, is typically decided through a mutual bargaining process between the two levels of government. This process is not driven by the results of performance assessment but rather such simple variables as population size and, maybe, composition (taking into account equity concerns between local governments), and transfers are typically given in block amount rather than as a calculated reimbursement. Moreover, national governments generally stay away from outcome monitoring at the local level. This is far from optimal.

Measuring outcomes and evaluating programmes

An improved governance structure also has an influence on the extent to which labour market authorities assess the impact of their labour market programmes and use this information to manage them better. A major challenge all across the OECD is the lack of data on the outcomes of active labour market policies for people with health problems or disability, and where data exist, the limited flow of information across institutions and governments. With the shift towards a more employment-focused disability policy, the need for better and more comparable data based on jointly-agreed standards is becoming ever more evident.

However, little policy-relevant evidence is collected or generated, and even less is shared with others. A few plausible reasons can be given for the lack of data accumulation and dissemination, such as the relatively short history of employment and rehabilitation measures for persons with disability; the untradeable and local nature of services; or the excessive demand for such services which will negatively affect the incentives of service providers to innovate and seek out information about better services elsewhere.

Where data are produced, *sharing* of information is another bottleneck for policy improvement. This is particularly unfortunate in federalist countries, like Canada and the United States, or countries where municipalities play a key role in organising and/or supplying services. These countries in theory have great potential for gradual policy improvement. Different regions all operating under the same system or policy environment can develop and trial their own, creative policy responses, and the outcomes of diversified approaches be shared among all regions in order to hasten the identification of optimal policy alternatives. This could generate a healthy race to becoming the top-performing region or locality, but in practice this happens too rarely. Denmark and Switzerland have addressed this "missed opportunity" recently and are currently trying to achieve better overall results by publicising and sharing process outputs and employment outcomes obtained by municipal job centres (in Denmark) and regional disability benefit authorities (in Switzerland), respectively.

In the absence of high-quality information, it will be both difficult and costly to develop better policies and programmes. Often in such a situation the only way to develop policies may be by trial-and-error. Trial-and-error can indeed be a useful approach as part of a strategy, and often is – *e.g.* countries trialing a new scheme or approach in a region, or in a few service units, before a country-wide roll-out, as is often done for instance in the United Kingdom. But in order to benefit from such an approach, and to minimise the probability of error when rolling-out the scheme, the trial needs to produce evidence on which the ultimate roll-out can build. To the extent possible, evidence should be based on rigorous scientific evaluation with a comparison/control group. For instance, a country may initially decide to set aside, say, 5% of total spending for programme evaluation, as was done as a part of general labour market policy reforms (the Hartz-reforms) in Germany earlier this decade. This has had a major impact on the amount of evidence available and, in turn, led to a complete overhaul of many labour market programmes.

6.2. Engaging with clients systematically and in a tailored way

To deliver the right service to the right people at the right time, a series of conditions need to be fulfilled. Potential clients should have easy access to supports that can help them and face no problems in identifying the right gateway to services. The authorities should have tools to identify, as early as possible, whether or not a client's sickness is at risk of developing into a more enduring work-capacity reduction and, therefore, demanding early intervention. They must have the means to procure a broad range of services tailored to the clients' needs as much as possible. Achieving this will in most countries require fresh resources or a considerable shift in resources towards employment programmes and away from passive benefits to ensure that service supply matches service demand.

Investing more to ensure that service supply meets service demand

Among the main weaknesses of disability employment services in most OECD countries are the low take-up of services, the low per-capita spending and the highly variable outcomes of services. These weaknesses are related to a number of things, including restrictive eligibility criteria which exclude too many and do not necessarily serve the right group of people, and a general under-investment in services. These limitations have to be addressed.

Table 6.1 briefly summarises, country by country, entitlement criteria to qualify for subsidised, supported and sheltered employment programmes. By and large, services require the existence of a rather significant disability. Often eligibility is linked to the relatively narrow status of legally-registered disability (see note 40) and with only limited recognition of the person's actual work capacity. The result of such tight criteria can be that many of those formally eligible might not have enough work capacity to move into the open labour market even with the help of a wage subsidy, for example, thereby reducing the measured impact of the support offered. At the same time, many of those with capacity that is reduced but not enough to qualify for comprehensive support may be excluded from several of these services.

Another problem is that in some countries certain types of intensive counselling and employment programmes are restricted to beneficiaries of a disability benefit. For example, until recently people not entitled to income support payments in Australia were only entitled to a more restricted set of services or often faced considerable waiting lists before they could access intensive re-employment services (OECD, 2007). With recent reform of its disability employment service, however, this is no longer the case. Linking of the eligibility for comprehensive services to disability beneficiary status can be especially problematic in combination with means-testing of income support and in countries with very tightly-controlled access to benefits.

On the contrary, as a general guideline, governments should make every effort to ensure that employment services reach all clients who want to and can work with the help of appropriate supports. In most OECD countries, such a situation can only ever be achieved with significant additional investment to equip the PES and, where applicable, other (sometimes private) service providers with the necessary funds. Today, on the contrary, many countries including e.g. Luxembourg and Spain have seen supply-demand mismatches of disability employment services due to a lack of human and/or budgetary resources. The result of this can be long waiting lists, or that people are offered inappropriate or in other ways not very useful services, in turn partly explaining the variable outcomes of these services.

Early identification of problems

Service intervention must come at the right time. In reality, disability employment services are only offered at a very late stage, typically after a person has been inactive for years and in many cases after a disability benefit has been granted; in short, at a time when people's mindset is no longer focussed on getting back into work. Timing is of the essence, especially at the early stages of a sickness absence. Chapter 5 discusses this issue and the respective roles for employers and the medical profession. However, benefit granting and employment authorities also have an important role to play, in particular but not only for people who do not, or no longer, have an employer.

Sickness absence monitoring of workers

Public authorities can support early identification and monitoring of sickness in many ways, and manage the services for the persons concerned. They can set the stages for doctors, employers and other players to play their parts, because most sickness benefit schemes in the OECD are institutionalised in the form of public social insurances.[2] The municipal caseworkers, responsible for the sickness benefit scheme in Denmark, for example, have at their disposal a series of tools to monitor their clients, including where necessary organising a roundtable discussion with physicians and employers.

There is a very strong case for public authorities to monitor sickness absence very closely and seek possibilities to intervene actively early on. Prolonged sickness benefit periods can easily become the main hindrance for beneficiaries' successful return to the workplace, or the labour force more generally. Long-term absence may effectively become a substitute for long-term disability benefit dependence and may preclude the sick person from the possibility to receive appropriate services. It is not surprising that, once a long sickness benefit period comes to an end, the sick person already cut off from the previous workplace frequently ends up claiming a disability benefit.[3] In this vein, countries have strengthened their systems and the monitoring role of their public authorities in different ways:

- Countries with hitherto unlimited sickness benefit duration have recently introduced time limits – two and a half years in the case of Sweden, and two years in Ireland.

Table 6.1. **Eligibility criteria for employment supports are very restrictive**

Eligibility criteria for subsidised, supported and sheltered employment

	Subsidised employment	Supported employment	Sheltered employment
Australia	Eligibility is assessed on the basis of minimum work capacity (of at least eight hours per week) and support needs; all eligible people with disability can approach service providers directly.		
Austria	Registered supportable disabled, *i.e.* at least 30% disability, unable to find job without such measures.	Severely disabled, most with mental or sensory disabilities or psychological disorders.	Registered disabled whose output matches at least 50% of that of an average productive worker.
Belgium	Long-term limitation in opportunities for social or professional integration and registered with the regional disability agency; some regions in addition require a minimum incapacity level depending on the type of disability.		
Canada	Provincial programmes, often with differing definitions; federal wage subsidies target unemployed persons having difficulties finding work; supported employment focuses on people with intellectual or developmental disabilities.		
Czech Republic	Acknowledged by the social security authorities as disabled or by the Labour Office as having reduced working capacity.		
Denmark	Ability to work permanently significantly impaired, normal employment impossible, possibilities of rehabilitation exhausted.	Permanent and substantial physically or mentally reduced functional capacity.	Considerably reduced functional capacity or special social problems, unable to get a job on normal terms on the labour market.
Finland	A disabled person is a worker referred by an employment office whose potential for gaining employment, job retention or career advancement has diminished significantly due to an appropriately diagnosed injury, illness or other disability.		
France	Assessed as disabled by assessment commission, work injury victim, disability benefit recipient or war veteran.		Assessed as disabled by assessment commision, owner of an invalidity card or non-contributory disability beneficiary.
Germany	"Registered severely disabled" (see next column) and registered as unemployed.	"Registered severely disabled", *i.e.* disability of at least 50% or equal status (*e.g.* 30-49% and unable to obtain a job).	Extent and type of disability makes open employment impossible, but able to do some productive work.
Greece	Disability percentage of at least 50% with limited potential for employment due to a chronic physical or mental or psychological disease or damage and registered as unemployed.		
Hungary	Reduction of working capacity at least 50%.		
Italy	"Registered disabled", *i.e.* 45% general work-ability reduction, or 33% work-related ability reduction, or military service disability, or visual/hearing/speech impairment ("compulsory placement list").		
Japan	Disability (physical, intellectual, mental or developmental) or intractable disease.	Considerable restrictions in vocational life because of a disability, or great difficulty in leading a vocational life over long period.	Those who have difficulties getting employed by usual establishments.
Korea	Considerable restriction in working life caused by disability for an extended period of time (medical definition).	Severely disabled or judged to have difficulty in finding proper work/need on-site support.	Severely disabled living in the community who are difficult to employ.
Netherlands	Classified as work disabled: current or former disability benefit recipient or on sheltered employment waiting list or passed the work disability test, which is valid for five years.		Severe disability, *i.e.* can only work under adapted circumstances.
New Zealand	Ill health and/or a disability that is likely to continue for a minimum of six months and to result in a reduction of independent function or social well being to the extent that support is required.		
Norway	Registered at the Labour and Welfare office as vocationally disabled.		Registered at the Labour and Welfare office as *severely* vocationally disabled.
Poland	Disability assessment carried out by local assessment teams – to determine degree of disability and identify appropriate training and employment measures; assessment obtained to receive social insurance benefits is also recognised.		
Portugal	Difficulty in either securing or retaining a suitable job.	Disabled in training at work (initial integration phase).	Inferior productivity, unable to work in open employment, registered with department.
Slovak Republic	Reduced capacity to carry out gainful activity owing to physical, mental or behavioural impairment as determined by a decision or by a statement of the Social Insurance Agency, or by an assessment produced by the Social Security Unit.		
Spain	Assessed to be handicapped, *i.e.* certified degree of handicap of at least 33% and registered as unemployed.		
Sweden	Registered vocationally disabled at regional employment office.	Registered as severely vocationally disabled.	Registered as severly vocationally disabled; can work half-time but cannot obtain any other work.
Switzerland	For early job retention measures: work incapacity and threat of invalidity. For measures to create conditions of a vocational rehabilitation: work incapacity of at least 6 months. For rehabilitation measures: (threat of) invalidity according to Invalidity Insurance Act.		Subsidy to institution requires 50% disability.
United Kingdom	Eligibility and suitability for a range of disability employment programmes (mainstream and special, supported and unsupported) is assessed on the basis of the type of benefit being claimed and individuals' employment aspirations and support needs.		
United States	Disability-label neutral, *i.e.* access is determined by programme characteristics.	Eligibility varies with the funding agency.	State programmes use their own configurations and criteria.

Source: Information provided by national authorities.

- Other countries, *e.g.* Finland and Denmark, have introduced a categorisation so as to better identify cases at risk of developing into long-term absence.

- Some countries such as France and Spain have strengthened controls by social insurance doctors of sick-leave certificates granted by general practitioners.

- Several countries have introduced clearly-set regulations as to when exactly certain steps will have to be taken by the authorities, including assessment of rehabilitation needs and the setting up of a rehabilitation plan (OECD, 2006, 2007, 2008 and 2009).

Health monitoring of unemployed and inactive people

Public authorities play a particularly critical role in health monitoring and early identification of rehabilitation and other service needs of sick people who are unemployed or inactive in order to minimise shifts onto disability benefits, for two reasons. First, rates of sickness absence have shown to be much higher for unemployed individuals than for workers; based on data for Austria, sick leave of the unemployed averaged 32.5 days compared with 12.5 days for the employed, with only around half of this gap being explained by a selection effect (Leoni, 2010). Secondly, long-term unemployment increases the likelihood of a transfer to disability benefits; in the United Kingdom, for example, more than one in five of those people coming from unemployment onto disability benefits had been on unemployment benefits for two years or more (OECD, 2007).

Case information gathered from various benefits or instruments that the unemployed or inactive person might have been enrolled in may help identify such cases. Especially in cases where a recipient is transferred from unemployment benefit to sickness benefit, a fortified monitoring process should kick in. Only a few countries have set up a special strategy for this group to address the issue of early identification.

- In the Netherlands, where the sickness monitoring responsibility for workers is predominantly in the hands of the employers, the employee insurance authority has exactly the same obligations (including to set up a rehabilitation plan, etc., see Chapter 5) for sick people without an employer.

- In Australia, after a certain period of prolonged sickness absence, the sick unemployed person is called in for an assessment of both work capability and support needs.

For people outside the labour force, early identification of employment-hampering health problems and subsequent early intervention will often be particularly important but difficult to accomplish. One such group is young adults who have not yet entered the labour market. In a number of OECD countries, including most of the Nordic and the English-speaking countries but also the Czech Republic, the Netherlands and Switzerland (Figures 2.A1.2), the share of young adults receiving a disability benefit is high or has increased considerably over the past decade. Many of those young people have not completed secondary education and they are in urgent need of educational, transition and guidance services to be able to access the labour market. School dropout is probably the best early signal for identifying those in need of services. Nonetheless, in terms of identifying and helping young people early in life, there is still a long way to go to close this action gap.

Earlier intervention to prevent disability benefit claims

There are a number of other stages at which monitoring and, where needed, intervention would help prevent long-term disability benefit dependency. One such marker is a disability benefit rejection, a rather frequent event (see Chapter 4). When applying for a disability benefit, people are typically already at a considerable distance from the labour market which is why many of the rejected claimants will reapply at a later stage and often end up on the disability rolls eventually. Denied applicants are an at-risk group in need of special scrutiny and more than usual support to get back into the labour force; hence, it is a missed opportunity not to target them.

The new redeployment procedure introduced in Luxembourg in 2002 is an example of a reform aimed at preventing a disability benefit application. For people ineligible for a continued sickness benefit payment (as identified through tighter absence monitoring) but nevertheless unable to return to their job, the new redeployment procedure kicks in – with considerable obligations for both the employer (who has to explore possibilities for internal job shifts) and the public employment service (in cases where it is impossible for the worker to stay in the company).

The main focus of the 2004 reform in Switzerland also was on earlier identification of health problems and earlier intervention if needed, in this case by the disability insurance, in an effort to reduce the inflow into disability benefit (OECD, 2006). Workers with disability themselves and all other actors involved, including family members, employers and doctors, are encouraged to report to the disability insurance cases where the health problem may need early intervention to prevent longer-term disability. New short and specially-focused services are offered to enable the worker to stay at the current workplace – a solution that is considerably cheaper than finding a new job which may require a whole new set of services including a new assessment, new training and possibly new accommodations at the new workplace. These efforts have contributed to the fall in disability benefit inflow rates in the past few years.

Identifying the right mix of services

Profiling service users

Clients identified as being in need of help, through timely and attentive monitoring, will in a next step have to undergo careful assessment to find out exactly what services could help most. The importance of accurate, activation-oriented assessment was addressed already, in relation to the benefit system. Employment and rehabilitation services need to profile their clients in line with the results of assessments. The profile should be sufficiently individualised and effectively bring together all the relevant information for each client, based on medical files, the employment history, and any services hitherto provided. At the same time, the profile should be sufficiently standardised so that its quality and homogeneity is independent from who had profiled the case and where it had been kept:

- Australia's Job Seekers Classification Index, which is performed when a jobseeker first registers with Centrelink for employment assistance, is an example of an individual but streamlined profiling approach. It recognises the jobseeker's labour market disadvantage, identifies people at risk of long-term unemployment and, especially for people with disability, may trigger a Job Capacity Assessment. The latter in turn has a dual role, i.e. to assess work capacity and refer the person to appropriate assistance.

- Norway, in 2008, introduced a work-ability assessment operated by the new Labour and Welfare Administration. This is a new profiling tool for all claimants, aimed at identifying those in need of more help at an earlier stage, assessing what measures would be required to maintain labour market attachment, and developing an individual action plan.

Ireland is one of those countries lagging behind in the development of employment approaches but aiming for ambitious change, through its National Development Plan 2007-2013. In the future, people of working age, whether unemployed, lone parents, or having a disability, will receive case management support, guiding them to education, training and employment. For the success of this Plan, elaborate customer-profiling at the first point of engagement is integral, and currently various pilot projects are under way experimenting, *inter alia*, with more advanced case management tools in line with the Plan.

Following the result of the assessment or profiling, clients should be channelled to the most appropriate service, or provider. The type and intensity of service will vary with the clients' needs, and also partly depend on the specific service environment in a country. In the following, a few issues in relation to the nature and structure of good service provision are addressed.

Flexibly adjusted services

Services need to be adapted to the needs of the client all along the process, not the needs of providers. Services should be designed and delivered in such a way to encourage clients to move into the regular labour market whenever possible. A close relationship with caseworkers should be maintained over the duration of service use, so that caseworkers can systematically refer their clients to the services needed at each stage and continue to help them adapt to the labour market. Critically, all negative incentives – for either clients or caseworkers – that may hamper such progress should be removed.

In this regard, conflicts of interests may arise for service providers, depending on the funding system in place. For instance, service providers may have an interest in keeping clients on their programmes. Such adverse effects can be reduced by a well-developed funding scheme focusing on *outcomes* rather than inputs or outputs (see Section 6.3). This is critical in countries with a weak PES or in poorer communities, where non-profit and private providers effectively assume the role of case-managers as well, thereby making it more difficult for the public authorities to oversee the process.

In a similar vein, sheltered employment – which was and still is widely used in many countries, most notably the Netherlands and Poland – can become a trap for people with more labour potential. For some people, sheltered employment will be the only option to do meaningful work. However, there is a risk that existing places are maintained because providers of sheltered employment tend to hold on to their best workers. Employees in sheltered workplaces rarely get the opportunity to develop their skills and knowledge to compete in the regular labour market. As such workplaces depend heavily upon public subsidies (for initial investment, working expenses, etc.), and maintaining them will often come at the expense of an under-development of new support strategies helping people into the regular labour market. In response to this challenge, Poland has extended its generous subsidies to non-sheltered workplaces; Hungary has introduced a better accreditation system and clearer subsidy rules, thereby providing persons with disability with services that better match their reduced work capacity; and the United States in their employment service funding regulations have eliminated sheltered employment as a measure of a successful employment outcome.

One particular issue in relation to the provision of flexibly adjusted services is the need in many cases to follow the previously inactive or unemployed all along their experience into sustainable work rather than interrupting services when a placement is achieved. This philosophy is important for several groups served by employment services but especially so for people in need of a multifaceted mix of health, employment and maybe also social services. One of the main characteristic of supported employment, or individual placement and support, models used in an increasing number of countries is to provide service (and also financial support) on an *ongoing* basis, in line with the individual's needs. Moreover, these models are used for placing people in competitive jobs in the open labour market. There is unequivocal evidence on the effectiveness of supported employment from a series of randomised controlled trials around the OECD, as summarised *e.g.* in Drake and Bond (2008).[4] However, because it is a resource and staff-intensive service, the number of people served in this way is still very small and many countries have yet to adopt such approach altogether. Supported employment is currently targeted predominantly on people with more severe health problems, while models have yet to be adapted *e.g.* to the large and growing number of people with often more moderate mental health problems.

Mainstreamed and specialised services

"Mainstreaming", *i.e.* giving people with disability access to generic employment programmes, is a policy used in many OECD countries. For instance, in Poland in 2005 disability beneficiaries became entitled to services hitherto restricted to those formally registered as unemployed. With the change in mind-sets and policy orientation, to seeing a person's ability rather than the disability, general labour market services were increasingly charged with offering services to people with disability as well. In some countries, including especially the Nordic countries, the PES or its complement became fully responsible for labour market integration of all people of working age. As such, not only are new services potentially accessible for jobseekers with disability, but also service procedures and objectives are harmonised with those used for other target groups in similar need of improved employability, such as the long-term unemployed, youth with incomplete education or older workers with outdated skills.

A first challenge is for mainstreamed employment services to ensure that new client groups are sufficiently represented on the various programmes. However, the ever stronger focus on targeting services to the individual implies that specialised services will also be needed. Denmark, for instance, has solved this by having one expert for disability employment in each employment office plus one specialised centre in the country providing advice to all communities. In this way, the merits of mainstreamed services – *e.g.* a stronger orientation and simpler gateways to the regular labour market – are harvested without losing the benefits from special services for special needs. Other countries, for example Australia, have kept the strict distinction between general and disability employment services so to ensure that services are provided by specialists, while at the same time harmonising the processes and funding regimes. Some countries, for example New Zealand, provide special funds to develop innovative services that can be more finely customised to the varying needs of persons with disability.

Ultimately, sufficient resources need to be provided to help people with chronic health problems or disability access the regular labour market. Without sufficient staff capacity and resources, countries will fail to provide employment supports for a sufficiently large number of people. Even in a country like Finland until recently but even more so, for instance, in some of the countries in southern Europe, the already heavy-burdened PES will not be able to take on the new caseloads or continue to focus on the traditional target group of unemployed clients. This can quickly turn into a big problem particularly during a job crisis like the current one, with a very rapidly rising PES caseload.

Work-first and train-first services

Generally, services more directly geared to the workplace are more successful in increasing employment than services focused on training. Most surveys of the programme evaluation literature have found that supports to regular employment (including wage subsidies, job coaching, workplace adaptation, and personal assistance) fared better than training programmes, including vocational rehabilitation, and workplace training better than general education programmes (e.g. Kluve, 2006; Martin and Grubb, 2001). This is equally true for the unemployed in general and for people with disability. These findings explain why some countries, e.g. Sweden, have in recent years gone through a transformation of their employment services, with a strong move away from education and towards work-first measures and wage subsidies.

Finland and Denmark offer interesting examples on the effectiveness of wage subsidies for people with disability. The small-scale, well-targeted system in Finland was shown to be effective, but it is helping very few people. To the contrary, Denmark's system of heavily and permanently subsidised flex-jobs is large-scale (offering employment to some 5% of the labour force), but comes with enormous substitution and deadweight loss – effectively subsidising a transition to part-time employment (see Chapter 5). Hence, the right balance needs to be found between the size and the degree of targeting of a scheme. This partly explains the high effectiveness of supported employment models, as described above, which also aim to place people into work first, followed by ongoing support on the job – for both the worker and the co-workers and management – by a job coach so as to ensure a sustainable placement.

On the contrary, outcomes from vocational rehabilitation measures have been mixed and ambiguous, with employment outcomes ranging between 20% and 70%. The effectiveness of vocational rehabilitation has been called into question by many studies which have identified creaming or selection effects as the driver for good results and lock-in effects (participants not looking for a job intensely during the rehabilitation period, hence, being locked into non-employment) for bad results. However, other researchers report positive results of educational measures on the probability of returning to work (e.g. Bach, 2007 and Westlie, 2008). In any event, there is a good argument for providing training (and also other social or medical programmes) to those people who cannot return to work immediately.

There is no clear-cut answer to the question whether work-first approaches are to be preferred over train-first approaches, and the answer will partially depend on the state of the economic cycle. The more important principle to tailor services to the clients' needs implies that job-ready clients will benefit most from ordinary employment-oriented services, while others in need of training and pre-employment services will benefit from vocational rehabilitation and other educational measures. Even so, however, existing vocational rehabilitation measures will often benefit from a stronger employment orientation, including a focus on trial work, as is being used increasingly for example in

Norway. The work experience programmes developed in some countries, like Ireland, are a move into this direction.

6.3. Addressing incentives for private service providers

Provision of disability services by private providers has long been an integral part of disability policy all over the OECD. Long before the new employment-oriented approach was established, NGOs and communities were already helping persons with reduced ability to reintegrate into the workforce. With the new work focus of policies, governments are now generally investing more resources in private providers, and seeking to build better networks with them. Traditionally, private providers used to be non-profit NGOs but more recently private companies are increasingly becoming involved in many countries, still operating predominantly on a non-profit basis. In a few countries, however, for-profit private companies have entered the market.

Whether governments should develop their own public service capacity or contract out most services to the private sector has been the subject of an ongoing debate (*e.g.* Zaidi, 2009). Proponents of contracting-out refer to cost-savings, efficiency gains and innovations, while opponents emphasise the risk of cherry-picking by private providers. The latter, however, can also be a problem where services are provided by PES offices. In some countries, including *e.g.* Ireland, the main policy issue is one of how to best resource the private, traditional NGO sector around which the service network has developed and which is strongly rooted in the local community. Other countries, including Australia and the United Kingdom, have chosen a different route and have over the past years outsourced employment services to the private sector, through a competitive tender process.

An issue in both groups of countries is the division of roles between private providers and public agencies, with the aim to get the best possible results. Contracting-out can potentially come with a number of risks at various steps of the process, including client intake, client assessment and case management, since in these phases the interests of private providers may be in conflict with those of the client.[5] Governments need to address this by enhancing the accountability of service providers so as to secure "value for (public) money". An *outcome-based* funding mechanism is the best-suited tool for doing so.

Towards outcome-based funding

Various funding methods have been and are being used to reimburse and reward service providers, including – from least differentiated to most differentiated – annual block grants, per capita grants, output-based, fee-for-service and outcome-based funding. The trend in many countries is away from block grants which preserve the existing service landscape and are often inflexible, towards outcome-based funding which can promote innovation and change. Outcome-based funding has been introduced in recent years for employment services in Australia, the Netherlands ("no cure-less pay") and the United Kingdom and for the vocational rehabilitation programme in the United States.

Outcome-based funding in terms of accomplishing the ultimate goal of raising employment of persons with disability is superior to other funding mechanisms for a number of reasons.[6] Outcome-based funding best addresses several of the potential weaknesses of privatisation. Since the providers are paid according to *how many persons they have successfully helped into employment* rather than *how many persons they have provided with services*, there is no reason for them to keep the clients in their services for longer than necessary and to offer inappropriate services. There is still a risk of cream-skimming in the intake phase, but this problem can be addressed by a carefully-adjusted funding structure. In Australia, fees are differentiated between clients depending on the assessed level of disadvantage in the labour market.

Quality, competition and service vouchers

A key concern in building a private, for-profit provider market is the quality of services delivered and the need to ensure continuous quality improvement. Australia offers an example of good practices in this area:

- Through its comprehensive *Star Rating* performance management system, Australia has gone furthest in monitoring the performance of service providers. A good rating is crucial for a provider to be included in the next round of tenders and thereby stay in the market. Employment outcomes for more difficult clients would raise the rating, for instance.

The United Kingdom has not gone as far as Australia in this regard, but uses a rigorous licensing system to ensure good-quality service. The Netherlands has so far chosen to leave this to the market itself to a large extent; a credibility check is the only control in the tender process, but many providers are registered with a branch association which grants a quality seal.

Competition is a strong tool for better accountability and, to a degree, also quality. In this sense, in countries outsourcing employment and vocational rehabilitation services to private companies the competitive tenders themselves can contribute to overcoming some of the quality risks involved – as long as the government manages well the bidding process; monitors and assesses the performance of the providers; and feeds the results back to the contract extension or renewal. Evaluation of the level of competition induced varies. The United Kingdom aims to have at least two competing providers in each of its employment zones. Findings for the Netherlands suggest that the level of competition has not helped providers with superior results flourish enough at the expense of those with poor results, but has been sufficient to generate a "race to the bottom" in terms of the price of contracts (Groot *et al.*, 2006). Outcomes in the United States show that, although beneficiaries have a choice of receiving employment services from private and/or public providers, almost 90% are receiving services from a state vocational rehabilitation agency.

Voucher systems aim to give customers control over the choice of service as well as provider. As such, service vouchers can stimulate further competition among service providers, who are not just seeking for the authorisation from the government but for the purchase of their services by the client as well. This requires, however, sufficient market transparency for clients to be able to compare and select suitable providers, either on their own or with the help of their case-manager. Service vouchers are still rare in the OECD and the two foremost examples provide interesting lessons:

- "Individual reintegration plans" introduced in the Netherlands in 2004 give people the possibility to decide on the best means for their own reintegration. These plans which have to be approved by the responsible authority seem to have been remarkably successful: They are now responsible for almost 70% of all reintegration trajectories due to enhanced client satisfaction, and employment outcomes are better.

- In the United States, since the phased-in rollout of the "Ticket to Work" programme, in 2002-04, disability benefit recipients can voluntarily use their Ticket to obtain vocational rehabilitation, job placement or other employment supports from registered providers. Contrary to the Netherlands, take-up of the ticket is low (around 2.4% of those who have received a Ticket) and so is, therefore, its impact – despite a number of incentives to use the Ticket.

The main explanation for the success in the Netherlands compared with the somewhat disappointing outcome in the United States is probably the different time of intervention: The Ticket targets (long-term) beneficiaries and is therefore coming too late, whereas the individual reintegration plans in the Netherlands will often be used by workers on extended sick leave. The Ticket is likely to have more impact, for both the person and the Social Security Administration, were it offered e.g. to rejected disability benefit applicants or people filing applications for other benefits where there is an indication that health conditions have contributed to the job loss or inability to work. Other countries like the Czech Republic and Germany are also experimenting with vouchers which give clients the possibility to buy the service they want.

Addressing problems for private providers

Virtually any reform efforts to strengthen the accountability of private service providers will involve more administrative and financial burden and workload for providers. For example, the Dutch "no cure, less pay" funding scheme has fuelled price competition between providers, which has led to less investment in long-term efforts to enhance the employability of clients. In reaction, the Netherlands is now experimenting with longer-term contracts which allow reintegration companies to invest. A similar problem of too-little long-term investment by providers has also been identified in three provinces of Canada that have been introducing project-funding schemes, which ordinarily require the service providers to report their performance results on an annual basis (OECD, 2010).

These issues become more acute in countries where individual service providers rely on a range of different sources – including e.g. different levels of government, the PES and/or the Social Insurance Authority, charities, etc. – which they have to combine or package together. Multiple sources will imply multiple and varying accountability, thereby increasing administrative costs for providers to an unhealthy level.

Notwithstanding its advantages, outcome-based funding schemes need to be developed wisely. Measuring employment outcomes, especially longer-term employment outcomes ideally including information on career development and the person's earnings path, is more difficult and complicated than monitoring outputs. Providers will find it burdensome to keep up with the requirements and the changing developments of a new scheme. Moreover, if a funding scheme becomes too complex and sophisticated, it might become unmanageable for the public authorities monitoring and procuring it; for instance, it will become difficult to judge if charges for individual service units are appropriately priced.

6.4. Conclusion

A complex and fragmented institutional setup, imperfect governance of service and benefit-granting institutions, and lack of co-operation across institutions and among various levels of government can contribute to poor outcomes of sickness and disability policies. Across OECD countries, the current welfare and labour market institutions are arranged in ways that provide either weak incentives to local institutions to assist disadvantaged clients in improving their employability, or strong incentives to shift people in need of assistance to another institution. Better co-operation and co-ordination among various stakeholders involved is critical to improve employment outcomes for people with health problems.

Recent efforts to overcome this dilemma include comprehensive mergers of different services and institutions into one-stop-shops that provide a single point of entry to joint services; adjustments to financing mechanisms in order to reflect the decision structure, hereby establishing direct implications of bad case management and over-generous use of benefits at the local or regional level; and improvements in governance of regional and local actors through better supervision and control from the national government, the national social insurance and the national public employment service.

In addition, progress is being made in many cases in providing services in a timely manner; and in identifying the right mix of flexible services including work-first and train-first elements. Ultimately, one of the biggest challenges will be to ensure that service supply meets service demand so that all those people who could work with appropriate support are helped into the labour market.

Notes

1. Most new claimants of this benefit are young people, often aged 18-19 years. However, the eligibility criterion is not age itself but the age at which the work-capacity-limiting disability was acquired. Hence, a person 50 years of age, just to give an example, can also qualify if it can be established that the disability originated before age 18.

2. The exceptions in the OECD are Korea and the United States. In those two countries, except for workers' compensation cases, sick leave and related payment are down to the individual employment contract between the employer and the employee. Switzerland also has no public sickness benefit scheme but instead mandates sick-pay regulations through private health insurance, comparable to those in other OECD countries.

3. Conversely, too-short sickness benefit periods – like the maximum of 15 weeks in Canada – can also be problematic. For instance, in a search for income security the sick person may instead of adapting to the new situation be pushed to apply for a disability benefit too early.

4. Drake and Bond (2008) is a Meta analysis of 11 randomised controlled trials from various states in the United States, Canada and Australia. On average, these studies show that the likelihood of open employment is 61% compared with 23% with more traditional interventions; the proportion of those working more than 20 hours is 44% compared with 14%; the time until the job placement is shorter and the average duration of a job some 50% longer.

5. Private providers may seek to avoid persons with severe disability and cream-skim those with milder conditions. They may prescribe services not in the best interest of the clients but which are more profitable for their business, offering easier or cheaper or available rather than the most effective service. Moreover, they may have an interest in keeping clients in their services longer than necessary (OECD, 2010).

6. Consider the alternative of *output-based* funding. Outputs are immediate actions or results of spending activities, while outcomes are the ultimate impacts of the activities that relate to the underlying policy goal. In this field of employment services for persons with disability, "people using a programme" is an example of an output while "post-programme employment rates" are an example of an outcome (OECD, 2010 and OECD, 2009a).

Bibliography

Bach, H., N.D. Gupta and J. Høgelund (2007), "Employment Effects of Educational Measures for Work-Injured People", IZA *Discussion Paper*, No. 2657, Bonn.

Drake, R. and G. Bond (2008), "Supported Employment: 1998-2008", Guest Editorial in the Special Issue on the 10th Anniversary on Supported Employment, *Psychiatric Rehabilitation Journal*, Vol. 31, No. 4, pp. 274-276.

Groot, I., D. Hollanders, J. Hop and S. Onderstal (2006), "Werkt de reïntegratiemarkt?", SEO publication No. 946, Amsterdam.

Kluve, J. (2006), "The Effectiveness of European Active Labor Market Policy", IZA *Discussion Paper*, No. 2018, Bonn.

Leoni, T. (2010), "Differences in Sick Leave Between Employed and Unemployed Workers. What Do They Tell Us About the Health Dimension of Unemployment?", WIFO *Working Papers*, No. 372, Vienna.

Martin, J.P. and D. Grubb (2001), "What Works and for Whom: A Review of OECD Countries' Experiences with Active Labour Market Policies", *IFAU Working Paper*, No. 2001:14, Institute for Labour Market Policy Evaluationn Uppsala.

OECD (2006), *Sickness, Disability and Work: Breaking the Barriers. Vol. 1: Norway, Poland and Switzerland*, OECD Publishing, Paris.

OECD (2007), *Sickness, Disability and Work: Breaking the Barriers. Vol. 2: Australia, Luxembourg, Spain and the United Kingdom*, OECD Publishing, Paris.

OECD (2008), *Sickness, Disability and Work: Breaking the Barriers. Vol. 3: Denmark, Finland, Ireland and the Netherlands*, OECD Publishing, Paris.

OECD (2009), *Sickness, Disability and Work: Breaking the Barriers. Sweden: Will the Recent Reforms Make it?*, OECD Publishing, Paris.

OECD (2009a), *Measuring Government Activity*, OECD Publishing, Paris.

OECD (2010), *Sickness, Disability and Work: Breaking the Barriers. Canada: Opportunities for Collaboration*, OECD Publishing, Paris.

Westlie, L. (2008), "Four Essays on Effect Evaluation of Norwegian Labour Market Policy", Department of Economics, Faculty of Social Sciences, University of Oslo.

Zaidi, A. (2009), "Welfare-to-Work Programmes in the UK and Lessons for Other Countries", *Policy Brief* October 2009, European Centre for Social Welfare Policy and Research, Vienna.

OECD PUBLISHING, 2, rue André-Pascal, 75775 PARIS CEDEX 16
PRINTED IN FRANCE
(81 2010 15 1 P) ISBN 978-92-64-08884-9 – No. 57531 2010